D0230432

Hilary Booker
May 1989.

THE MEMOIR OF MARCO PARENTI

THE MEMOIR OF MARCO PARENTI

A Life in Medici Florence

MARK PHILLIPS

HEINEMANN
LONDON

William Heinemann Ltd
Michelin House, 81 Fulham Road, London SW3 6RB

LONDON MELBOURNE AUCKLAND

First published in Great Britain 1989

British Library Cataloguing in Publication Data

Phillips, Mark, *1946–*
The memoir of Marco Parenti: a life in
Medici Florence.
1. Italy. Florence. Social life, 1300–1796
I. Title
945′.5105

ISBN 0 434 58814 8

Printed in Great Britain by
St Edmundsbury Press Ltd, Bury St Edmunds, Suffolk

CONTENTS

PREFACE

THIS BOOK arises out of my discovery of a lost fifteenth-century Florentine historical memoir, an extensive account of a patrician revolt against the Medici regime shortly after the death of Cosimo de' Medici in 1464. I came upon the anonymous manuscript because, having completed a study of the sixteenth-century historian Francesco Guicciardini, I was looking for links connecting him to earlier traditions of vernacular historical writing in Florence. This new manuscript provided the sort of evidence I sought of the continued vitality in the mid-fifteenth century of this vernacular or nonclassical tradition—a kind of history writing that had long served Florentine citizens as a primary vehicle for expressing political commitment.

In time a further interest took shape, and it stands behind much of the present book. The great majority of the medieval or Renaissance historical narratives we have remain anonymous fragments of an almost irrecoverable experience. Even when the author's name is known, the effective anonymity of the document cannot be breached. But in this case, once Marco Parenti's authorship was established (see Appendix), a detailed personal record book and a substantial family correspondence were available in the Florentine archives. Through these materials we can capture a sense of the ordinary citizen's experience of political life and explore an important context for the interpretation of Renaissance historical writing. Thus my purpose here is to lift this memoir from the accident of its anonymity and to restore to it some part of the intricate web of story that surrounds every work and every life.

Marco Parenti was—if we can put it this way without oversimplification—an ordinary bourgeois of Renaissance Florence. Keeping family, civic, and historical records was a long-standing tradition for men of his class, and the various types of record keeping often overlapped. At its deepest level, history writing was an act of citizenship, the expression of pragmatic commitments to the public world. In the absence of a body of formal political theory, historiography served as the major literature of political commentary. For this reason, the tradition of historical writing Parenti exemplifies is an essential background to the later flowering of political thought in the generation of Machiavelli and Guicciardini, both of whom had roots in this civic tradition. At the same time, because works like Parenti's *Memoir* were pragmatic expressions, interpretation must often begin with the concrete circumstances, both familial and public. Hence biography becomes a method of intellectual history.

Marco Parenti left behind three quite different records of his life: the *ricordanze* or record book, the correspondence with his exiled in-laws, the Strozzi, and the *Memoir* itself. The record book is a detailed ledger of family expenses and contains a wealth of information about such matters as dowries, wedding feasts, and construction costs. Here the focus is on the immediate household. The correspondence with the Strozzi, on the other hand, is dominated by the concerns of this once powerful family, exiled from Florence since the initial triumph of the Medici in 1434. The perspective is wider and the subject is often political, but the framework is always the interest of the patrician family. Finally, we have the *Memoir* itself, a fully public history with only an occasional autobiographical reference. Each of these records is centered in its own sphere of life—the household, the wider family (or lineage), and the public world. But these spheres were never entirely separate. They overlapped or intersected in ways that gave Parenti's life—and the patriciate's experience of politics—its particular shape.

These three spheres also correspond to the main divisions of this study. Part I, drawing heavily on the *ricordanze*, assembles the circumstances of Marco Parenti's life as a householder and citizen. Part II follows in detail the story told in his correspondence of 1464–1466 of the campaign to repatriate his brothers-in-law, an effort that quickly became entangled and eventually was overwhelmed by the deepening political crisis in the city. Part III analyzes the *Memoir* itself, its political arguments and its historiographical form and tradition. These three sections connect to one another and yet must remain distinct. Marco Parenti's commitments as a private and a public man do not converge in a single, simple pattern, nor is it easy to hold their variety in simultaneous focus. But if we move in sequence through the principal records of his life and layer each upon the others, we carry away some sense of the order and depth of his experience.

I had first expected a simpler design. As an intellectual historian interested in historiography I hoped that whatever biographical details emerged would support my own focus on the *Memoir*. But the letters refused to serve as footnotes to the history, and gradually I came to see this as an enlargement of the problem rather than an obstruction. To deal with the central question of why this rather ordinary man briefly aspired to be the historian of Florentine liberty I would have to give substance to his separate activities without merging them into one; I would have to posit the unity of his life but accept its diversity.

Let me draw a contemporary analogy. In the morning, setting out for my office, I see a man in working clothes painting a front porch. Later in the day I encounter him again, differently dressed, and lecturing a class on the prosody of "Samson Agonistes." Finally, that same evening I find him attending an antipollution rally. Such discontinuities are a commonplace of urban life and ordinarily we give them little thought. We know that our lives are lived in several dimensions and would likely react with amusement to anyone who found the juxtaposition of paint, prosody, and politics bizarre. Yet a foreigner—or a historian—who could not so easily intuit a connection between these activities might well find these disparate images a starting point for examining contemporary North American civic culture. If so, the observer would have to take all three seriously, neither conflating all into one nor abandoning the assumption of an underlying unity.

Two themes stand out in Marco Parenti's biography. The

first is his devotion to his wife's family, the Strozzi, an attachment that is written on every page of his long correspondence with his brothers-in-law in Naples. A second commitment is only hinted at in these letters, though it dominates the *Memoir*. This is Parenti's dislike of the restrictive, oligarchical character of the Medici hegemony and his hopes for a more open regime. At a critical period of Parenti's life—the years chronicled in his *Memoir* and examined here—these two commitments seemed at first to converge, but in the end they ran counter to each other. Cosimo de' Medici's death was followed by a political crisis that excited expectations for both a liberalization of the regime and the repatriation of the Strozzi. With Parenti as his willing agent, Filippo Strozzi intrigued with both opposing factions to secure the right to return. Ultimately, Piero de' Medici proved stronger than his patrician opponents, and it was the triumph of the Medici, not their defeat, that brought the Strozzi back to Florence. For Marco Parenti this resolution must surely have been bittersweet; long efforts had finally borne fruit, but in a melancholy season.

It is obvious that Parenti held conflicting interests in the events of 1464–1466 which he chose to make the subject of his history. If we ask for his "view" of this crisis, then, the answer has to be more complex than either his *Memoir* or his correspondence taken separately would suggest. Each of these records proves selective when examined in the light of the other. The correspondence with the Strozzi gives little hint of Parenti's wider views or commitments; the *Memoir*, for its part, is silent on a whole history of family dramas and intrigues detailed in the letters. Thus the letters, although seldom offering a direct corrective to the account given in the *Memoir*, are certainly a corrective to the anonymity that would otherwise isolate the text.

Marco Parenti does not invite a conventional biography. In no sense a figure of the first rank, he acted primarily as an agent for others, an advisor, a conduit for news and impressions. The documentation of his life, though rich and expressive in places, is selective and sometimes sparse. Even the

Memoir, though it was apparently planned on a fairly ambitious scale, comes down to us only as a fragment. We see Parenti largely as he observed others, so that his biography becomes a sort of group portrait, and we learn to know him more through the quality of his intelligence than through his own actions. But if these limitations are accepted, Marco Parenti's acquaintance is worth making. Secondary figure that he was, he is all the more able to lead us into the common experience of Florentine citizens. He lived in interesting times and was well placed to observe them. His education was classical as well as mercantile and he played a small part in the intellectual ferment of his day. His intelligence is calm and sympathetic and, whether turning his attention to the proper apprenticeship of his youngest brother-in-law or the failures of the anti-Medici faction, he tells us something worth knowing, both about himself and his times.

It will inevitably be asked, "How typical was Marco Parenti?" I cannot give an exact sociological answer—though chapter 1 gives grounds for a rough financial ranking. But whether or not Marco was statistically typical (and there are reasons for thinking that his value as a witness owes something to his not being the typical patrician), the evidence at hand is sufficient to make him intellectually and socially specific. This specificity is the basis for the final chapter, which places his political and historical views in relation to an important civil intellectual tradition and a central problem of the patrician class.

It has been said that anything sufficiently specific one can say about an individual acquires a kind of generality. In my experience as a teacher as well as a student of Florentine history, I have often found a craving for a degree of human particularity that is seldom satisfied by contemporary historical writing. For me the writing of this book has been an exercise in generalizing the specific and specifying the general. I hope that for my students and others like them the story I have to tell will serve the same purpose.

It is a pleasure to be able to acknowledge at least a few of the many people and institutions that helped to make this work possible. My research for this book has been generously supported by several grants from the Social Sciences and Humanities Research Council of Canada. Time to write was afforded me by the Marston LaFrance Fellowship of the Arts Faculty, Carleton University, and by the Institute for Advanced Study, Princeton. It is a pleasure to have the opportunity to acknowledge the kindness of Felix Gilbert and John Elliott during my year at the Institute. To other friends and colleagues—especially Robert Goheen, Blair Neatby, Isabel Huggan, Charles Wittenberg, and Silverio Lupi—I am grateful for continued advice and support. I am indebted to Joanna Hitchcock and Elizabeth Gretz of Princeton University Press, thanks to whom this book now floats a little higher in the water. My greatest debt is to the companionship of my wife Ruth; to her and to Sarah and Emma—who would not be left out—I dedicate this book.

NOTE ON ABBREVIATIONS AND SOURCES

A.S.F.	Archivio di Stato, Florence
B.N.F.	Biblioteca Nazionale, Florence
CS	Carte Strozziane, A.S.F.
Lettere	Alessandra Macinghi Strozzi, *Lettere di una gentildonna fiorentina del secolo XV ai figliuoli esuli*, ed. Cesare Guasti (Florence, 1877).
Memorie	Marco Parenti, *Memorie*, B.N.F., Magliabecchi XXV, 272.
Ricordanze	Marco and Piero Parenti, *Libro di ricordanze*, CS ser. 2, 17 bis.

IN CITING Marco Parenti's correspondence, reference is made to the *Lettere* as well as to the manuscript source whenever appropriate. Guasti's excerpts are often brief, but I have made no attempt to indicate how much of the given letter is quoted in the *Lettere*. I have given the date of each letter, but since all of Parenti's correspondence, with a solitary exception, is with the Strozzi brothers—and principally the elder, Filippo—I have not indicated the recipient.

In citing Alessandra Strozzi's letters, I have given only the printed reference and the date. Again, all the letters were directed to her sons in Naples. When other correspondence or documents are cited from the *Lettere*, I have simply given the page number, omitting dates or other collateral information.

I have tried to keep footnotes to a minimum; where extensive use is made of a source—the letters, *Ricordanze*, or *Memorie*—reference is given at an early stage and subsequent quotation or paraphrase can be assumed to come from the same place until a further primary source is noted. In the case of the coded letters, decoded phrases are placed in parentheses;

where there is some doubt of the meaning of the code, I have left the ciphers in the text or indicated the uncertainty with a question mark.

All dates have been given in the modern rather than Florentine style.

THE MEMOIR OF MARCO PARENTI

Perhaps I am doing a bold thing to bespeak your sympathy on behalf of a man who was so very far from remarkable,—a man whose virtues were not heroic, and who had no undetected crime within his breast; who had not the slightest mystery hanging about him, but was palpably and unmistakably commonplace. . . . Yet these commonplace people—many of them—bear a conscience, and have felt the sublime prompting to do the painful right; they have their unspoken sorrows, and their sacred joys; their hearts have perhaps gone out towards their first-born, and they have mourned over the irreclaimable dead.

—GEORGE ELIOT, *Scenes of Clerical Life*

For as all Action is, by its nature, to be figured as extended in breadth and in depth, as well as in length; that is to say, is based on Passion and Mystery, if we investigate its origin; and spreads abroad on all hands, modifying and modified; as well as advances towards completion,—so all Narrative is, by its nature of only one dimension; only travels forward towards one, or towards successive points: Narrative is *linear*, Action is *solid*.

—THOMAS CARLYLE, "On History"

INTRODUCTION

AUGUST 1, 1464: THE DEATH OF COSIMO DE' MEDICI

★

> What followed we have already narrated at the start of these memoirs, which we began at the death of Cosimo de' Medici in the belief that in the future it would be our task to write about the affairs of a free city and of men who would become better citizens because they were tired of the servitude of previous times. In this I have not succeeded. I waited for the time that this liberty would come, and it approached, but did not succeed entirely, and so was completely lost. My spirits grew weak, and the difficulty of knowing the truth when those who govern keep secrets to themselves drew me back from diligence and from the idea that I had formed. And so these memoirs are very uneven, and discontinuous in describing everything that went on, though sometimes more and sometimes less according to the times.[1]

THIS IS THE voice of Marco Parenti, sometime silk merchant, ordinary citizen, and would-be historian. His apology comes after seventy pages of manuscript in which, as he says, he had attempted to narrate the course of events in Florence after the death of Cosimo de' Medici in 1464. Another forty pages completed the text as we have it in the anonymous copy through which some later Florentine gave a second, though obscure, life to Marco Parenti's observations. In all, the *Memoir* follows the events of only three or

[1] *Memorie*, pp. 69–70.

four years in detail; it begins in the late summer of 1464 when Cosimo died, describes the rise of the anti-Medici faction in 1465 and its decisive defeat in 1466, and ends with the confused aftermath of the following year. To this is added, however, a substantial retrospect on the careers of Cosimo de' Medici in Florence and his ally Francesco Sforza in Milan, which comes in the middle of the manuscript.

We have, then, only a fragmentary work, one that may not even represent the full extent of Parenti's original composition, though given the mood of dejection into which he had apparently fallen after seventy pages it would not be surprising if he simply abandoned the project. Nonetheless, Marco Parenti's *Memoir* is a historical text of real interest. Though in the end events proved him wrong in expecting that Cosimo's death would bring a renewal of liberty, Parenti was not mistaken in sensing the tide of republican feeling. Nor was he deceived in presuming that the years he had chosen to chronicle would be eventful and perhaps decisive in the history of the Medici domination. Confirmation of this can be found in Machiavelli, who wrote that after the defeat of the anti-Medici party in 1466, legitimate opposition within Florence was no longer possible and all that remained was the path of violent conspiracy.[2]

As an observer Parenti was well placed and receptive. His connection by marriage to the Strozzi widened his access to the inner circles of Florence, whether inside the regime or among its opponents. He was also on friendly terms with a number of the leading intellectuals of the city, who evidently accepted him as a man with a cultivated mind. These circumstances played their part in fashioning Parenti's narrative, making it a work that, though fragmentary, is intelligent, critical, and well informed. But there is another attraction here: the voice of the man behind the work, a voice most clearly heard in the apology with which we began. Ostensibly this interjection after seventy pages of narrative is meant to

[2] N. Machiavelli, *The History of Florence*, intro. W. Dunne (New York, 1960), p. 356.

explain the broad digression that the author had seen his history take to include the background of Francesco Sforza and his connection with Medici power. It is clear, however, that added to the sorrow he felt over the public events of his day as chronicled in his own account, there was also a more private sense of failure. Thus he confesses not simply to a certain untidyness in his text but to a sense of inadequacy as a historian that grows out of personal disillusionment.

Marco Parenti's personal voice draws us on to a curiosity about the man and his motives. It can quickly be learned that he was a person of comfortable means, though no great wealth, a member of a small parvenu family without either political prominence or social prestige, a sometime silk merchant with an interest in humanistic studies, a relation by marriage to the exiled Strozzi family. Taken by itself, however, none of this tells us very much about why a rather ordinary citizen of Medicean Florence was inspired by the death of Cosimo de' Medici to attempt a history of his city, nor how the unfolding of subsequent events touched him personally.

Extraordinary minds create worlds of their own, so that biographical detail is secondary and often distracting. But if we are to appreciate a man like Parenti, whose life has about it always the dimensions and attractions of the commonplace, concreteness is essential. Fortunately, enough detail survives to trace large parts of the story to which the *Memoir* belongs, so that its composition becomes a specific act in an individual life. Let us begin where he himself began the *Memoir*, with the character of Cosimo de' Medici and the impact of his death on August 1, 1464.

★

Cosimo de' Medici was both the greatest and most prudent of Florentine politicians. The successful leader of a faction in a notoriously factious city, he built a strong and effective regime that lasted his thirty years and thirty years more before being overthrown, only to be reestablished in the next century on more permanent lines. Yet during his lifetime at least, the regime always retained the provisional character of personal and factional rule. Institutionally Florence changed very slowly: a republic in name, a narrow and tightly controlled oligarchy in fact.[3]

The Medici regime in the fifteenth century is best thought of as an oligarchy rather than a consolidated princely state. It was an alliance of great families and powerful men, united by self-interest and the undeniable prestige of the Medici family. This alliance was not static, however, and its leading family had more to fear from potential rivals within the politically dominant class than from those outright enemies Cosimo had succeeded in dismissing into lifelong exile when he first took power in 1434.

Cosimo devoted all his enormous political tact and a great deal of his personal wealth to keeping this family of families in line. This was his greatest achievement, and within his generation-long tenure of power, Florence moved measurably closer to the principate it would eventually become. Still, the potential rivalries remained and after his death they became urgent. Even a politician as skillful as Cosimo could not prevent a succession crisis. For politically engaged Florentines, whatever their allegiance, Cosimo's death was sure to be a significant marker.

As Cosimo grew into old age, the anticipation of his death preoccupied many Florentines, including Cosimo himself. Vespasiano da Bisticci, the Florentine bookseller who retired to write the biographies of the "illustrious men" of his day, draws a revealing portrait of Cosimo as an old man:

> In his latter days Cosimo fell into irresolute mood and would often sit for hours without speaking, sunk in thought. In reply to his wife who remarked on his taciturnity he said, "When you propose to go into the country, you trouble yourself for fifteen days in settling what you will do when you get there. Now that the time has come for me to quit this world and

[3] The fundamental study of politics and the constitution under the early Medici is N. Rubinstein, *The Government of Florence under the Medici* (Oxford, 1966).

pass into another, does it not occur to you that I ought to think about it?"[4]

Cosimo's thoughts were not all so philosophic, however. In these long silences he also had plenty of opportunity to think about what he was leaving behind him in this world. Vespasiano again gives us an image of Cosimo's concerns:

> knowing well the disposition of his fellow citizens, he was sure that, in the lapse of fifty years, no memory would remain of his personality or of his house save the few buildings he might have built. "I know (he said) that after my death my children will be in worse circumstances than those of any other Florentine who has died for many years past; moreover, I know I shall not wear the crown of laurel more than any other citizen."[5]

It seems surprising at first that Cosimo should voice such gloomy prophecies, which seem more like the hopes of his critics than his own expectations. But Cosimo was above all things a shrewd observer of the marketplace. He knew that although Florence might, a little grudgingly, acknowledge the *virtù* of a merchant prince, it had no room as yet for a philosopher king. "He spoke this," Vespasiano writes, commenting on Cosimo's pessimistic prophecy, "because he knew the difficulty of ruling a state as he had ruled Florence, through the opposition of influential citizens who had rated themselves his equals in former times."

As Vespasiano seems to suggest, no one was better schooled in the realities of Florentine politics than Cosimo. No one knew better the fragility of his own achievement and the odds against its permanence. He fully understood the competitive, sharp-eyed character of his countrymen and their deep attachment to the form, if not the entire substance, of their communal traditions. He appreciated all this, in fact, because he was himself in so many ways the outstanding exemplar of this commercial citizenry. His penchant for covert or indirect

[4] Vespasiano da Bisticci, *Vite di uomini illustri del secolo xv*, ed. P. D'Ancona and E. Aeschlimann (Milan, 1951), translated as *Renaissance Princes, Popes, and Prelates* by W. George and E. Waters (New York, 1963), p. 234.

[5] Vespasiano, *Renaissance Princes*, p. 223.

control, his public modesty, the friendly relations he cultivated with foreign princes, the bourgeois marriages he arranged for his children, his outstanding liberality, his patronage and influence in every corner of civic life—what was this careful mix of operations if not the political equivalent of prudent mercantile diversification? How different, on the other hand, was his friend Sforza, who banked heavily on military skill to establish his house in Milan.

Cosimo belonged more to the world of his own detractors than to the visions of his courtly eulogists. Although he more than anyone was responsible for setting Florence on the new course that was taking it away from republican tradition, he still valued and practiced the old republican virtues—and he wanted his fellow citizens to know it. So, when his beloved second son died in 1463, he forbade public demonstrations of mourning. And a year later, his own funeral showed the same sober spirit, as described in the opening page of Parenti's *Memoir*:

> Cosimo di Giovanni de' Medici, preeminent citizen of Florence whether in wealth or prudence or authority or power, died on the first day of August, 1464, around the 22nd hour, aged a little less than 76 years, in his villa called Careggi. The next day, putting aside the customary pomp of funerals of great citizens, with little display, as he wished, accompanied only by the priests of San Lorenzo and the friars of San Marco and the Abbey of Fiesole, churches he had built, and a few citizens who were relatives and friends walking behind the corpse, he was buried in San Lorenzo in Florence in a low tomb in the ground under the tribune.[6]

This was not the splendid public ceremony that Machiavelli later imagined, "conducted with the utmost pomp and solemnity, the whole city following his corpse to the tomb . . . on which by public decree he was inscribed Pater Patriae."[7] Cosimo's standing may well have justified a state funeral with

[6] *Memorie*, p. 1.

[7] Machiavelli, *History*, p. 319. Parenti's picture of a more modest funeral is confirmed by a letter of his brother-in-law, Giovanni Bonsi, in *Lettere*, p. 327.

appropriate ceremony, but that was not Cosimo's wish. He must have understood that for men like Parenti, the most impressive thing would be the austerity of the occasion: the lack of "customary pomp," the "low tomb," the mourning procession restricted—as though for a simple, private citizen—to family and a few friends, thus making the presence of the priests and friars of several churches all the more telling a symbol of Cosimo's many philanthropies. Evidently Cosimo had wished his last public appearance to be governed by the same tactful deference to the republican traditions of Florence as the rest of his long and highly successful career.

Pater Patriae: for Machiavelli this classical eulogy, carved in the marble of Cosimo's tomb, was the culminating honor of the funeral. In fact, however, he had telescoped events. Though a committee was established within a week of the funeral to discuss ways of honoring the dead leader, it was not until the next year that the title was actually bestowed.[8] Presumably this accounts for its absence from Parenti's description of the funeral, which must have been written soon after Cosimo died.

What did the eulogy really mean? It was a splendid compliment. Rich with classical resonance, it draped the shrewd banker in the toga of the Roman statesman and set him beside the immortal Cicero—himself an ambitious party politician. This was a fitting reward for a man whose wealth had gone so generously to support the architects and humanists who were transforming modern Florence after their image of ancient Rome. But the title was as fitting in its cloudiness as in its dignity, its lofty ambiguity nicely matching the real ambiguities of Medici power.

The truth is that, as Florence's first citizen, Cosimo could easily afford modesty but could ill afford its opposite. A certain ambiguity was essential to the preservation of his power. As a self-confessed realist, he was inclined by temperament and self-interest to exercise his authority with as little ostentation as possible. "Cosimo used to say," Vespasiano wrote,

[8] Alison Brown, "The Humanist Portrait of Cosimo de' Medici, Pater Patriae," *Journal of the Warburg and Courtauld Institutes*, 24 (1961): 195n.

"that in most gardens there grew a weed which should never be watered but left to dry up. Most men, however, watered it instead of letting it die of drought. This weed was that worst of all weeds, Envy."[9]

The avoidance of envy was, in fact, the central tactic of Cosimo's political career. No doubt he would have appreciated the high-minded evasion posthumously tagged to his name, but his own strength lay in more common language, alternately forceful or slyly indirect. This gave him a useful reputation for homely wit. A good example is the realistic dictum, quoted approvingly by Machiavelli, that "two yards of rose-colored cloth could make a gentleman."[10] The frankness of this estimate from so grand a gentleman is disarming and seems at first disinterested, until we consider how many yards of fine cloth—and how many gentlemen—his patronage could buy.

A second example comes from Vespasiano. When confronted by an angry rival, Cosimo is reported to have said: "You concern yourself with infinite, I with finite affairs. You raise your ladder to the heavens, while I rest mine upon earth lest I should mount so high that I may fall. Now it seems to me only just and honest that I should prefer the good name and honor of my house to you. So you and I will act like two big dogs who, when they meet, smell one another and then, because they both have teeth, go their ways."[11] This picture of sniffing hounds brings us closer to the substance of power in fifteenth-century Florence (or anywhere else) than does the loftiness of the Latin epithet. But there was cunning in this street idiom, too. Precisely because he saw himself as a realist—as a man whose ladder rested on solid earth—Cosimo valued his pose as plain-spoken citizen. No prince, after all, would have expressed himself this way.

For their part, the Florentines were equally gratified by the deception. As Machiavelli observed in the *Discourses*, "in reading the history of republics we find in all of them a degree of

[9] Vespasiano, *Renaissance Princes*, p. 234.
[10] Machiavelli, *History*, p. 317.
[11] Vespasiano, *Renaissance Princes*, p. 225.

ingratitude to their citizens."[12] The Florentines were well aware—as the citizens of democracies have always been from the days of Themistocles to those of Winston Churchill and General MacArthur—that a great man is both the glory of the state and its dearest enemy. The disappearance of a great man is never simply a loss; it also comes as a relief.

Cosimo understood this too, as we know from his gloomy prediction to Vespasiano about the future of his house. About his own posthumous fame he was, of course, wrong: in memorializing him as Pater Patriae, Florence did indeed offer him "the crown of laurel." But it is fair to say that in large measure Cosimo won this wreath after his death because he had so studiously avoided seeming tempted by a crown while he lived. As much as any of his more substantial achievements—the regime that he organized, the peace that he secured, the monasteries, churches, palaces, and monuments that he built or extended—it was this self-protective modesty that earned him his honors after death.

Cosimo's calculated modesty did not prevent his praises from being sung during his lifetime, still less after his death. To the princes of Italy and of Europe beyond the Alps, the Medici looked like princes. When Cosimo died they sent Piero, his son, their princely condolences. "His life," Pope Pius II wrote, "was full of honor, his glory extended beyond his own city to Italy, nay, to the whole world." From France, Louis XI offered his own consolations, adding to them permission to Piero de' Medici and his descendants to emblazon the Medici coat of arms with the royal fleur-de-lis. Piero himself collected a volume of consolatory letters in which a long list of notables and fellow citizens praised his father's magnificence and offered renewed loyalty to his heir. Even Piero's young sons, Lorenzo and Giuliano, offered condolences on the death of their grandfather in formal Latin.[13]

[12] Machiavelli, *The Prince and the Discourses*, trans. L. Ricci (New York, 1950), bk. 1, ch. 28.

[13] A.S.F., *Mediceo avanti il Principato*, 163. The book opens as a conventional *ricordanze*, with an invocation to the saints, and then records Cosimo's death and the funeral expenses. Piero himself penned a fine eulogy to his father,

The Florentines themselves had not been slow to recognize Cosimo's fame. For thirty years his political and commercial genius had dominated the city. His astuteness both in business and government, his wide-ranging patronage, his prestige abroad as well as at home, his wealth and conspicuous liberality, all these had combined to make him the first citizen of Florence. Even during his lifetime he had begun to attract a variety of literary tributes from citizens, humanists, and poets, and after his death he was celebrated in ever more exalted ways.[14]

Among those who joined in this chorus of praise, the most moderate and disinterested were Cosimo's fellow patricians. They shared his love of the city and his enthusiasm for the revival of ancient glories. To such citizens, the city was a theater of virtue, and the virtue they extolled in Cosimo was his liberality in beautifying Florence and supporting its learned men.

A younger generation of poets and philosophers was less restrained. They lacked the patricians' social independence as well as their commitment to the values of republican citizenship. For these literati, Cosimo's combination of statesmanship and learning inevitably suggested the Platonic image of the philosopher-ruler. Marsilio Ficino, whose Platonic academy was supported with generous gifts from Cosimo, confessed that he owed as much to the daily example of Cosimo's virtue as to the ideas of Plato himself. To his benefactor's grandson, Lorenzo de' Medici, he offered this salutation and punning advice: "Farewell, and just as God formed Cosimo in the image of the world, so you should model yourself, as you have begun, on the image of Cosimo."[15]

---

which is followed by transcriptions of the consolatory letters, beginning with the pope and other ecclesiastical dignitaries. I am grateful to D. Kent for a reference to this document. On the condolences of the pope and the king of France, see also J. R. Hale, *Florence and the Medici: The Pattern of Control* (London, 1977).

[14] For what follows on the eulogists of Cosimo I am indebted to Alison Brown, "Humanist Portrait."

[15] Brown, "Humanist Portrait," pp. 203–204.

Florentines remained in awe of Cosimo's fame long after his death. Even Machiavelli, hardly a Medici apologist, felt the overwhelming attraction of Cosimo's reputation and gave him a long and splendid eulogy in the *Florentine History*. In doing so, Machiavelli acknowledged, he had "rather imitated the biographies of princes than general history," but he justified this unusual attention to a single life by arguing that "of so extraordinary an individual I was compelled to speak with unusual praise."[16]

Ordinary Florentines were apt to take a less exalted view of Cosimo's life and to react rather differently to the news of his death. Against the cosmic flatteries of Ficino or the eulogies of princes and later historians we must set the concerns of contemporary citizens. For many, the immediate worry was simply security. Cosimo alive seemed a guarantee of public order and continuity in government, but now that reassurance was gone. "Since he died, things continue smoothly," one man wrote, "and I believe that those who have been in power will continue to be so. May God keep them united and let them manage well."[17]

The author of these words was Marco Parenti's brother-in-law, Giovanni Bonsi, and one can only assume that his anxiety, so tentatively expressed, was the undertone of many conversations in Florence in the late summer and autumn of 1464. His mother-in-law (and Marco's), Alessandra Strozzi, was a touch bolder. She allowed herself to speculate that undoubtedly "a number of citizens" would be entertaining thoughts among themselves about how the city was to be governed. "But for the moment one hears nothing," she wrote, "since the thing is so recent."[18]

Marco Parenti's own immediate reactions are lost to us. We know from his *Memoir* that he saw Cosimo's death as a point of departure, both for himself and for Florence. For Parenti, Cosimo was certainly an important figure, though not for reasons encompassed in the eulogistic literature. It was not

[16] Machiavelli, *History*, p. 319.
[17] *Lettere*, p. 327.
[18] Ibid., p. 321.

that Parenti wished to deny Cosimo's greatness, but he felt it a burden on Florence that death had now lifted. Thus Parenti composed a deliberately lustrous description of Cosimo's achievements and the benefits he brought the city in his last years, only to make these praises a preamble to his celebration of civic renewal:

> Not for many years had this city been so prosperous. For this reason many festivities were celebrated, jousts, spectacles, weddings, balls, and banquets, with the finest decorations and the women magnificent in dresses of silk, embroidery, pearls, and jewels. At these festivities the women were numerous and the youths were dressed in varied and very rich liveries. Men of all ages dressed themselves ordinarily in the finest clothes in beautiful cloth of rose color, or violet, or black, and every color of silk and rich linings. There was a great deal of building, both inside [the city] and out, and very elegantly done. Cosimo, who because of his great wealth could outdo everyone else, exerted himself more than anyone else to construct buildings that were large and beautiful, as did his sons. The arrangements of his household were properly civil, but very fine. So too there were a great number of worthy citizens who maintained fine households according to their way of life, as regards decoration, servants, horses, and similar matters having to do with rank.
>
> Florence stood in this happy condition during the life of Cosimo de' Medici, until the first day of August 1464. And although this prosperity was owing to the goodness of the times, due to the league and the peace that held throughout Italy, nonetheless Cosimo made every effort to maintain it [i.e. the peace], arranging it for the well-being of Florence and bringing it into effect by means of his authority in Florence. And nevertheless, on his death everyone rejoiced, such is the love of and desire for liberty. It appeared to the Florentines that from his way of governing they had experienced a certain subjection and servitude, from which they believed his death would liberate them. This they desired and in this they delighted, putting off thought of any other good which they enjoyed.[19]

Marco Parenti's belief that Cosimo's death was welcomed

[19] *Memorie*, pp. 68–69.

by most Florentines may be as open to question as Machiavelli's contrary assumption that "the regret was universal." Most likely the fundamentally unpolitical anxieties of men like Giovanni Bonsi represented the mood of the majority. There is no mistaking, though, the strength of Parenti's personal conviction, which stimulated him to begin to chronicle Florentine affairs in what he clearly anticipated would be a new era.

Others, too, had reasons for sharing these hopes. The Medici regime, like its predecessor, was not always gentle. In the intimate circle of civic politics competition was inevitable, personal, and harsh. Cosimo came to power in 1434 after a year of exile and, in turn, banned or exiled his enemies. Many prominent individuals and families suffered fines, loss of political rights, confiscation, or banishment. The list is long. It includes, to name only some of the best known, the Albizzi, Altoviti, Bardi, Brancacci, Castellani, Gianfigliazzi, Guadagni, Lamberteschi, Panciatichi, da Panzano, Peruzzi, Ricasoli, and—most important to Marco Parenti—the Strozzi.

Subsequent swings of political fortune brought periods of relaxation and a return to communal traditions. In the end, however, the result was always stricter oligarchical control. In 1458, widespread pressure for reform had resulted in a sharp reaction from the oligarchs. Only a few prominent opponents were exiled, but penalties against earlier enemies were renewed and extended and a new council was created to centralize power and consolidate the regime. Nicodemo Tranchedini, the Milanese agent in Florence, summed up the situation in a letter to his duke:

> The chief authorities here yesterday banished the citizens named in the enclosed list. I do not think they will take other measures for the time being. They have punished the young tom-cats in order to frighten the lions, and if these refuse to be tamed their turn is sure to come. However, they appear to be trembling with anxiety and assert that they will behave like good children.[20]

[20] Quoted in C. Gutkind, *Cosimo de' Medici, Pater Patriae* (Oxford, 1938), p. 137.

In these ways direct opposition to the Medici oligarchy became less and less possible. Those whose loyalty seemed less than total might find themselves harshly treated. Others lost favor or political rights simply because they were connected by marriage to the exiles. Among these was Marco Parenti.

Undoubtedly Parenti's sense of the political mood in Florence in 1464 was a reflection of his own situation and a projection of personal desires. Many others—as many as subscribed to the exaggerations of the eulogists—must have felt the same stirrings. For all of them, Cosimo's death would be a signal. Only a few years earlier, the Milanese agent in Florence had reported that Palla Strozzi, a leading exile, had refused to join in a new conspiracy against his old enemy, because time itself would soon bring everything they wanted: "He said these were vain thoughts and plans, since while Cosimo lives it is impossible to stop him, but once he is dead, in a few days things will change of their own accord towards their [i.e. the exiles'] own needs and desires."[21]

Palla Strozzi's expectations were overly optimistic, as the views of exiles tend to be. But Marco Parenti, though more moderate and better informed, did not fundamentally disagree. There was no alternative but to accept the reality of Cosimo's power. One could also concede his greatness and pay tribute to the benefits he had brought Florence, as Parenti did. Yet it was easy to believe that at last time was running out on Cosimo. In 1463 he had suddenly lost his younger, more vigorous son; the other, Piero, was already ill and elderly. Cosimo's own death, long anticipated, would surely open a new chapter. Writing "in haste" from Cosimo's deathbed, Nicodemo reported that "in extremo" Cosimo repeatedly asked Sforza's protection for his son, and the Milanese agent concluded with a plea of his own "to support Piero's authority [riputatione] as soon as you can."[22]

★

[21] Quoted in Rubinstein, *Government*, p. 136n.

[22] B. Buser, *Die Beziehungen der Mediceer zu Frankreich wahrend der Jahre 1434–1494* (Leipzig, 1879), pp. 422–23.

In concluding his recollections of Cosimo de' Medici, Vespasiano da Bisticci was acutely conscious of how much more could still be said about this famous man. "Many other things might be told of Cosimo . . . ," he wrote; "I leave all the rest to anyone who may undertake the work of writing the life of so worthy a citizen, the ornament of his age."[23] It is all the more striking, therefore, that about Cosimo's son and heir, Piero, Vespasiano had almost nothing to say. In a compilation as broad and in some ways unselective as the *Lives of the Illustrious Men of the Fifteenth Century*—a collection that includes Spanish, Portuguese, English, and even Hungarian churchmen, along with minor humanists and second-rank Florentine politicians—Piero de' Medici's *vita* is missing. What little space is given him, in fact, comes mostly in the life of one of his principal rivals, Agnolo Acciaiuoli, whom Piero banished in the troubles of 1466.

Even to his own contemporaries, apparently, Piero was lost in the shadows of his father's fame. His time as head of the family and leader of the city was brief. Already forty-six when his father died, he lived only five more years before dying of the gout that afflicted the entire family. During these final years Piero was rarely entirely well. The crippling disease made him irritable, as his son Lorenzo complained, and he was often confined to bed or a litter. This not only limited his effectiveness but provoked new resentments that piled on top of those already directed against the Medici and their policies. Nor did the adverse economic climate help. A wave of bankruptcies hit Florence, and the Medici bank itself had entered the period of its decline, as Piero discovered when he ordered a financial review after Cosimo's death.

Despite all this Piero managed to bring the regime through its most severe, widespread, and prolonged challenge, and when he died in 1469, he was able to hand on the power built by his father to his son. In August of 1464, however, it was far from clear that this would be so. To ordinary citizens like Giovanni Bonsi or Alessandra Strozzi, the future was worrisome and the desire of a number of powerful men to force

[23] Vespasiano, *Renaissance Princes*, p. 234.

changes seemed obvious. One of these put the matter frankly to the Medici's ally in Milan: "While Cosimo was alive, decisions were left to him; now those who remain at the head of the regime are Piero and a number of citizens supporting him, who were brothers to Cosimo and who will now be fathers to Piero."[24]

The history of this confrontation will occupy us in Part II. In the meantime there is no better summary of Piero's position in 1464 than the passage with which Parenti introduces him in his *Memoir*:

> He [Cosimo] was survived by his son, Piero, aged 46; he held great authority, like his father, with many supporters, wealth, and power, almost the same as he had already enjoyed during the lifetime of his father, with whom he had shared authority in the care and governing of the city. Like his father, he was ill with gout, so that he no longer rose from his bed. For this reason it was necessary for all other citizens that had need of him to go to his chambers; similarly the Magistrates, who did not presume to take decisions on serious matters without his consent. Likewise foreigners, ambassadors, and Seigneurs that had any business to do with our city were obliged to find him there. Thus his chambers were almost always crowded with men of every sort of various errands, and often it was difficult to speak with him.
>
> This difficulty, added to the resentment of his excessive power, stimulated in the minds of many citizens a great hatred, and the greater and more generous of mind they were, the more insupportable they found it. And among the others there were three men of the highest prestige who showed themselves openly to the people as being impatient of bearing this arrogance any longer, believing it to be almost servitude for themselves and for other citizens. These were Messer Luca Pitti, Messer Dietisalvi Neroni, and Messer Agnolo Acciaiuoli. They let the people know, along with many others of every sort who were their followers, that Piero should not succeed to this power. Nonetheless, though fearful, he pursued his purpose and assumed the leadership [principato] like his father.[25]

[24] Quoted in Rubinstein, *Government*, p. 137.

[25] *Memorie*, pp. 1–2.

Clearly Parenti's political commitments went deeper than Giovanni Bonsi's anxiety for order or Alessandra Strozzi's vigilance for any change that might offer hope to her exiled sons. Marco's horizons were wider and included the prospect of a new political order—or perhaps a return to an older one. In taking up his *Memoir* he was affirming these hopes, and in putting it aside some years later he acknowledged their frustration. The *Memoir* is more than a record of a few years of severe political crisis. It is also an expression of ambitions and commitments that, being widely held, made some such crisis, sooner or later, inevitable. To understand this wider sense we must go beyond the text and explore Parenti's life in both its private and public dimensions.

PART I

FAMILY

Marco Parenti and the Strozzi

CHAPTER I

HOUSEHOLD

★

IN A LETTER of August 24, 1447—almost two decades before the events we have been discussing—we find our first description of Marco Parenti, already a young man of twenty-five. The letter announces the betrothal of Caterina Strozzi to the son of Parente Parenti. It was written by the young girl's mother, Alessandra Strozzi, the widow of a man exiled in 1434 by the Medici, and was addressed to her eldest son, Filippo, living in Naples. Eventually Filippo would become one of the richest men in Florence and the builder of the grandest private Florentine *palazzo* of his century. In 1447, however, all this was a distant dream, and Alessandra emphasized the pragmatic considerations that underlay her decision to accept Marco Parenti as her son-in-law.

Alessandra gave a succinct summary of his attractions. He was a "worthy and virtuous young man, and he is the only son, and rich, 25 years old, and keeps a silk workshop; and they have a little political standing—'un poco di stato'—since only recently the father was in the Colleges." The dowry was to be one thousand florins, a substantial sum but not a brilliant one, and she readily admitted that for four or five hundred more she could have found her daughter a husband "in greater estate or more noble." Alessandra was more than willing to find justifications for a decision taken out of necessity. Marriage to a better-placed family—one with an older name and more frequently found in high communal posts—might only bring unhappiness for her daughter. After all, prestige aside, office "brings no return, and there are many expenses. And I decided, all things considered, to see the girl well established and to pay no attention to other things."[1]

Her mother's rationalizations notwithstanding, Caterina clearly was marrying "down." In himself the young man seemed an attractive prospect. But marriage was more than a coupling of individuals; it was an alliance of families. Marco's father had only "un poco di stato." Taken as a whole, his family had even less. Even granting the twin disabilities of widowhood and exile, Alessandra obviously did not regard Marco's family as measuring up to her own.

There was no business more serious than marriage for Florentine families. In a dozen ways it not only measured but affected social status. A favorable match might signal advancing fortunes, open up a valuable commercial connection, or bring the protection of a political alliance. And for no one was this truer than for the widow of Matteo Strozzi, left alone to raise her family with few means and little room for maneuver. We can be sure that every item in Alessandra's description of her future son-in-law had been thoroughly gone over in her mind before she decided to accept him.

Giovanni Parenti, Marco's paternal grandfather, had in fact been a man of some political impact, though it was of a sort that only underlined the family's lack of social distinction. He was one of the leaders of the popular party in the 1370s, when the tensions between this faction and its aristocratic opponents in the Guelf party led the city into the upheaval of the Ciompi revolt. As a member of the armorers' guild, Giovanni Parenti was a minor guildsman, a representative of a large number of men, many of them "new citizens," who were struggling for political authority in a regime hitherto dominated by the major guilds and patricians. Florence in the period after the Black Death was a more open society than it would later become, and Giovanni sat six times on the Signoria, the highest council of the commune. This prominence was also his undoing. In 1371 he was able to win acquittal against a charge that he was a Ghibelline, a favorite weapon used by the Guelf

[1] *Lettere*, pp. 3–5.

party. Seven years later the Guelfs attacked him again and he lost all political rights.[2]

Giovanni Parenti's career was not of the sort to recommend his memory in later, more oligarchic days. The echoes of his politics may be traceable in the republican sympathies of his grandson and great-grandson, but as the family climbed in social status they were probably more than happy to forget their recent past. Alessandra Strozzi, at least, seems to have had no notion of this grandfather whose name she mistakenly gave as Piero.

By the early part of the fifteenth century Giovanni's two sons, Stefano and Parente, were able to improve the family's economic and social position, though without any prospect of playing the sort of role in the upper class that their father had enjoyed in the lower. Matriculation in the silk guild raised them to the ranks of the major guildsmen, a decisive jump in status. Silk manufacturing also brought them a fair share of prosperity. In 1403 the Parenti were not among the 150 wealthiest households in the San Giovanni quarter, the area of the city that centered on the cathedral. A similar list for 1427, however, ranks Stefano's household—in which Parente was included—as eighty-seventh, and in a less wealthy quarter they would have ranked somewhat higher. Stefano's net capital of 3,739 florins was certainly not a great fortune, especially if divided between the two brothers. Compared to the 79,000 florins declared by the wealthiest man of the quarter, Giovanni de' Medici, it seems modest indeed. On the other hand, Stefano's net worth was not so far behind the 4,396 florins recorded by Matteo Strozzi, whose eldest daughter Marco would eventually marry.[3]

In political terms as Alessandra acknowledged, Marco's father did not have a brilliant career. At the time of the betrothal in 1448 he had gone no further than a recent term in the

[2] Giovanni di Piero Parenti's political career and problems are outlined in G. Brucker, *Florentine Politics and Society, 1343–1378* (Princeton, 1962), pp. 69, 263n, 323–24. The family history and Marco's biography are reviewed briefly in L. Martines, *The Social World of the Florentine Humanists, 1390–1460* (Princeton, 1963), p. 346.

[3] See Martines, *Social World*, appendix 2.

Colleges, a respectable post, but second in dignity to the Gonfaloniere and eight priors who made up the Signoria; and two years later, already over seventy, he was rewarded by being selected as a prior.[4] As a merchant, on the other hand, Parente Parenti must have experienced steady prosperity, and Alessandra did not hesitate to pronounce his heir a rich man. Parente's tax return for 1446, made out in his name but clearly in the hand of Marco, gives a reasonably clear picture of the wealth he would pass on to his son. Following the prescribed form of such declarations, Parente first listed his house on the Via del Cocomero—the modern Via dei Ricasoli running north from the cathedral to Piazza San Marco—a nontaxable asset. In addition he owned four farms in the *contado* (the neighboring countryside) and a small house that was rented. Like most Florentines of his class, Parente had also invested in the Monte, the public debt, and the combined value of the shares he listed came to a little over 4,900 florins. From such assets the tax law allowed a personal deduction of two hundred florins for each dependent—or, to use the more expressive term of these documents, for each "mouth." Parente listed only three persons: himself, aged seventy; his wife Mona Tommaso, forty-eight; and Marco, then twenty-five. A younger daughter, Lessandra, for whose dowry a previous declaration listed a little over one thousand florins invested in the Monte, apparently was already married.[5]

As the only son, Marco inherited Parente's house, business, and properties. His tax report of 1457 shows many continuities with his father's of a decade before—and with the whole series of declarations made by both Parente and Stefano going back to the first *catasto*, a new, more accurate form of tax assessment begun in 1427.[6] Real estate was the most stable form of wealth. From time to time, property might be bought or sold, but most often families were either rounding out an

[4] On his father's election to the Signoria, see Marco's letter of 24 Oct. 1450; CS ser. 3, 131, fol. 58^{r-v}.

[5] A.S.F., *Catasto* 679.

[6] A.S.F., *Catasto* 827. Earlier declarations are to be found in *Catasto* vols. 498, 625, 679, 715.

existing holding or dividing one previously held in common. No wonder that when the boundaries of a property are described, a brother or cousin is often listed as one of the neighbors.

The house on the Via del Cocomero is a case in point. In the early *catasti* it is listed in the name of Stefano, Parente, and a nephew, Giovanni. Often such joint households were a temporary expedient following the death of the original owner; this was unlikely to have been the case here, however, since in 1433 Stefano gave his age as sixty-four, Parente's as fifty-five, and Giovanni's as thirty-one. Nonetheless, the house was eventually divided, for in 1457 Marco listed his cousins, the sons of Giovanni Parenti, as his immediate neighbors. On both sides of the household a new generation was coming into possession.

Subdivision of the common household has sometimes been taken to signify the fragmentation of the family and the growth of individualism. Perhaps so, but since Marco and his cousins remained his closest neighbors, it would be surprising if the same family feelings—and family tensions—did not remain. It simplified matters that Marco was an only son. A more prolific family would have had to face the difficult choice of overcrowding itself in its old house or sending its sons out to find a new one. Even so, most sons chose to build, buy, or rent as close to home as possible, thus continuing to enjoy the sociability of the family and its ties to longtime neighbors.

In the countryside, where residence was not involved, arrangements were more flexible. Farms, if they were large enough, could be legally divided; more simply, the produce, already shared between the urban proprietor and the peasant who actually worked the land, could be divided once again among the common heirs. Marco listed three farms in the Mugello in his report of 1457, all of which had been in Stefano's name in the first catasto, and in one of these his cousins were joint owners. This left Marco the possessor of a quarter of this farm's production of grain and "corn of various types." Of the two pigs, one was his, plus "a sucking pig." But, he reported, "there is no wine to be gathered at all."

A large part of Marco's inheritance came in the form of shares in the Monte. He declared 8,869 florins listed in his father's name, of which some 2,170 florins had been converted to funds for the dowries of his daughters, Ginevra and Lisa. This left 6,694 florins, against which Marco pleaded for some reduction, since "there still remains Agnoletta, for whose dowry I have done nothing." Beyond this already substantial sum, Marco listed 4,765 florins inscribed in his own name and 1,000 "with stipulation" in that of Giovanni Parenti.

These were considerable holdings, even when one has taken into account the fact that the market value of the shares would have been far less than the nominal value. It is striking, too, that Marco's declared holdings on the Monte exceeded those his father had listed in 1446 and 1451. Where had this additional capital come from? The most likely explanation is that both Parente and Marco had withdrawn capital from their business and put it into the safer, less entrepreneurial form of shares in the public debt. This is suggested by another part of the declaration. "I rent," Marco wrote, "from the friars of the Charterhouse a workshop in the Por Sta. Maria for forty florins a year . . . where we used to work in silk. Now it is approximately ten years I have retained it, although I no longer exercise the trade." Apparently he did not wish to cut himself off entirely from the silk business; he chose instead to keep up his rights to the shop in order "that I not lose the use of it."[7] But Marco had effectively entered the class that the Florentines called *scioperati*—men who kept up their guild membership for social or political reasons rather than for trade. Since unearned wealth always carries with it a certain prestige, this in some ways represented a jump in status. By withdrawing from the occupation of his uncle and father, Marco

[7] A new five-year agreement had been drawn up only a year before. It is not clear when precisely the Parenti abandoned silk manufacture, but it may have been soon after Marco's wedding. At that time Marco gave his bride a gown described by Alessandra Strozzi as being made of the finest material and a product of his own shop. In his catasto declaration of 1451, Marco's father declared, "I have neither trade, nor shop, nor earnings" (A.S.F., *Catasto* 715).

had taken their efforts to raise the family into the upper class of Florentine society one step further.

It would be wrong, however, to think of Marco as rich and carefree; at least, he did not want the notaries of the catasto to think so, and he filled his declaration with lists of debts and responsibilities. In the first place there were the eight mouths he had to feed: himself, aged thirty-seven, Caterina, his wife, twenty-six; Piero, his first-born, now eight; Gostanza, aged five; Marietta, three and a half; Ginevra, two; Lisa, one; and Agnoletta, only a month old. At 200 florins apiece, these dependents amounted to a deduction of 1,600 florins.

As head of this rapidly growing family, Parenti no doubt had many expenses. He owed the banker, Bono Boni, 120 florins, but there is no indication of the purpose of the loan. A second item was the 230 florins it cost to buy a neighboring house to enlarge his own. There were smaller sums as well: 10 florins to a tailor, 5 to a workman, and 5 more to a wet nurse called Bionda di Bruno—Blonde, daughter of Brown. Finally, a deduction was allowed for properties both in the city and the countryside that had once been held in the family and had since been "alienated."

His mother's death had left Marco with responsibilities of a different sort. By her will he was charged with a series of small charitable expenses. Simona, her niece, was to have clothing to a value of 15 florins. Several convents, the prisons, and a hospital had to have 10 florins apiece, and the canons of the cathedral, the friars of Santa Croce, and the seven friars who had witnessed the will received smaller sums. Finally, the friars of San Francisco in Fiesole were endowed with 4 florins per annum so that every year in perpetuity they could say an office for the soul of the departed.

Viewed from the distance of so many years, the exact size of sums spent in honoring the dead or in enlarging a house for a growing family is not critical. These details provide a focus for the imagination and a reminder of the reassuring ordinariness of life in any period. The catasto officials, on the other hand, took a less detached view of these matters, and they filled the margins with figuring and cross-references to other declarations where Marco's might be corroborated. When all was added in, they figured Parenti's total wealth as 3,689 florins, against which they allowed deductions of 1,837 florins, leaving a taxable "surplus" of 1,852 florins. Florentines paid a standard rate of .5 percent, a figure that seems remarkably low until one remembers that it is based on total wealth, not yearly income, and that it could be levied as often as the government saw the need.[8] In all, including a small head tax, Marco was assessed fi.9 s.11 d.3.

By itself the figure is not very helpful, but fortunately, the records for 1457 are unusually complete and a table showing the distribution of tax assessments has been worked out that allows us a reasonably accurate guide to Parenti's economic status. In that year there were 317 households that were assessed between 5 and 10 florins, representing approximately 4 percent of the 7,636 households paying taxes. In all, 97 percent of Florentine households paid 10 florins or less; only 227 households paid more. In short, Marco, with his assessment of a little over 9½ florins, probably stood just outside of the top 3 percent of taxpayers.[9]

Backed by these statistics, our estimate of Marco's economic status seems fairly secure. In 1457, however, Marco was still a young man and his responsibilities were considerable. It would be a reasonable guess that his income at that time was relatively low, a suspicion that can be confirmed by checking figures for other years. Marco listed his own and his father's previous assessments at the beginning of his 1469 declaration:

[8] On the operation of the catasto, see R. De Roover, *The Rise and Decline of the Medici Bank* (New York, 1966), pp. 23–25; and D. Herlihy and C. Klapisch, *Les toscans et leurs familles* (Paris, 1978).

[9] If we take into account paupers who paid no tax, the percentiles would be higher still. See De Roover, *Bank*, pp. 29–30. De Roover refers to the families paying from 1 to 10 florins as the "so-called 'middle classes.' Those paying 10 florins or more are the rich." By this breakdown, Marco Parenti stood at the top of the "middle classes" and at the threshold of the 2.13 percent of the population who were the "rich."

1427.	Stefano and Parenti di Giovanni Parenti	fi. 19	s. 11	d. 10
1451.	Parente di Giovanni Parenti	23	5	—
1457.	Marco di Parente Parenti	9	11	3
1468.	Marco	17	1	9

To this list we can also add the assessment found at the end of the 1469 declaration itself—fi. 19 s. 7 d. 3—and the much reduced figure for 1480 of fi. 9 s. 2 d. 6.[10]

Parenti's declaration for 1457 provides a rather low estimate of his financial status when compared to the figures for subsequent years. It seems clear that although Marco never equaled Parente's highest assessment, over the course of a lifetime he did not lag too far behind his father. There had been some fluctuations, but these were natural to the life cycle of families. Marco was able to maintain the family fortune and see a new generation safely launched.

By mid-century—the years of Marco's early manhood—the Parenti had found a place in the Florentine upper class. In two generations they had risen out of the ranks of the artisans and "new citizens" for whom Giovanni Parenti had been a spokesman, into the class Giovanni and his companions had opposed. In this new status the Parenti never achieved real prominence or power, but at least they had arrived. Thus in 1472, when Benedetto Dei, the crankiest of Florentine private chroniclers, compiled a list of leading Florentine families, whose presence was an ornament to the city and a "confusion to our enemies," the Parenti found a place.[11]

The commercial energies of his uncle and father had lifted

[10] The 1469 declaration is in *Catasto* 926; 1480 is in *Catasto* 1019.

[11] B. Dei, *La cronica*, ed. R. Barducci (Florence, 1984), p. 80. But one must be a little cautious regarding Dei's inclusion of the Parenti. Later in the chronicle Dei compiles another one of his endless and wonderful lists, this time of the richest families. Then he turns to the other side of the coin, asking rhetorically "where is the wealth" of a number of families. Here too the name Parenti occurs, though it does not seem likely that the reference is to Marco's family, but to the heirs of Michele di Ser Parenti, a wealthier lineage. Since Dei does not distinguish these two families, one cannot be sure that he had Marco Parenti in mind in the earlier list.

the family into this new niche, but it was Marco who inherited the benefits. First among them was the marriage to Caterina Strozzi. Marco's letters of the time show his pride in being connected to this old and prominent house, and in later years, as the Strozzi brothers rebuilt their fortunes, the connection became more prestigious. Equally, Marco was still a young man in 1454 when he was selected to the Signoria, an honor for which his father had waited until the end of his life. In education, too, Marco seems to have been privileged beyond his parents, and he became part of a circle of well-educated and socially prominent young men.

In a sense, though, the most notable of the privileges Marco inherited was the freedom to withdraw from the silk business that had created his family's prosperity. Of this important decision nothing is said either in his letters or in his private record book, but its significance seems clear. Marco was then a young man, recently and advantageously married. His father, nearing the end of his life, presumably was no longer able to direct the business, which would have to survive on the energies of the young—energies that were directed instead to establishing a household and raising a family, to the first steps of a political career, and to the literary and political interests of Marco's circle.

Seen against the background of his family's struggle to establish itself, Marco's decision to withdraw from the silk shop seems both a denial and a fulfillment. His was a familiar evolution, reenacted by men in every generation: the transfer of commercial capital into less risky forms of wealth, the eagerness of the sons of merchants for other enterprises, the acceptance of newer families into older political and cultural elites. By the same token, in the society at large, other compensating changes also occurred to maintain commercial vitality. Thus—contrary to what was once the assumption of historians—it is generally recognized that fifteenth-century Florence did not undergo any widespread withdrawal from commerce. While Marco was turning toward civic interests, his brother-in-law, Filippo Strozzi, was working with great determination to create one of the great commercial fortunes of the age.[12]

In a society so thoroughly mercantile, it would have been hard for anyone to detach himself from commercial concerns or the commercial outlook, nor had Marco any apparent desire to do so. Though no longer active in silk manufacture, he remained a member of the silk guild, the Por Santa Maria, and served several terms as a guild officer. Likewise, he twice served in the financial offices of the commune. His intimate connection with the Strozzi brothers was another link to the commercial world—and probably a source of some income—and his correspondence shows that he was called upon to assist them with a variety of commissions: usually personal, familial, or political, but also on occasion commercial.

In the closely kept pages of his ricordanze, his personal record book, Marco left a chart of his life as a bourgeois. Here we find the preoccupations of the householder and the persistence of mercantile habits in the silk merchant's son.

★

Marco's *Libro di ricordanze* is a particularly good example of a type of personal document characteristic of the Florentine upper class. Scores of them have survived in Florence, though elsewhere in Italy these private record books are almost unknown. The precise origins of the ricordanze are not clear.[13] One source was probably the *libro segreto*—the merchant's "secret book" in which he kept information of special significance to himself and his heirs. A second model was the no-

[12] See R. Goldthwaite, *Private Wealth in Renaissance Florence* (Princeton, 1968).

[13] On the origins and distribution of ricordanze, see G. Brucker, *Two Memoirs of Renaissance Florence* (New York, 1967), p. 9ff.; A. Sapori, *The Italian Merchant in the Middle Ages*, trans. P. A. Kennen (New York, 1970), p. 97ff.; C. Bec, *Les marchands ecrivains* (Paris, 1967), pp. 49–51; and A. Petrucci, ed., *Il libro di ricordanze dei Corsini* (Rome, 1965), introduction. Ricordanze have been extensively used recently by social historians. See especially W. F. Kent, *Household and Lineage in Renaissance Florence* (Princeton, 1977).

tarial protocol. Notaries played a key role in Italian commerce, since contracts, loans, property transfers, and obligations of all kinds were registered in their official books. It is reasonable to think that the individuals involved would want parallel records of their own. "Always when you have a paper drawn up," advised Paolo da Certaldo in his miscellany of rules and cautions, "have a book of your own and inscribe in this book the date, the name of the notary who registered the document, and the witnesses; write also the import of the document, so that your children, if they have need of it, can find it."[14]

However ricordanze originated, the keeping of such a record came to be seen as a kind of duty for the head of the household. "Be sure that in your books everything you do is described at length and that you never spare your pen and that you pay strict attention to your book," wrote Giovanni Morelli. The reward would be prosperity and the avoidance of many pitfalls; "you will not need to fear having to make restitution or that it will be demanded of your sons, and you will live freely, being firm and sound in your estate and without care."[15] Such fatherly instruction was itself a sort of inheritance, a practical wisdom that was handed on, like other, harder assets, for the benefit of future generations.

The core of these notebooks was evidently the need to keep personal affairs in good order. But good order is a wide and flexible concept and the head of a family had much to keep in mind besides his financial assets and obligations. The record book was a logical place to register whatever seemed of importance to the family. It became a record of births, deaths, and marriages in the immediate family, including such important ancillary information as the size of a dowry, the names of the brokers in a marriage contract, or the list of godparents to a newborn child. Civic honors and offices, too, even when no financial gain or obligation was involved, were often recorded; and from this it was a fairly simple step to make note

[14] Paolo da Certaldo, *Libro di buoni costumi* (Florence, 1945), p. 245.

[15] Giovanni di Paolo Morelli, *Ricordi*, ed. V. Branca (Florence, 1969), pp. 228–29.

of important events one had seen, especially while holding a public office.

The civic honors and offices that a man earned set his family's prestige as well as his own. Thus the head of a family who kept track of his own magistracies was helping to enhance the name of his descendants; similarly, he might search his family papers for evidence of such honors in generations past. Some ricordanze begin with a sort of genealogy, and at times this expands into large-scale family history. The best-known example is the "domestic chronicle" of Donato Velluti, a fourteenth-century Florentine who accumulated information on scores of his relatives, living and dead. Two centuries later the greatest of all Florentine historians, Francesco Guicciardini, began his career in history writing with his "Family Memoirs," a history of the Guicciardini family.[16]

These last examples seem far removed from the commercial "secret books" or notarial protocols. But it is not easy to insist on precise definitions here, as can be done with more public and literary genres. When a young patrician in the sixteenth century like Francesco Guicciardini set down the items of his personal affairs in much the same order as his grandfathers did, he was continuing their practice, but not in any conscious sense imitating a tradition. The notebooks express long-felt needs and habits in a society deeply imbued with both commercial virtues and family pieties.

This marriage of commercial reasoning and family spirit is celebrated in the most famous fifteenth-century discussion of family life, the *Book of the Family*, a dialogue written by Marco's brilliant contemporary and business associate Leon Battista Alberti. Though an architect and humanist, Alberti did not disdain the commercial virtues of his merchant forebears. Better than any practicing merchant he expressed the merchant's pride in his orderly and diligent life, and nowhere more pointedly than in a passage describing the young wife's first introduction to the ways of the household:

[16] N. Rubinstein, "The *Storie fiorentine* and the *Memorie di famiglia* by Francesco Guicciardini," *Rinascimento* 4 (1953): 171–225.

> After my wife had been settled in my house a few days, and after her first pangs of longing for her mother and family had begun to fade, I took her by the hand and showed her around the whole house. . . . At the end there were no household goods of which my wife had not learned both the place and purpose. Then we returned to my room, and, having locked the door, I showed her my treasures, silver, tapestry, garments, jewels, and where each thing had its place. . . .
>
> Only my books and records and those of my ancestors did I determine to keep well sealed both then and thereafter. These my wife not only could not read, she could not even lay hands on them. I kept my records at all times not in the sleeves of my dress, but locked up and arranged in order in my study, almost like sacred and religious objects.[17]

In his study, alone with his books and papers, a man is most fully the head of his household, most clearly the living representative of the family spirit.

★

Individual ricordanze have been most studied as they depart from the general form and purpose of the private book. The diaries of Morelli and Pitti, the domestic chronicle of Velluti, or the miscellany of Rucellai have become well known because they seem to leave behind the routine world of the merchant's daily life to approach autobiography, chronicle, or homiletics. Marco Parenti's book of ricordanze, on the other hand, is none of these things, and its interest is that it takes us directly into the thick of his commonplace concerns.

As a good Christian, Marco begins with an invocation:

> In the name of God and his virgin mother, St. Mary, and of St. Nicholas, angel and archangel, and of St. John the Baptist and of the Evangelist, and of St. Peter and St. Paul and St. Mark, and of St. Mary Magdalene and St. Catherine, and of all the Apostles and Evangelists and saints, male and female, of God; and may this book in its beginning, middle, and end be to their honor, and by their mercy may it please them to

[17] L. B. Alberti, *The Family in Renaissance Florence*, trans. R. N. Watkins (Columbia, S.C., 1969), pp. 208–209.

> give me grace so that what I will write in this book may be to the benefit of my soul and of my body and my goods.[18]

Above this is written, in Roman numerals, the date: 1447. Below we read: "This is the book of Marco Parenti, son of Parente di Giovanni Parenti, in which I will write all my records [ricordi] and debtors and creditors, and it is marked A."

The *Libro di ricordanze*, utilitarian instrument though it may have been, was not for that reason in any sense casual or negligible. The young man who solemnly inscribed MCCCCXLVII across the first page of his blank notebook felt that he was beginning the chronicle of his adult life, which might be said to date from this moment. In asking grace for this book he was asking it also for the life it would record, and he was not apt to separate the prosperity of his soul from the health of his body or the wealth of his possessions.

That life is a book is a time-honored metaphor, though there can be few cultures that have taken it more literally than these Florentines did. It seems doubtful, too, that these men could open any book without being reminded somehow of the widest meanings of these still scarce and potent objects: the book of life, the book of memory, the book of nature, above all *the* book itself, the Bible. In this sense, the simple personal account book becomes simultaneously the book of my life, the book in which I will make an accounting of my life. No wonder then that soul, body, and goods are all involved; no wonder either that, though still in his twenties, Marco looks so far forward, asking "may this book in its beginning, middle, and end be to their honor."

Subsequent pages, filled with columns of figures or the records of a thousand trivial purchases, seldom recollect the solemn invocation of the opening page. But, following Marco's hint that the book of life must have its closing as well as its opening, let us turn to the final pages of his ricordanze. Here there is an entry written in a new and looser hand:

> MCCCCLXXXXVII. I record this 9th day of June that Marco di

[18] *Ricordanze*, fol. 1^r.

> Parente di Giovanni Parenti came to this end and died, leaving me, Piero, his legitimate and natural son, since there was no will, his universal heir; he granted me and required me that I should continue to write in all his books in my own hand as matters occur. And so, executing his will, I will begin here, as will be seen.[19]

Obedient to his father's instructions, Piero began his own entries. His first duty was to enter a notice of the exact time of his father's death and the details and expenses of the funeral honors, performed "as his rank and mine merited."

The same mood of filial piety guided him in performing another, less obvious duty in making good one considerable omission in his father's records. Though Marco had noted from time to time his involvement in civic office, especially the high honor of a term on the Signoria, he had never set down a full list of these. It seems he thought this outside the stricter purposes of the ricordanze, except where expenses or obligations were involved. Piero, however, wanted his father's honors to be recorded, and he did so on a blank half-page near the end of his father's entries, though unfortunately his list is without information about dates or numbers of terms served, for which Piero must have lacked the necessary details.[20]

With this retrospective listing of his father's offices, Piero was performing the same duty toward his father that Marco over the years had performed for him, as for all the members of the family. For each of them, Marco had annotated the first entry of their names with the briefest outline of subsequent events—usually death or marriage, but occasionally something more—turning the first pages of the ricordanze into a very rudimentary family chronicle. With Marco's death, the ricordanze came full circle and passed into the hands of a new generation. Turning to the first page of the notebook, where his father had written his long invocation to the saints, Piero now added his own name to the statement of ownership: "And continued by me, Piero di Marco Parenti, his son and heir *ab intestato*, as appears on page 85 and 86 of this book."

[19] Ibid., fol. 86^{r}.

[20] Ibid., fol. 20^{v}.

Marriage and family take up the first pages of Marco's notebook, as they did the first years of his adult life. His first entry gives the particulars of his betrothal. "I record," he wrote, using the universal introductory formula of these documents,

> that on the 4th day of August, 1447, I took for my wife Caterina, daughter of the late Matteo di Simone di Filippo di Messer Lionardo degli Strozzi, and of Madonna Alessandra, daughter of the late Filippo Macinghi, his wife. And on the said day I swore in Sta. Maria Sopra Porto; and I am to have one thousand florins in dowry in the following manner: that is half, which is 500 florins from the said Mona Alessandra in money and gifts, and the other half, which is 500 florins, from the Monte del Comune of Florence inscribed in the name of the said Caterina, my wife, that will come due on the 30th of June, 1448.[21]

It is in the nature of ricordanze to tell us much more about the financial obligations of matrimony than the human ones, and Marco was not the sort to leave to chance or memory the many details of expenses or credits that clustered around the marriage. First there was the payment of the dowry itself, five hundred florins of which were due at the time of marriage. Five hundred more would come when Alessandra's investment in the Dowry Fund (Monte della Doti) matured. Marco listed four payments from Alessandra between late October and early January, when the wedding took place, and two more the following spring. In addition a considerable part of the five hundred florins was to come in the form of gifts. Most of them consisted of cloth and clothing. There was a long overgown (*cioppa*) done in white damask and trimmed with the fur of marten; another of embroidered woolen cloth, also trimmed with marten; still another; a dress called a *gamurra*, in white and blue silk with green velvet sleeves; another in a deep blue color. There were also sixteen braccie (roughly eleven yards) of cloth in a rich red dye; seventeen shirts that had been "worked"; ten towels; thirty kerchiefs and thirty more handkerchiefs; two large towels; and a single braccia of

[21] Ibid., fol. 2ʳ.

white damask. Other personal ornaments and furnishings made up the rest, including a string of large corals; two silver-handled knives; six silk caps for a man; a dark grey belt decorated with light silver; a devotional book; and a basin ornamented with the Strozzi arms and his own.[22]

These were only the major gifts. There were also the "unappraised gifts" and these followed the same pattern, being largely items to wear, though of smaller value. They included an embroidered kerchief; two ivory combs; nine hanks of hemp or flax; twenty-four bonnets; some ribbons; three pairs of red hose; two pairs of shoes or slippers; a pair of scissors; and two lady's collars made of linen.

The gifts would go to equip Marco's household as part of the comforts with which he and his wife would begin their life together. The items have a certain fascination as signs of their expected style of living. There is no mistaking the accent on personal ornament and luxurious dress—a luxuriousness that cannot entirely be explained as the kind of showiness that gift giving requires. Such ostentation is a reminder of how much of a man's wealth was carried on his back and of how much the gulf between rich and poor was made a matter for daily spectacle. No wonder it seemed so saintly a thing to exchange cloaks with a beggar. And yet, scanning the lists again, we are also reminded of how empty and uncomfortable their "palaces" often were, with rooms so chill and bare by comparison to their richly furnished bodies.[23]

Furnishings were not entirely neglected, though. Matching *cassoni*, or marriage chests, were a standard part of the bride's trousseau. In this case the arrangements were made by Marco, perhaps because he could better afford the expense. The painter he chose was one whom he had dealt with before—another reason for Marco undertaking it himself. This was Domenico Veneziano, an important Venetian artist who spent

[22] Ibid., fol. 3^{r}. A convenient discussion of Renaissance dress, including a glossary, can be found in J. Herald, *Renaissance Dress in Italy, 1400–1500* (London, 1981).

[23] See A. Schiaparelli, *La casa fiorentina e i suoi arredi nei secoli xiv e xv* (Florence, 1908).

some time in Florence and whose Santa Lucia altarpiece is one of the treasures of the Uffizi.[24]

Domenico was paid fifty florins for his work, including the cabinetry and gilding that would have been done by other craftsmen. Because this was well above the average price for these chests, they must have been large and well made. These particular cassoni have not survived, but we have some idea of what they would have been like: large wooden chests, probably raised on carved feet; a single long, painted panel on the front surrounded by carved moldings and pilasters; similar but smaller panels at each end; and a flat wooden lid, also painted inside and out. The decorations and depictions on cassoni were varied but conventional. The large panels may have shown an allegory—the seven liberal arts, or the cardinal virtues—or they may have illustrated a scene from ancient history, the Bible, or Italian *novelle*. The smaller panels on the end probably showed just a figure or two and perhaps armorial decorations, while the lid might have been painted with reclining youths symbolizing love, or just decorated with tile or tapestry patterns; and everywhere gilding would have been liberally employed to give an effect of sumptuousness.[25]

Marco's cassoni were meant for display as well as utility, and with them came smaller coffers, also decorated, and a mirror. Together these made up the largest item of furnishing, but others also followed. Marco ordered a bed made of walnut, decorated with his and the Strozzi arms done in intarsia. He also made payments for another bed, for a new headboard with sculpted capitals, for some small chests to go at the foot of the bed, a footboard, and a pair of walnut *cassapanche*—chests that doubled as benches. All this came from a woodworker or cabinetmaker, but there are also payments for several items from a blacksmith, including a bell and a pair of andirons. And a lesser-known painter, Stefano di Francesco

[24] *Ricordanze*, fols. 5^{r}, 9^{r}. On Domenico Veneziano and Marco's patronage, see H. Wohl, *The Paintings of Domenico Veneziano* (London, 1980), pp. 19–23.

[25] On *cassoni*, see Callman, *Apollonio di Giovanni* (London, 1974), ch. 2 and 3.

Magnolini (the brother of Masolino), was commissioned for five and one-half florins to make a polychromed Virgin Mary in relief.

These were not small items. To an artisan, thirty-odd florins for a bed would have seemed a large expenditure. But in comparison with the rest of Marco's own expenses at this time, it is striking how little went into durable furnishings of this sort and how much was spent on cloth, clothing, and jewelry. As his father's only son and heir, Marco would inherit the family house on the Via del Cocomero. All the more reason to spend liberally on dressing his Caterina, and so folio after folio of the ricordanze is covered with the particulars of these lavish gifts.

From his own workshop he bought a large piece of crimson silk velvet. This was for a *giornea*, a sort of gown or underdress. At three and one-half florins a braccia it was expensive cloth, and the twenty-four and one-half braccie (or sixteen yards) he needed cost more than eighty-five florins. Beyond this, there was the lining, also in red and probably in cotton, ordered from another clothmaker, thirty-two ringlets or eyelets from the goldsmith, soft leather or fur trimmings for the edgings, and a relatively small sum to the tailor. In all, the giornea cost more than 101 florins, twice what Marco had paid Domenico Veneziano for the marriage chests.

In the same accounts we find that eighteen braccie of the same crimson silken velvet went for a kind of cloak or overdress called a *cotta*. One hundred and twenty gilded ringlets or eyelets went on the front of it, and another one hundred smaller ones decorated the sleeves, which were also embroidered. Soft skins or furs went on the hem and a fringe in gold and green, as well as silk ribbons and braid. This cotta, being less full than the giornea, cost somewhat less: a little over seventy-three florins.

A third gift was "a garland of peacock tails embellished with silver and pearls." It was less expensive than the two gowns, but must have been even more splendid. In this account he noted payment for five hundred "eyes" of select peacock tail feathers, and a second sum for three hundred more. The peacock feathers were complemented with artificial ones—golden *tremolanti*—and enameled flowers in red and blue. Sums were spent for gold leaf, for six ounces of pearls, and for tinsel and brass. The whole wonderful assemblage was completed with "eleven rosettes made of peacock feathers."

One might well stop to wonder how anyone would wear, between dress and cloak, forty-two braccie of heavy velvet—some twenty-eight yards, if we can trust the standard equivalences. Nor is it easy to imagine the sight of eight hundred peacock feathers on a girl's head. But for the mother of the bride-to-be there was nothing but pride and delight. Writing to her son far off in Naples, Alessandra luxuriated in the richness of Marco's gifts. The cloak and dress would be made of "the most beautiful cloth to be found in Florence," a product of Marco's own *bottega* (workshop); and she was no less pleased by the "garland of feathers and pearls, costing 80 florins," or her headdress with "two tresses of pearls, worth 60 florins or more." "When she goes out," wrote Alessandra, "she will be wearing more than 400 florins." And more clothes had been ordered for the time of the wedding. "He cannot do enough for her," she concluded.[26]

★

With Marco's ricordanze in hand, we might go on for some time window-shopping in this gallery of Renaissance luxuries. But the notebook has something to tell us about more mundane expenses, too. Five florins went to the marriage broker, who was paid a percentage of the total of the dowry and so profited from what was clearly an inflating market. The commune, too, had a claim on the dowry and Marco paid a gabelle on each portion. And when the second half of the dowry came due, Marco recommitted it to the Monte, receiving a credit of 2,500 florins for the 500 invested. Apparently, despite his expenses at this time, he had no immediate need of the cash; and the fact that he chose to invest in the Monte rather than

[26] *Lettere*, pp. 5–6.

in his business tells its own story. Finally, before we get completely away from Marco's gifts to Caterina, one last item should not be omitted: a note, dated November 1490, of the resale of a number of these pieces of cloth and linings to a *rigattiere*—a dealer in used clothing—for the considerable sum of sixty-eight florins.

The chief, most serious business of these early years was beginning a family. Immediately following the notice of the betrothal, Marco entered the births (and often the deaths) of his children. Given the language and format of the account book, they were, in a sense, subsequent items in the account he held with Caterina.

Caterina proved to be fertile, though unfortunately, given the prejudices of the age and the necessity of providing dowries, mostly with females. Their children were: Piero, born January 1451; Maria, born August 1451, died 1452; Gostanza Maria, born June 1452, and subsequently married; Maria Magdalena, born May 1454, also married, died in 1493, leaving six children, three male and three female; Ginevra Matea, born September 1455, died 1463; Lisa Tomasa, born January 1457, died 1458; Agnoletta Margherita, born February 1458, died 1458; Lisabetta Maria, born March 1459, later married.

These names and brief histories filled the folio at the beginning of the notebook that Marco had reserved for this purpose, and a note directs us to one last birth recorded many pages later:

> I record that up to this day, the 17th of June, 1463, I have had eight children, between males and females, from Caterina my wife, as appears in this notebook on page 2. And on the said day, Friday, at the tenth hour, was born to me a male child by the said Caterina my wife; and I gave him for a first name Giovanni and for a second name Parente, and so he was baptized in S. Giovanni in Florence; and my companions [godfathers] were Ser Grifo di Giovanni Griselli, notary, and Vespasiano di Filippo [da Bisticci], bookseller. May it please God to give him in this world a happy life and grace and in the other life eternal glory, Amen.[27]

[27] *Ricordanze*, fol. 57^{v}.

In the margin next to this entry—so characteristic a mixture of accountancy and prayer—we read a second, added soon after: "And on the 7th day of September, 1463, in the morning before daybreak, he left this life, and was buried in Sta. Reparata. May God have received his soul."

The loss of this second, late-born son must have been a particular grief, but the formulae of birth and death vary only a little. For the girls the place of baptism and of burial is recorded, but nothing is said of godparents, if there were any. Marriage or death, the two events that ushered them out of the family and beyond Marco's protection, is all there is of a life history, though a note directs us to another page where the details of betrothal and dowry can be found.

In the case of Piero, firstborn and heir, Marco's entry is a little fuller. He was born away from the city "in the Mugello, at Ronta, in the house of the sons of Giovanni Parenti [i.e. Marco's grandfather] where in that year we had fled the plague." As a result the baptism was in the local church and most of the godparents, "except two from Florence," were local people. Listing them on the facing page, Marco put the two Florentines—Tanai de' Nerli and Mona Caterina, the widow of Benedetto Bianciardi—at the top of their respective lists, carefully bracketing off the others as being "from Ronta." Finally, he noted his own age and that of his wife at this auspicious moment: he was twenty-eight years and eight months old, she eighteen years and eight months.

The marginal annotations for Piero are also a little more informative than for his sisters. We learn that in April of 1467 he was "veduto de' Signori"—nominated for the priorate, a civic honor that showed he had come of age politically. A second note, undated, indicates that Piero married and points to the page where this is entered. Finally, in July 1482, Piero, like Marco and Parente before him, was seated as a prior. But the fullest of these marginal notices is not Piero's. It belongs to Caterina herself:

> On the 8th day of May, 1481, on the 9th hour, she passed from this life, to me so very joyous and happy. May God have received her soul, as I certainly believe because of her kindness

> and the worthiness of her life and the great honesty and grace of her ways. She was 50 years old exactly. I buried her in our grave at Sta. Maria del Fiore as honorably as one can according to the law.[28]

This is almost all we have to tell us of the companionship between Marco and Caterina, and given the nature of ricordanze it is rather remarkable that we have even this much. Though historians of the family have sometimes forgotten it, the function of these notebooks was not, after all, to document the emotions. Even an entry as affecting as this one still obeys the rule and format of the account book. Marco's little eulogy is placed exactly at the side of the initial entry recording the betrothal that had made her his own. Like the transverse lines that score out a debt once it has been paid, in effect this notice of Caterina's death sorrowfully cancels an obligation taken on so eagerly more than thirty years before.

This growing family necessarily left its traces in Marco's book. Now wet-nurses, dowry investments, and wedding arrangements take up more and more space, and the inevitable lists of tailor's bills (never again so exuberant in their detail) increasingly include such items as "a gamurra, rose-colored, embroidered in silk with sleeves of green velvet, for Gostanza."

Gostanza (or Constance) was Marco and Caterina's eldest surviving daughter, and a review of the brief items concerning her can serve for all. Under 1452, the year of her birth, we find expenses for a wet-nurse with whom she stayed only four months, at a cost of five and one-half lire per month. For reasons not stated, Gostanza was then given to another woman who lived "outside of the gate of [Santa] Croce," who nursed her for sixteen and one-half months for only five lire a month.

The infant was hardly weaned before it was time to start providing for her future. In September of 1454, when she was little more than two years old, Marco invested 140 florins in her name in the Dowry Fund. The money was invested for fifteen years at 14 percent and would ensure her a dowry of

[28] Ibid., fol. 2r.

one thousand florins when it matured. Marco duly noted the provisions: "In case said girl should die, may God save her, before she marries, I must notify the Monte officials within one month and they are obliged to return the capital to me, that is fi. 140. But if she lives and marries, may God give her good fortune, the fifteen years having elapsed, which will be in September of 1469, and the marriage having been consummated, the officials of the Monte must pay to her husband, whoever he is, 1,000 florins."[29] Finally, a little more than a year later, Marco added a further two hundred florins to the girl's eventual dowry with a small second investment to mature in November 1470.

Gostanza was one of those lucky ones who survived the awful toll of childhood disease, and she was doubly lucky in that her family's advancing fortunes brought her a husband with one of the oldest of Florentine names. He was Filippo Buondelmonti—a member of the family whose marital feud two centuries before was remembered by Florentines as the origin of the fierce rivalry between the Guelfs and Ghibellines. But there is no need to go back to the chronicles to sense the prestige of the connection Gostanza was making. "I record this day the 15th of March 1472," Marco wrote, "that I married Gostanza, my daughter, to Filippo di Lorenzo di Messer Andrea di Messer Lorenzo Buondelmonti; and it was sworn that day in Orto San Michele; and the arbiters were Messer Luigi di Piero di Messer Luigi Guicciardini for their side and for ours Lorenzo di Piero di Cosimo de' Medici, with a dowry of 1,400 florins di sugello."

Clearly this was an alliance negotiated at the very highest level of the Florentine patriciate. In addition to the two illustrious arbiters, Marco names Piero di Neri Acciaiuoli and Lorenzo Carducci as playing the part of go-between, and Lorenzo de' Medici himself personally presided over the arrangements. The time wouid come when some Florentine patricians would resent Lorenzo's close attention to their marriage plans—one of the ways in which his regime began to look,

[29] Ibid., fol. 40v.

in their terms, more princely than civil. But it is most unlikely that Marco harbored any such feelings about the young Lorenzo, only recently brought to power by his father's death. The marriage was too advantageous, the attention too flattering for one of Parenti's social position to resent it. Well might he conclude, "let us give thanks to God, from whom all good comes"—though he may have added in some mental footnote that being a good and loyal brother-in-law to Filippo Strozzi, for so long a dubious honor, had finally paid off.

As far as the family record is concerned, Gostanza's marriage was both a climax and an abrupt conclusion. After this point we hear no more of her in the ricordanze, though relations between the two families must have remained cordial since Filippo Buondelmonti, her husband, appears several times acting for Marco and the family. He was, for example, one of the arbiters named in connection with her brother Piero's wedding. But for Gostanza herself, marriage effectively removed her from the family, placing her beyond Marco's protection, unless by misfortune she should become widowed and so return to her family.

For Piero, on the other hand, the opposite was true. As only son and heir, he remained at the center. For him marriage was only a step toward renewing the family and inheriting its assets and obligations, as symbolized by his continuation of the ricordanze. His marriage in 1480 to Onesta, the daughter of Antonio degli Alessandri, brought him a dowry of 1,500 florins and a long list of children—a list begun by Marco and continued by Piero himself. The firstborn was baptized Marco, and just as he had done at Piero's birth, Marco solemnly recorded Piero's age and his own. Piero was thirty-two years and eight months old; Marco himself was sixty-one years and five months.

As a male, Piero also had opportunities and obligations beyond the family, and several of these were entered in Marco's book. In 1477, for example, the city sent an embassy to Naples to congratulate King Ferrante on his marriage and Piero Parenti accompanied them as one of the *giovani*—young men not yet able to be ambassadors themselves but worthy of the honor of filling out their train. For the young man's father, it was an expensive apprenticeship. Not including the horse and trappings Piero bought for his father in Naples, Marco spent 225 florins. Nearly a hundred florins went just to outfit Piero for the trip.

On another, less ceremonial occasion, Piero was elected Podestà of Lari, one of Florence's subject towns, where Marco also had served a term. These appointments were usually for six months and required establishing a temporary household away from Florence. Marco made Piero a loan of the necessary household goods, but this time Piero would have a salary and there was no question of a gift. Marco listed all the items in his book and had them properly evaluated, entering it all as a debt against his son's name. A typical item was "three good white coverlets, that is 2 'da signore' [suitable for the master] and 1 'da famigli' [for servants]." Another reads "6 spoons and 6 forks in silver, weighing 11 ounces; two large plates of tin, 2 others a little smaller; 2 more lesser plates; 4 small plates; 6 serving dishes; another similar; 6 large soup bowls; 6 medium bowls; 4 bowls with a straight border; 12 fine little bowls; in all 45 pieces in tin, weighing 64 pounds."[30]

Since his father was long-lived and his wife fertile, Piero soon needed to establish a household of his own. Again Marco provided the necessities and—leaving little to chance or charity—carefully listed and appraised them. Most of the inventory consists of beds, mattresses, and chests, but there are one or two of greater interest: "a hoist with rope and two buckets for the well" along with some kind of lye toilet and a "painted *desco da parto*"—a wooden tray used in childbirth and usually decorated with a Nativity or perhaps a Triumph of Love or Chastity. All this, Marco recorded, belonged to "my house, next to Bernardo Rinieri, and consigned to Piero, my aforementioned son, for his residence and that of his family."[31]

The house that Piero had taken over was not a separate unit, in the modern fashion. Over time families like the Parenti both acquired and subdivided properties, so that the "palace"

[30] Ibid., fol. 68ᵛ.

[31] Ibid., fols. 79ᵛ, 80ʳ.

of a wealthy Florentine was not really one house, but several. In his childhood Marco had been part of a joint household belonging to the heirs of his grandfather, Giovanni Parenti. Their house, like their silk shop, was shared between the two brothers and a nephew: Stefano, Parente, and the younger Giovanni. Since then the property had been severed, but as the ricordanze shows, Marco had also been buying bits and pieces when he could. One of these was the house now in Piero's hand.

The house had been bought many years before and in a somewhat curious manner. Since it lay between his own property and that of his near neighbors, Bernardo and Filippo Rinieri, both sides had an interest in it and were "in competition" to acquire it. The house had been part of a charitable bequest to the Hospital of San Matteo, and the consuls of the Cambio Guild who administered the hospital chose to sell it in a blind auction: "The said offer of the said house in contention between Filippo Rinieri, above-mentioned, and myself, each of us was to make a secret bid on a slip of paper. Because said Filippo Rinieri offered with his slip to the above-mentioned consuls and their notary 221 florins, and I offered with my bid 230 florins, the said house remained with me and is mine."[32]

Marco's shrewd bid had won him a neat victory. But the Rinieri, an old and proud family, were now immediate neighbors—"neighbors with a common wall" as the saying went—and twice more there would be some contention between them. In 1472 Marco recorded in his notebook that Bernardo Rinieri had "built a covered wooden terrace on the common wall between his houses and mine above his roofs and mine; this terrace juts out and drips on my roof, which by rights he cannot do."[33] The matter was settled by an agreement on Rinieri's part that the terrace would only remain on Parenti's sufferance and could be removed at his own expense whenever Marco wished.

A second dispute was not so easily settled. This time Marco

[32] Ibid., fol. 56ʳ.

[33] Ibid., fol. 70ʳ.

was the apparent transgressor and Bernardo the aggrieved neighbor, and Bernardo insisted on seeking satisfaction in court. "I record," wrote Rinieri on the seventh of July, 1487, in his own ricordanze, "that on the 6th of said month, that is yesterday, Marco di Parente, my neighbor with a common wall, hastily had constructed a window on the garden wall, or truly the wall overlooking my courtyard; and I was forced to go to the Palace of the Podestà to secure a claim against him."[34] And below he recorded a favorable judgment requiring Marco to rewall the window and pay costs.

It must have been a tempting spot for a window, since Rinieri noted that many years earlier the same issue had arisen with the previous occupant and the Tower Officials had several times forbidden it—a fact that Rinieri was sure Marco was aware of but deliberately chose to disregard. But of course Marco had his own version of the incident, which he in turn confided to his ricordanze. He claimed that he had obtained a favorable opinion from the Tower Officials and had hoped to bring the case before them. In such cases, he asserted, the Tower Officials use common sense, not the "sophistical" reasons of the Podestà. Unfortunately Rinieri had been able to "fix" enough votes at the Tower so that he had no hope at all of having the case transferred; "and so, having made only a negligent defense at the Palace of the Podestà, I received a judgment against me, in which I suffered a great wrong, since all Florence is full of similar examples."[35]

But Rinieri won his case and the last word belongs to him. In his mind there was no explanation for the incident except his neighbor's fractious character. Marco had obstinately disregarded the prohibition enforced against the former occupant many years earlier "because he is a disgraceful person with a perverse nature—"uomo schandoloso e di perversa natura."

[34] A.S.F., *Conventi soppressi*, 95, fol. 173^{r}. On fol. 164^{v} there is a reference to the earlier dispute. The families were not always at odds: at the same time as the dispute over the window, Rinieri recorded that he stood as *compare* to a daughter of Filippo Strozzi, though by the time he wrote down the entry, he seems to have forgotten the infant's name (fol. 173^{r}).

[35] *Ricordanze*, fol. 81^{r}.

Fortunately not all of Marco's additions or alterations to his property resulted in such contention. A poor neighbor was bought out in classic fashion. Since she was in need of money, Marco lent her a substantial sum, with half of the property as security and the proviso that he would have first rights if the house were sold. A year later the house was his. Along with these extensions of his property, Marco also invested considerable sums on rebuilding and renovation; and—to judge by the folios that he covered with the details of accounts with masons, woodworkers, and smiths—he devoted considerable time and thought as well.

No enterprise since his marriage occupies so much attention in the ricordanze. There is a feast of payments: to the brickmakers for bricks, flooring tiles, and roofing tiles of all sorts; to the Opera del Duomo, the building yards of the cathedral, for beams, rafters, and joists; to the blacksmith for hinges, latches, bars, mullions, and those great iron hooks or hitching rings that still adorn Florentine *palazzi*; to the stone cutter for slabs and paving stones for stairways, door jambs, window sills, and thresholds; to the master mason for his daily labor and that of his workers; to other workers for sawing, plastering, painting, or cleaning up the rubble.

The profusion of detail is bewildering, while the vocabulary is often technical beyond the resources of the best dictionary. (Is any other language so rich in words for brick and tile?) And in the end we learn more about the price of nails and bricks or the daily wages of skilled and unskilled masons—information more useful to the economic historian than the biographer—than we do about Marco's intentions.[36]

But here and there items stand out as clues to the shape of Marco's rebuilding. Doors and windows were being cut or refitted, several of the doors being described as "all' antica" or "in arco all' antica"—that is, in the form of a Roman archway. Some or all of these must have been interior doors, but another is described as "a door on the street 3 braccie wide and 5 high" with considerable attention being paid to its stone jambs, cornice, threshold, and moldings. Another payment

[36] R. Goldthwaite, *The Building of Renaissance Florence* (Baltimore, 1980), p. 441.

was for raising the roof of the kitchen and the adjoining wall and "to raise the whole roof of my low house equal to the house beside" and to construct a new eave on the large roof. The doorway to the garden was also reworked, so too the garden and courtyard walls, and a pergola was built in the garden. Bells were bought for the doors and a large bell for the street door. Inside, a wall was taken down in the ground floor room and the enlarged room retiled and plastered, and much new material went into two stairways, including the ornament of a black marble ball.

It is not easy to visualize all these details, but the overall intention becomes a little clearer. Marco's first interest, apparently, was in the outward face of his house. The enlarged and decorated street entrance, the raising of the roof, and construction of a new eave for the whole indicate that he was probably trying to bring the several parts of his house together behind a single façade. At the same time his courtyard and garden—the private side of the house—would also be made more attractive. The house would gain a grander entrance, a larger hall on the ground floor, new stairs, and doorways in the proper classicizing style.

Rebuilding projects of this sort were a common preoccupation of wealthier Florentines in this period. The central inspiration was the great palace faced with rusticated stone that Michelozzo built for Cosimo de' Medici. But with few exceptions—notably Luca Pitti and Filippo Strozzi—the builders of these bourgeois "palaces" had to work within the limitations imposed by their crowded ancestral neighborhoods. Adjoining houses were difficult to acquire and costly to raze and rebuild. It was easier and more economical to reuse and harmonize old structures, a practice followed even by as rich a citizen as Giovanni Rucellai in the construction and extension of his famous palazzo.[37] Marco's own project was certainly more modest. Nonetheless, the indications are that he was playing his part in the great campaign of private building that swept through Florence in his generation.

[37] B. Preyer, "The Rucellai Palace," in *Giovanni Rucellai ed il suo Zibaldone*, ed. A. Perosa, vol. 2, *A Florentine Patrician and His Palace* (London, 1981), p. 175.

CHAPTER 2

EDUCATION AND POLITICS

★

MARCO PARENTI'S practical training in business is not likely to have been all the education he received. Scattered references in his own records and in the writings of a number of Florentine intellectuals point to his familiarity with some of the leading intellectuals of his day. It is fair to assume that Marco must have been conversant with their ideas and interests as well, and for this reason he has sometimes been included in the ranks of Florentine humanists. It remains difficult, however, to draw these fragments of evidence together into any clear picture of his formal education or intellectual attainments.[1]

To his mother-in-law, the young Marco certainly seemed a man of refinement. Alessandra described him at the time of his betrothal as "vertudioso," that is, as her editor comments, "Buono e colto," well mannered or well educated.[2] Later in her correspondence she also called her son-in-law "studious" and remarked on his penmanship—in those days especially a desirable accompaniment of a good education.

[1] Marco Parenti is included in Lauro Martines' sample of humanists in his study of the social standing of the Florentine humanists. "Nothing is known about the identity of Marco's teachers," Martines writes, "Della Torre believed that he was to some extent an auto-didact. He was, at all events, exceptionally well-trained in Latin and philosophy." Martines, *The Social World of the Florentine Humanists, 1390–1460* (Princeton, 1963), p. 346.

[2] *Lettere*, pp. 3, 10.

Alessandra—like all but the most exceptional women of her day—had little formal education, but other, more cultivated minds shared her assessment of Marco. At one time or another intellectuals of the stature of Filelfo, Donato Acciaiuoli, Alamanno Rinuccini, Cristoforo Landino, and Benedetto Colucci paid brief compliments to his learning. Filelfo found Marco "learned," as did Rinuccini, who also remarked, however, on his ignorance of Greek. Landino gave Marco a minor part among the Aristotelian disputants of his Camaldolese Disputations. More substantial, perhaps, is the evidence of Donato Acciaiuoli's friendship and his invitation to Marco in one letter to exchange ideas on active and contemplative virtue.[3] Marco had a relationship of a different kind with another leading humanist intellectual, the architect Leone Battista Alberti, for whom he acted as procurator (or business agent) in the 1450s.[4]

A more revealing, though still fleeting, glimpse of Marco's intellectual interests and associations comes from the biographies written by his friend Vespasiano da Bisticci. Parenti was not one of the "illustrious men of the fifteenth century," even by Vespasiano's generous standards, but he is mentioned in the *vita* of Franco Sacchetti. In describing the character of this virtuous patrician and friend of learning, Vespasiano composed a loving description of the meetings of a circle of young Florentines who during the 1450s gathered occasionally at Sacchetti's villa just outside Florence. Here we find the young Marco, still in his twenties; here too we seem to find the ideal ambience that nourished the more liberal side of the minds of these young men.[5]

[3] See A. Della Torre, *Storia dell' Accademia platonica di Firenze* (Florence, 1902), pp. 320–21; E. Garin, *Medioevo e Rinascimento* (Bari, 1966), pp. 232–34.

[4] G. Mancini, *Vita di L. B. Alberti* (Florence, 1911), pp. 258–59, 414, 451; A. Parronchi, "Otto piccoli documenti per la biografia dell' Alberti," *Rinascimento*, 2d ser., 12 (1972): 229–35.

[5] Vespasiano da Bisticci, *Vite di uomini illustri del secolo xv*, ed. P. D'Ancona and E. Aeschlimann (Milan, 1951), pp. 431–34; translated as *Renaissance Princes, Popes, and Prelates*, by W. George and E. Waters (New York, 1963), pp. 403–405.

Sacchetti's guests included a number who were important to the cultural and political life of their city. The guest of honor was not a Florentine but a Byzantine Greek, Argyropulos, "a pilgrim in this country, having lost his own." Argyropulos had been brought to Florence largely through the efforts of Donato Acciaiuoli, the patrician intellectual now best remembered for his translation of Leonardo Bruni's *History of the Florentine People.* Acciaiuoli was afraid that with the disappearance of Bruni's generation the revival of learning would fade, and in Argyropulos he found a teacher of Greek and philosophy who would exercise a considerable influence on the men of his own generation.[6] Acciaiuoli, too, was one of Sacchetti's circle, and Vespasiano described him as "learned in Greek and Latin and an excellent philosopher in both philosophies." A similar figure in many ways was Alamanno Rinuccini, likewise "learned in Greek and Latin and an excellent philosopher." Among the others present were Pierfilippo Pandolfini, another student of Greek and philosophy, and his brother Pandolfo, who was "well read and of excellent manners and high respect." As we will see at the time of his death, Pandolfo Pandolfini seems to have been a particular friend of Parenti; so too was Vespasiano himself, who modestly names himself last "among the number of such worthy men."

It was an impressive company, and Marco's position among them seems more than respectable. Among Sacchetti's dozen guests he is listed fourth, after Argyropulos himself, Pandolfo Pandolfini, and Alamanno Rinuccini. A better indication of Parenti's acceptance in this circle is the brief description at-

[6] On the influence of Argyropulos, see J. Seigel, "The Teaching of Argyropulos and the Rhetoric of the First Humanists," in T. K. Rabb and J. Seigel, *Action and Conviction in Early Modern Europe* (Princeton, 1969), pp. 237–60. Seigel lists Parenti himself, along with Antonio Rossi, Andrea Alamanni, Alamanno Rinuccini, Donato Acciaiuoli, and Piero Acciaiuoli, as being among the faction supporting the appointment of Argyropulos against his rival Landino. On Donato Acciaiuoli, see E. Garin, "Donato Acciaiuoli cittadino fiorentino," *Medioevo*, pp. 211–87; M. Ganz, "Donato Acciaiuoli and the Medici: A Strategy for Survival in Quattrocento Florence," *Rinascimento*, 2d ser., 22 (1982): 33–73.

tached to his name, as to each of the other participants. Marco was, it seems, literate or well read, and skilled in natural philosophy—"litterato e con buona perizia di filosofia naturale."

Given that Vespasiano knew Marco well enough to stand as godfather to one of his children, this description seems at first disappointingly uninformative. Vespasiano's job, of course, was not easy. He had a dozen men, all very similar in certain respects, to record and somehow characterize. It would be best not to read too much into this brief tag, but at least we can gather something about the direction of Marco's interests. His knowledge, it seems, lay in the area of natural philosophy, what we would now call the sciences.

For most humanists, or intellectuals influenced by humanism, natural philosophy was definitely secondary to moral philosophy. "The other part of philosophy," as Leonardo Bruni put it, "is our concern."[7] Often the indifference spilled over into hostility, as in this prescription from Matteo Palmieri's *Vita Civile*:

> It consists in the investigation of the secrets of nature; certainly in itself a not unworthy study, but none the less one of much less service to mankind than that of moral wisdom, upon which is based the well-being of the race. Therefore admitting that the causes of rain, hail, snow, and ice, the origin of the colors of the rainbow, the secrets of lightning and thunder, are in themselves matters of marvellous significance, and deserve enquiry, we hold them still of the minutest interest in the supreme task of solving the problem of how to live.[8]

There is no telling just how far "the secrets of lightning and thunder" attracted Parenti. It is clear, however, that he was knowledgeable about those parts of Aristotle from which the fifteenth century still took its ideas of nature and natural history. The cultivation of this interest points back to the influence of Argyropulos himself and his lectures on Aristotle.

[7] E. Garin, *Italian Humanism* (New York, 1965), pp. 41–42.

[8] Quoted in W. H. Woodward, *Studies in Education during the Age of the Renaissance* (New York, 1967), p. 76.

In Parenti's account book there is a record of an order for a copy of Aristotle's *Physics* in Argyropulos' translation; the bookseller was Vespasiano da Bisticci.[9]

A little more can be gathered if Vespasiano's description of Marco is examined with an eye to the whole series of characterizations. The intellectual center of the group, Argyropulos, was "dottissimo," very learned. Among the Florentines, Rinuccini, the two Acciaiuoli brothers, and Pierfilippo Pandolfini were all learned in both Latin and Greek—"dotto in greco e in latino." By comparison, Marco himself was simply "litterato," literate or well read. In this he was like his friend Pandolfo Pandolfini and several others. Parenti could not be regarded as "learned" because he knew no Greek; his knowledge only extended to Latin—since literacy in the *volgare* was no literacy at all.

In a similar sense, we can reexamine Marco's reported "skill" in natural philosophy in relation to the claims made for others in his circle. Argyropulos, the learned foreigner, was essentially beyond comparison. He was simply "greco uomo dottissimo," a very learned Greek. Rinuccini, however, was rated as "an excellent philosopher." More explicitly, Donato Acciaiuoli, his brother, and Pierfilippo Pandolfini were each seen as "an excellent philosopher in both philosophies." Marco, by contrast, seems not to have been an excellent philosopher, yet he had considerable knowledge or expertise—"buona perizia"—in one branch of philosophy, natural philosophy. Evidently this put his knowledge beyond that of several others who, though "well read," were not philosophic at all. Pandolfo Pandolfini was a man of "excellent manners and high respect," while Carlo d'Antonio di Silvestro's "costumi" (manners) were "laudable," and Banco da Casavecchia had an excellent wit. Finally, regarding his own Greek, philosophy, manners, or wit Vespasiano, the author, keeps silent.

Apparently Marco Parenti did not cut a poor figure in the company of some of Florence's brightest and most serious young men. His ignorance of Greek and the limitations of his

[9] *Ricordanze*, fol. 47^r. But the order had to be canceled when it could not be filled.

philosophical knowledge did not place him at the bottom of the list of Franco Sacchetti's guests. In fact, the place of honor among the young Florentines went to the virtuous but unphilosophic Pandolfo Pandolfini. This is an important point because it is a clue to the wider significance of this circle. Only when we have understood a little better the common qualities and interests that brought these men together can we make full use of Vespasiano's brief characterization of Marco.

The key figure to notice is Franco Sacchetti himself. Sacchetti came from "an ancient and noble family in the city of Florence" that had produced many worthy men. He was "learned in both Greek and Latin," "the friend of all the learned men of his age, and a great lover of virtue." He had attained all the honors in the city that a citizen could have and conducted himself in these with great modesty. The result was that he was universally liked, "no small thing," as Vespasiano remarked, "in a democratic state."

Sacchetti was one of those men in whom family pride, civic obligation, and classical inspiration combined to revivify sober Roman ideals of senatorial virtue in fifteenth-century Florence.

> Franco lived entirely on his income, which was a meagre one. He followed no calling, but devoted himself exclusively to letters. He lived an upright life without ostentation, satisfied with little and always living within his own income—narrow as it was—rather than trench upon that of other men, as is the fashion of those who are not troubled with an over-delicate conscience.

It was natural that such a man would attract to himself and to his house a group of like-minded men in imitation of the intellectual banquets of the ancients. These were the symposia to which Parenti and his friends came—and it is worth noting that Vespasiano still found it necessary to insist upon the spirit of seriousness that sharply distinguished these gatherings from lesser entertainments:

> His custom was to invite ten or twelve men of letters twice a year to his villa, where he would entertain them handsomely

> for two or three days. In all aspects the life he led was very fine and proper. Those that went to his house were all amongst the first men of the city, well-read and well-mannered and entirely free of vice. In his house no games of any kind were played, as is done in most villas. The entertainment given was the discussion of literature or of the governing of republics or worthy matters. He received all his guests with easy familiarity and welcome, and his house was home to men of worth. He was always anxious to invite Giovanni Argyropulos, along with all or most of his students, and in that house no man spoke a dishonest word.

Evidently Sacchetti's circle was not devoted primarily to academic erudition. Their first concern was with virtue in a setting of letters. Sacchetti himself appears simultaneously—indistinguishably—the model man of letters, the model patrician, the model citizen. Among his friends too—all of them, we are told, leading men in the city—virtue was as prized as intellect, and their talk was equally about literature and the governing of republics.

The meetings at the Sacchetti villa were not frequent and one might want to discount their real importance, thinking these gatherings an escape or an indulgence. But Vespasiano insists this was not so, that the bonds of love formed among these young men were brought back into the city and carried through everyday life. His own evident emotion in telling the story makes it easy to believe that for the others as well this circle of friends was formative:

> All those that went to this house were men of respect [autorità] in the city and beyond. They were sent as ambassadors, from which they brought back the greatest honor to the city. I will declare here how great is the power of virtue in everything. Between the men named above was born a bond of love so strong that one could describe them as several souls in a single body. These are the fruits of true friendship. So great was the friendship joining such worthy men and the likeness of their customs that rarely did a day pass that they did not meet together. They acquired a very high reputation in the city, and there was very little that they wished, either for themselves or their friends, that they could not obtain.

These last words can hardly be accepted literally: Marco, for one, soon faced a major political setback, so that it cannot be said that there was little he wished that he could not obtain. But there is an invaluable truth in these recollections of Vespasiano that lies beyond points of literal detail. It is plain that Vespasiano recollected these virtuous days of his early manhood with nostalgic affection, and in the preface to this little trio of lives he admits as much.[10] The result is certainly a kind of idyll in which the clarity of virtue, the light of learning, and the seriousness of youth combine in the warmth of friendship. But to recognize the element of the ideal in what Vespasiano remembers is not to deny the importance of his testimony.

Seen through Vespasiano's eyes, the Sacchetti villa emerges as the perfect setting of quattrocento classical republicanism, a prefiguring of the discussions in the Rucellai gardens that in a later generation nourished Machiavelli's passion for republican Rome.[11] For Vespasiano, everything that happened in that villa took on a special luminousness, honesty, and conviction. Hence his feeling declaration at the close of this *vita* that "this brief record of Franco Sacchetti has cost me no pains, his life and customs being of a sort about which it is impossible to be wrong."

It is impossible to be sure how far Marco's experience of these gatherings matched Vespasiano's, or whether in later days he recollected them with the same warmth. We do have a kind of substantiation in the evidence of his friendships with Donato Acciaiuoli, Pandolfo Pandolfini, Alamanno Rinuccini, and Vespasiano himself. On the other hand, as more than one scholar has noted with some puzzlement, Marco's letters

[10] Vespasiano da Bisticci, *Le Vite: Edizione Critica*, ed. A. Greco (Florence, 1970), 2: 459: "pensando meco quanto il governo di questa città era mutato rispetto a quello lo ricordano ne' tempi mia. . . ." Vespasiano's nostalgia in his rural retreat blends with a muted note of political criticism. This reinforces the impression that Vespasiano shared common ground with his friend Marco Parenti.

[11] See F. Gilbert, "Bernardo Rucellai and the Orti Oricellari," in Gilbert, *History, Choice and Commitment* (Cambridge, Mass., 1977), pp. 215–46. As it happens, Bernardo Rucellai was the dedicatee of these three *vite*.

to the Strozzi show no traces at all of humanist influence or activity. Intelligent and lucid though they are, these letters were firmly tied to the pragmatic and political concerns of the family. They are the letters of a political observer, a concerned citizen, a merchant, a family man, but not of a humanist intellectual.

Should Marco's name be withdrawn from the list of Sacchetti's guests? Here the rediscovery of the *Memoir* is helpful, because it points to a middle ground in which both worlds—that of the Sacchetti villa as well as that of Strozzi family politics—have some influence. The *Memoir* by no means establishes Parenti as a humanist, if by that is meant someone who had a strict classical training and wrote or taught in classical traditions and genres. On the contrary, it is a vernacular work that draws primarily on local, Florentine concerns in politics and history. Nonetheless, in its criticism of Medici tyranny and in its liberal and republican spirit it is reasonable to see the influence of those days spent in "discussion of literature or of the governing of republics or other worthy matters."

The evidence at hand does not support the identification of Marco as a humanist,[12] but the development of humanist culture by men professionally engaged in intellectual work is only one part of the story. It is just as important that men of substance in society accepted the new culture and lent it their patronage and prestige. These men—merchants, citizens, heads of families—found in the language of humanism a way of expressing and refining their own needs and hopes, that sprang in the first place not from academies or books but from the life of the city and the marketplace.

Sacchetti's villa is a symbol of this reeducation of the political class of Florence—a process that went on for genera-

[12] For this reason, I question Martines' inclusion of Marco Parenti in his sample of humanists cited in note 1 above. Martines' failure to distinguish between men of private wealth like Marco Parenti and the professional literati, like Bruni and Poggio, leads to a confusion between an investigation into the wealth of humanists and one concerned with the prestige of humanism among the wealthy.

tions, not only in Florence but all over Europe.[13] With the exception of Argyropulos, their teacher, the men gathered there represented first and foremost a circle of citizens. They were all, to repeat Vespasiano, "among the first men of the city." They brought their political influence and social standing with them, the product not of their erudition but of families, money, and offices, and in turn, they came away with the influence of Sacchetti's patrician virtue and Argyropulos' learning.

Marco could hardly fail to feel the influence of such friends. As we will see, in his first real opportunity for political action he carried their spirit of public virtue into a brief term of office, at some cost to himself. A decade later he placed his hopes on the anti-Medici opposition and set himself to be the historian of Florence's liberation, only to be disappointed again. In this he was like another member of the circle, Alamanno Rinuccini, whose chronicle and "Dialogue on Liberty" were protests against tyranny. Both men could well say—echoing a phrase from Vespasiano's preface to the Sacchetti *vita*—that they had been contemplating how much the governing of the city had changed in their time.

To understand the motives behind Parenti's *Memoir* it is important to keep Sacchetti and his friends in mind, as much for the broad ideals they represented as for the specific information about Marco himself. The ideals of early manhood may be tempered or subverted by experience, but they are not easily replaced by others.

★

In political life, as in business, Marco was his father's heir. The honor of the priorate which Parente had received so late came to Marco at an early age. In the spring of 1454 when Marco took his place on the Signoria he was young and comparatively green. A term as a magistrate in the Florentine dominion and two on the Council of the People was the sum of his experience of public life. The administration of the

[13] See J. Hexter, "The Education of the Aristocracy," in Hexter, *Reappraisals in History* (New York, 1963), pp. 45–70.

subject communes in Tuscany was the staple of Florentine government; the Council of the People was one of two large assemblies that voted on measures proposed by the Signoria before they became law. Though minor offices, such positions provided useful exposure, especially for a young man from an insignificant family. Nonetheless, the Signoria, made up of eight priors and the Gonfaloniere (or Standard Bearer), was the select center of government; upon entering it, Marco must have felt that he had begun a new phase of life.

He was fortunate in achieving office at an interesting time. The years around the mid-century had seen a good deal of conflict and a major realignment of the Italian powers.[14] The death of the last Visconti duke of Milan provoked a three-way struggle for the succession. Milanese republicans found themselves caught in a losing battle against the expansionism of Venice and the dynastic ambitions of Francesco Sforza, son-in-law of the old duke. Sforza, the leading condottiere of his day, triumphed in the end, thanks in part to the financial and political backing of Cosimo de' Medici. For the Florentines the consequence was that an alliance with Milan, the traditional enemy, replaced one with Venice, a longtime ally; a second consequence was that, after several years of conflict, a general peace—known as the Peace of Lodi—was arranged between the Italian states. Afterward, these states bound themselves together in the Italian League, pledged to maintain the peace and, in effect, the balance of power in the peninsula.

Marco belonged to the Signoria of April 1454 to whom it fell to pronounce Florence's official ratification of the peace. Such was his excitement that for once he violated the purely private character of his ricordanze. Between the day-to-day expenditures, he inserted a brief account of the ratification of

[14] See G. Pillinini, *Il sistema degli stati italiani 1454–1494* (Venice, 1970); G. Soranzo, *La lega italica* (Milan, 1924); F. Catalano, "La Nuova Signoria; Francesco Sforza," in *L'Eta Sforzesco dal 1450 al 1500, Storia di Milano*, Fondazione Treccani degli Alfieri (Milan, 1456), vol. 7, chaps. 1–3; F. Catalano, "Francesco Sforza e la pace di Lodi," in *Gli Sforza tra la Francia e Machiavelli* (Milan, 1981); V. Ilardi, "The Italian League, Francesco Sforza, and Charles VII, 1454–1461," *Studies in the Renaissance* 6 (1954): 129–66.

the peace and explained his own role in the affair. He even decided to decorate the covers of his personal record book with the articles of the peace, thus symbolizing in the clearest possible way his sense of personal identification with these events.[15]

For a brief two months Marco Parenti had become a public man, a magistrate of Florence. The intensity with which he responded to the events he saw can be taken as prefiguring the feeling of public involvement that later led him to write his history. But beyond the elation he evidently felt, it is hard to recover from the ricordanze a more specific sense of his political experience as a prior. For this we must turn to a short and initially rather puzzling recounting of these same events in the pages of his *Memoir*, written perhaps a dozen years after Lodi:

> The news reached Florence on the 11th [of April] at the 15th hour. Everyone marveled because the discussions being highly secret almost no one knew anything except for those few who negotiated it. In Florence there was great celebration by people of every rank. The exception was Cosimo who hoped for the war to continue the next summer because he thought the duke would take Brescia and Bergamo from the Venetians, a great loss to them and boost to us. And perhaps he was not wrong, but weariness decided the issue.[16]

[15] *Ricordanze*, fol. 39^{v}: "con questi patti e titoli honesti chome in detto contratto apparisce per 36 capitoli chome n' aparisce copia nella coverta di questo libro."

[16] *Memorie*, p. 62. Parenti may have distorted Cosimo's attitude toward the peace. According to Capponi, who was in a better position to know, Cosimo agreed to the necessity of seeking an end to hostilities. Despite the widespread opinion that the Venetians were not in a position to carry on fighting, he wrote, Neri and Cosimo "conclusono che ciascuno di loro scrivesse al Duca, confortandolo della pace" (*Comentarii, Rerum Italicarum Scriptores* [Milan, 1723–51], vol. 18, col. 1215). Marco Parenti's willingness to believe the worst about Cosimo's war plans confirms his general attitude of suspicion toward Cosimo's authority. But Parenti was not alone in his misunderstanding. Capponi reports that a little earlier, when the *Ten* sent Otto Niccolini to Rome to join the peace talks, almost everyone thought that he had gone to disrupt the negotiations, and the boys on the street sang, "La pace è fatta se Messer Otto non la guasta."

Curiously, the date on which the peace would officially be proclaimed seems to have become an issue. Florentines were divided, Parenti wrote, over whether the peace should officially be made before or after the fifteenth of the month and arguments "for good and for ill" were raised on both sides. Marco himself, as he recorded with pride, played a role in deciding the issue: "I, finding myself one of the Lord Priors, on the 14th of the said month, Palm Sunday, it seemed to me a day most suited to peace and auguring well; and considering that, in truth, the peace had been made before the 15th day, I thought to have it proclaimed that said day, the 14th. Thus, the matter being put to my companions, it was carried."

Vernacular diarists often moved from public to private matters without the slightest hesitation, but this is one of the few "intrusions" of autobiography in Marco's history—the exact counterpart to the insertion of the story of the peace in his private notebook. At first glance, his emphasis on what seems so minor an issue as the dating of the peace appears odd and out of proportion. Was the symbolic value of Palm Sunday really so compelling as to need this much attention? More than a decade after Lodi, was Marco still so taken with his brief hour of office that he could not let it go unnoticed?

Without a doubt Marco was impressed by the aptness of the occasion and in a second passage he linked the durability of the peace to the auspicious date on which it was officially declared. But there is a larger political meaning to this apparently trivial question that only gradually emerges from his reticent and puzzling account. At the start, Parenti had declared that the Florentines were divided over the issue of whether to promulgate the peace before or after the middle of the month, but focusing on the symbolic date and his own role in the discussion, he neglected to explain why this division existed. Later he writes that those opposed to an early proclamation—that is, before the fifteenth—argued that Sforza's negotiations with Venice on Florence's behalf were carried out "without our authentic commission."[17] But the formal

[17] Literally, those to whom a peace made before mid-month was injurious: "A chi noceva la pace fatta innanzi mezo aprile. . . ."

proclamation established Florence's adherence to the articles and "thus removed any quibbling," and the result was a "very great saving of expense to our people." It seems that the Signoria had earlier proposed a tax to support the war, but since peace talks were already going on, a condition was attached to ease its passage, namely "that if peace were to come before mid-April, this tax would be annulled." The proclamation of the peace on the fourteenth meant both the annulment of the war tax and the early termination of the office of the war commissioners, the Ten, "since they were lacking the intended funds."

But it is evident that Marco believed the issue was wider than the powers of the Ten, that it concerned the authority of the regime as a whole.[18] In fact, the year following Lodi brought a pronounced liberation of Florentine politics, and Parenti carried his narrative from the making of the peace to the unsettling of the regime as if they constituted a single episode. The very next group of priors to take office annulled the Balìa, the special council the Mediceans used to protect their electoral interests; later the power of the electoral officers (accoppiatori) to elect the Signoria "by hand" was removed and the traditional method of selection by a blind lottery reinstated. "Never before," writes a modern historian of these events, "had there been so abrupt a reversal of the electoral policy of the Medici regime."[19] Marco's judgment was less dispassionate. "It seemed to the citizens," he wrote in his *Memoir*, "a recovery of some measure of liberty, being freed from the servitude of the accoppiatori, whom the priors they themselves had selected were bound to support. The accoppiatori and those who backed them having lost their authority, the others lost their fear and they dared from time to time to do something worthwhile on their own, without first asking

[18] The underlying issue was the power of Cosimo and his link to Francesco Sforza. Parenti describes an earlier moment during the war when Cosimo urged Sforza to go on with hostilities against Venice, while opponents of the Medici urged peace, hoping to reduce the power of Sforza and thereby diminish Cosimo's, which was "concatenata con la sua" (*Memorie*, p. 57).

[19] N. Rubinstein, *The Government of Florence under the Medici* (Oxford, 1966), p. 22.

those whom they were accustomed to regard as the chief citizens [principali]."[20]

This verdict on the events of 1454–1455 was written at least a decade later, but it seems reasonable to take it as a reflection of Marco's own experience on the Signoria. As one who had qualified for office when the electoral controls were still in full force, he obviously knew at first hand the timorousness of the priors in face of the "servitude of the accoppiatori." By the same token, his celebration of the priors' new freedom to act on their own for the public good brings us back to his own single recorded act as prior. By intervening when he did to have the peace ratified promptly, Marco claimed to have put an end to quibbling and to have saved the public from an unnecessary tax. In taking this initiative, he does not appear to have checked first with the "principali"; on the contrary, there is a strong implication that his action went against their interests, and especially Cosimo's. He and his colleagues had thrown off the habitual timidity of the priors and resisted the tyrannical demands of faction. In a memoir that is explicitly a chronicle of stunted hopes for freedom, it is a significant moment.

How much of this was in Marco's mind in the spring of 1454 it is impossible to know without correspondence from the period. The resurgence and defeat of the anti-Medici forces in 1465–1466, which stirred him to compose the *Memoir*, must have broadened his perspectives on the earlier episode. Still, it would have been naive on Marco's part to think that the regime could be opposed without cost; and even if he were capable of such innocence, others were not. Though the accoppiatori had been deprived of their extraordinary power to elect the Signoria "by hand," they retained their original authority to screen those qualified for office and make up the purses. In June of 1455 they summarily removed the names of nineteen men from the ballot bags, alleging the need to protect the "peace and quiet" of the republic. Marco Parenti was one of them.[21]

[20] *Memorie*, p. 63.

[21] Rubinstein, *Government*, p. 45n.

Marco's reaction is unknown. He made no mention of the incident either in the ricordanze or the *Memoir*; nor can we gather much from the public record or the other victims. Like Parenti, they were men of modest status, an indication either that the regime, in its present weakness, felt unable to take action against anyone better connected or that the opposition genuinely was a grass-roots movement among the middle ranks.

Alternately, as was shrewdly observed about disturbances a few years later, it might be that they had "punished the tomcats in order to frighten the lions." The exception among the tomcats was Giovanni Rucellai, a wealthy patrician. He, too, was connected by marriage to the Strozzi, a parallel that strongly suggests Marco's marriage to Caterina did him no good in the eyes of the powerful. Rucellai's identification with the exiles of 1434 was far clearer, however, and he later recorded that, "for 27 years, that is from 1434 to 1461, I was not welcome, but suspect to the regime." Rucellai, however, could afford to look back on the vicissitudes of political fortune with some detachment. A wealthy but politically unambitious man, he eventually rehabilitated himself and sealed his success by marrying his son to a sister of Lorenzo de' Medici. With evident satisfaction he noted the perils he had avoided, a recognition that even for a Rucellai success was far from automatic. "I was required to navigate most carefully and without a mistake," he wrote, but in the end adversity only made his triumph "more sweet."[22]

For Parenti the prospect was certainly bleaker. In the next ten years he served in a number of secondary positions. Often a member of the Council of the Commune or the Council of the People, he also had a term on the Regulatores, an important fiscal body, and another as captain of the prestigious

[22] *Giovanni Rucellai ed il suo Zibaldone*, ed. A. Perosa (London, 1960), p. 122. A third man with Strozzi connections was also removed from the electoral purses (*borse*). This was Iacopo di Tommaso Sacchetti. See H. Gregory, "A Florentine Family in Crisis: The Strozzi in the 15th Century" (Ph.D. diss., London University, 1980), p. 118. I am grateful to her for permission to cite this work and for many helpful discussions in the archives.

Guelf party.[23] These responsibilities kept him in touch with the political world; and as the Strozzi fortune grew, he gained access to powerful men as Filippo's proxy in Florence. In his own right, however, he never again came so close to the political center. His early success in reaching the priorate was not repeated, nor was he ever a member of the Council of 100, which after 1458 became the core of the Medici oligarchy. He was destined to be an observer, not an actor, in Florentine politics; but in this role there was some advantage in being an onlooker, and the critical stance that had barred him from high office could find a use.

[23] In the *Ricordanze* Piero di Marco listed his father's offices (fol. 80ᵛ):
De' Regolatori [1456]
De' Capitani di Parte Guelfa [1458]
De' Signori priori di libertà
De' Consoli dell' arte di Porta Sta Maria tre volte [1476, 1481]
De' Sei della Mercatantia [1475]
Camarlingo [bursar] di detti Sei di Mercatantia [1488]
Camarlingo dell' arte di Porte Sta Maria [1478]
Camarlingo d' Or San Michele e Bigallo
Capitano d' Or San Michele [1474]
Delle X Uficiali della Torre [1471]
Delli Uficiali di Bancho per prestare ff. V mila al Comune di Firenze [1478]

In a separate column he also lists six posts in the *dominio* in which his father served as *podestà, capitano,* or *vicario,* and that Marco had been "electionario del potestà di firenze [1489]." Piero Parenti did not and probably could not date these offices, and Marco himself states that he only recorded offices in his ricordanze where financial obligation was involved (cf. *Ricordanze,* fol. 75ᵛ). I have added the dates of the offices where I have been able to find them in the electoral registers of the *Tratte.* These show that Parenti was a member of the Council of the Commune or the Council of the People, two lesser councils, in 1451, 1453, 1455, 1456, 1458, 1460, 1462, 1463, 1465, 1467, 1468, 1469, 1471, 1474, 1481, and 1485. It is clear that after his term as prior and subsequent removal from the *borse,* Marco did not regain political favor until the 1470s, when Filippo Strozzi had returned to Florence.

CHAPTER 3

THE STROZZI

★

A MAN who marries a woman "above himself," a prominent Florentine preacher once warned, "can be said to have been sold to a woman and to her family."[1] Looking at Marco Parenti's life from the outside, a cynical observer might well take this view of his marriage to Caterina Strozzi. He had certainly married a woman "maggior di se," and the result was his long absorption in her family's struggles. In a sense, Marco seems to have become a Strozzi more than Caterina a Parenti.

Flattered by the social advantages of the marriage, Marco took on the burdens of a connection that in a practical sense often seemed far from advantageous. But this he did willingly, knowing that in more prosperous times the Strozzi would never have considered such a match. Eclipsed by exile and political disfavor, the family was in a reduced state, unable to offer either money or family connection as the reward of an alliance. Alessandra was a widow and very much in need of the sort of support that male relatives alone could give. Here was a role that suited Marco and that he gradually came to occupy—with evident eagerness on his part and some reluctance on hers.

Marco's contact with his mother-in-law was both personal

[1] G. Dominici, *Regola del governo di cura familiare*, ed. D. Salvi (Florence, 1860), p. 177, cited by H. Gregory, "A Florentine Family in Crisis: The Strozzi in the 15th Century" (Ph.D. diss., University of London, 1980), p. 195.

and frequent, though not always easy. She was not, however, his only connection with his wife's immediate family. Of growing importance were his relations with his absent brothers-in-law, Filippo and Lorenzo. Marco's long and regular correspondence with them, men a little younger than himself, testifies to a steadier and more straightforward relationship, which need and loyalty soon built into friendship. For Filippo the elder, more ambitious son, Marco was an ideal contact in Florence, well informed, dependable, and self-effacing, and in later years Marco proudly described himself as Filippo's closest relation in the city.

Though Marco must also have corresponded with others, no other letters remain, with a single exception. Only the wealth, continuity, and family pride of the Strozzi ensured the preservation of this one fragment of Marco's life. Even the hundred-odd letters we have are only a fraction of what must have been a considerably larger total, but what survives is enough to reveal a great deal of his story, especially when set by the side of Alessandra's own letters. Inevitably the result is as much a group portrait as an individual one. We see Marco primarily as he presented himself to the Strozzi and as he responded to their demands. The focus remains on their problems, their hopes, their tragedies, not his own.

*

Though her date of birth is uncertain, Alessandra could not have been thirty when exile and death turned her life upside down. In the aftermath of the victory of the Medici faction over their Albizzi rivals in 1434, her husband, Matteo Strozzi, was banished to Pesaro. To guarantee his compliance with the terms of his confinement, there was the threat of a fine of two thousand florins, for which five Florentines were made to stand surety. Alessandra, whom Matteo had married twelve years earlier, followed her husband into exile with their seven children.[2]

[2] The biographies of Alessandra and her children are outlined in Guasti's introduction to the Strozzi letters. For the circumstances of the exile and the dates of birth of the children, see especially *Lettere*, pp. xxff.

Alessandra and the children were not themselves directly subject to the ban of exile—it would not be extended to the sons of the exiles of 1434 for another two decades—and legally they might have chosen to remain in Florence. Once in Pesaro, however, their communication with Florence and travel to the city were restricted by the magistrates of the Eight of Ward. In the event, their stay in Pesaro proved unexpectedly short. Within two years Matteo and three of the children died in an outbreak of plague, and the young widow returned home. Her eldest surviving child, Filippo, was only eight years old when his father died; the youngest was born only after Matteo's death and was given his father's name.

Though he had enjoyed some time in office, Matteo Strozzi was not a leading figure in Florentine politics. His family's prominence in the Albizzi ranks, not his own, led to exile. He had neither the wealth, experience, or prestige of his famous cousin Palla Strozzi, one of the great men of his day, who also lost his homeland in 1434. In a brief but laudatory *vita*, Vespasiano da Bisticci, who was well acquainted with the younger generation of Strozzi, pictures Matteo as a man more given to literature than to political strife, so much so that exile came as a complete surprise:

> Matteo di Simone degli Strozzi was of the highest birth. He possessed a wide knowledge of Latin letters, but not contented with this, he devoted himself to philosophy, and together with . . . other citizens with whom he was intimate, heard the lectures of Messer Giannozzo on the *Ethics* of Aristotle. In the city he won all the civic honors within his reach, and bore himself in a way which gained for him a good name. He devoted himself entirely to letters, was a man of the soundest judgement and widest views and was also of most generous mind. And as the fateful happenings of '34 were distasteful to him and to others not inflamed by factious spirit, he deemed that, as he had always borne himself temperately and had never supported any upheavals in the city, he had deserved well and never dreamt of exile.[3]

[3] Vespasiano da Bisticci, *Renaissance Princes, Popes, and Prelates*, tr. W. George and E. Waters (New York, 1963), p. 245 (translation slightly

Even the generous and garrulous Vespasiano, however, could find little else with which to fill out Matteo's brief "Life." Accordingly he grouped it together with a more substantial biography of Messer Palla, prefaced it with some remarks on the famous men and worthy customs of Rome, and dedicated it all to Filippo Strozzi with the pious thought that "in this life there is nothing one can give that is more welcome than to make men immortal through the memorial of letters."

As for Matteo's widow—whom Vespasiano must have known quite well—it is unlikely that it ever crossed his mind to single her out. Women scarcely figure in the *Lives* and only one is given the honor of a *vita*. How much it would surprise the worthy biographer to know that of all the Strozzi the one who remains most alive to us now is not the eminent, wealthy, and philosophic Messer Palla, much less his more obscure cousin Matteo, but that unfortunate man's widow, who survived him by thirty years, raised his children, and oversaw the first steps in the rebuilding of his family. And this posthumous fame has come to her literally through "the memorial of letters." Indeed, her unschooled but vivid and attractive letters have made Alessandra perhaps the most memorable bourgeoise of her time.

Vespasiano's neglect of women in the *Lives* did not go unnoticed, and he began a parallel work in praise of women: the unfinished and little known *Libro de le lode e comendazione de le donne.*[4] Though an odd and unsuccessful work, it is unexpectedly valuable because in it Vespasiano tells us something essential about the framework of ideals within which women were expected to live their lives. In this way, without ever mentioning Alessandra Strozzi, the biographer provides us with a useful, if indirect, introduction to this woman whose life exercised such an influence on Marco Parenti's.

The idea of doing justice to exemplary or famous women apparently proved far more difficult than Vespasiano had

modified); "Proemio a Filippo Strozzi," in Vespasiano da Bisticci, *Le Vite: Edizione Critica*, ed. A. Greco (Florence, 1970), 2: 429–33.

[4] Vespasiano da Bisticci, *Libro delle lode e comendazioni de le donne*, ed. L. Sorrento (Milan, 1911).

imagined. He did manage to work his way through a long and dull compilation of the lives of classical and biblical heroines. Among his contemporaries, on the other hand, he found only a handful to eulogize. Still it would hardly have mattered if Vespasiano had managed to double or treble the numbers of contemporary heroines, since each is so much like the others. They are all pious and chaste, but also strong and determined. Afflicted by the double trial of exiled menfolk and early widowhood, they suffer and endure, raise families, dedicate themselves to duty, and put aside all temptations. All, in short, could be taken for the sisters in adversity of Alessandra Strozzi. Thus if Vespasiano tells us nothing about Alessandra as an individual, he tells us something almost equally helpful: he establishes her as a type.

The men of Vespasiano's *Lives* are singled out for their learning, public service, courage, or witty sayings. Even so obscure an "illustrious man" as Matteo Strozzi could take public action and seek public recognition. But their female counterparts remain fixed forever in their domestic roles and domestic virtues. Despite widowhood and exile, they keep a strict dedication to their assigned duties. Giving themselves entirely to their families, they spurn the possibility of remarrying, and a number finish their lives in the assured piety of the convent. No wonder that the book is really less a collection of biographies than, as the title says, a eulogy "in praise and commendation of women."

It is easy to see why exile and widowhood play such an important part in this scheme of praise. These tragedies were all too frequent a part of the circumstances of fifteenth-century Florentine life. Such women, left unsupported and solitary, were suspected of being prey to sexual temptation, as even a girl late in marrying was thought to be.[5] They were also faced with unusually wide domestic responsibilities as guardians of their children. Most of all there is an underlying pattern of

[5] When Lorenzo Strozzi proposed to marry Marietta di Lorenzo Strozzi, Filippo objected (among other things) that she was older, an orphan, and beautiful. Thus it "would not be remarkable if there were some blot [on her reputation]" (*Lettere*, p. 594).

normal life that these women, by their unusual dedication, confirm. Since the only image of female virtue that could be imagined was domestic, extraordinary virtue consisted of practicing these ordinary virtues despite great odds. Thus exile and widowhood provide the setting for an exercise of heroic domesticity.

Vespasiano found no way to bring his general admiration for suffering womanhood down to particular cases, and as a result his book on women entirely lacks the copiousness and curiosity that makes his earlier collection a favorite guide to fifteenth-century life. But the biographer's failure will not matter much to readers of Alessandra Strozzi, because in her vivid letters Vespasiano's abstractions come to life. Though we will concentrate on the individuality of Alessandra Strozzi, it is well to be reminded that she was far from unique in her struggles.

★

She was born a Macinghi, a prosperous but "new" family not to be compared to her husband's in prestige. Her mother had been an Alberti, also one of the great Florentine clans, but of them we hear nothing in the letters. Even the Macinghi seldom figure, though as a widow Alessandra might have fallen back on them for help. Rather, Alessandra looked toward the Strozzi and mentions dozens of her late husband's relatives in her correspondence. She adopted the perspective of her sons, and her sons, of course, were Strozzi. In very direct ways their welfare would depend on the fortunes of the wider family. Their Strozzi cousins, trading in Naples, Barcelona, and Bruges, gave them their start in business, and in politics too the fate of the several branches of the family was likely to be linked.[6]

Even her own daughters could not really compete with Alessandra's fiercely concentrated concern for her sons and

[6] The financial career of Filippo Strozzi is traced in R. Goldthwaite, *Private Wealth in Renaissance Florence* (Princeton, 1968), p. 52ff. See also Gregory, "A Florentine Family."

their future. Not that she neglected them or lacked affection. In describing the preparations for Caterina's marriage to Marco, for instance, she dwelled on the splendid figure the young girl would cut, but added fondly that it was no more than her daughter was due: "In truth, there isn't another girl in Florence like her, and in the opinion of many she has all the right qualities." Still, Alessandra did not hide from herself or Filippo that Caterina was making a lesser match. Caterina's good fortune would have been her brothers' loss; a larger dowry, Alessandra confided to her son, would have meant "my undoing and yours."[7]

Two years later Alessandra was looking toward the marriage of her second daughter: "If God grants me a few more years of life and Lessandra leaves the house," she wrote to Filippo and Lorenzo, "I will provide you with so much linen that you will really be well off. For it is true, alas, that as long as there are girls at home, nothing is done that isn't for them."[8] By contrast, when the time came for her youngest son to leave home, she faced the separation with terror, put it off as long as she could, and only gave way to the combined counsels of the family with deep distrust and forebodings of death.

Alessandra's attention to the welfare of her sons—their work, their morals, their prospects for marriage or career—was more than either simple personal preference or social convention. The family had suffered in the previous generation and its chances in Florence seemed poor. When these boys left home it was not, like their sisters, to settle comfortably near, but to be apprenticed to a life of trade in distant centers. Her sons did not bear the responsibility for the family's future in equal measure, and Alessandra did not give herself in the same way to all three. Filippo, the eldest, assumed the full impact of her hopes and anxieties. Of the second son, Lorenzo, dominated by his older brother and

[7] 24 Aug. 1447, *Lettere*, pp. 4–5.

[8] 6 Dec. 1450, *Lettere*, p. 100. See L. Martines, "A Way of Looking at Women in the Renaissance," *Journal of Medieval and Renaissance Studies* 4 (1974): 22–23 and passim.

sheltering behind him, we hear much less. The youngest was Matteo, her husband's namesake, and for him she reserved her tenderest feelings.

At the time of Alessandra's first surviving letter, dated August 24, 1447, Filippo was already in Naples, which was to be his home for the next twenty years. Born in July of 1428, Filippo left Florence at age thirteen and was now just nineteen. His brother Lorenzo, born two years later, was then in Avignon, after a stint in Barcelona, and from there he went to Bruges before finally being reunited with Filippo in Naples. There the two began trading independently sometime in the 1450s and quickly established a modest fortune; in the meantime they were under the tutelage of their employers, their father's cousins, Niccolò, Filippo, and Iacopo Strozzi.[9]

The main news of this first letter was the betrothal of Caterina to Marco Parenti. These good tidings aside, her words are a characteristic mix of blunt admonition and intense longing. Apparently Filippo's journey to the Tuscan port of Livorno had raised her hopes of seeing him, but he came no further. As she wrote, "there are things that one can say by word of mouth that cannot be written in a letter. May it please God that I see you healthy before I die." But whatever more tender sentiments she may have reserved for a meeting with her son, the written words of her letter were hardly gentle. Like every mother's son, Filippo was admonished to write more often—"by every courier even if only to say that you are well." She also begged him to mend his ways: "Above all, my son, see that you behave well, so that, though last year you gave me such pain with your bad ways, you bring me consolation." No specific offense is named, but she obviously felt that he lacked the proper gratitude to his cousin, protector, and employer: "and considering your condition and all that Niccolò has done for you, you should feel worthy of kissing the ground on which he walks. And I say this out of love for you, since you are more obligated to him than to your own father or mother."[10]

[9] Goldthwaite, *Private Wealth*, pp. 53–55.

[10] *Lettere*, pp. 8–9.

Such rough chiding and the abrupt reminder that "you are no longer a child" would have been hard on any young man, perhaps harder for Filippo than for many others. Cesare Guasti, the editor of the Strozzi letters, describes the young Filippo as having a "resentful and aggressive nature."[11] He gives the appearance of being an inflexible, closed sort of man, sharing his mother's determination, but without her expressive and forthright personality. In later years, his cautious and determined character would serve him well in avoiding political hazards while steadily acquiring one of the century's great fortunes. And if his late-born son and biographer is to be believed, this same combination of inflexible will and tight emotional control was the key to the greatest ambition of his life, the building of the Strozzi palace. The success of this massive project, especially for a family still tainted by its political past, depended on avoiding any appearance of challenging the prestige of the Medici. Thus, as the story goes, Filippo managed to pretend a complete lack of interest in building a great family mansion and had to be urged to begin the project—his dearest, but secret ambition—by a civic-minded Lorenzo Magnifico.[12]

Although Filippo preserved a large part of his mother's and Marco Parenti's correspondence, almost nothing that went the other way has survived. On the slim evidence we have, it seems that the cautious note in Filippo's make-up took time to develop, while determination, even arrogance, was there from the start. Reading an early letter from Filippo to his mother, one is struck by his clarity and confidence as he looked to the future.[13]

At the time Filippo was expecting a move from Barcelona to Naples and welcomed the change, "since I will be closer to there [i.e. Florence] and I will be in a more beautiful city than this; and it is a courtly city. Besides there are many Florentines there." But for all his wanting to be closer to home

[11] *Lettere*, p. xxix.

[12] *Vita di Filippo Strozzi il Vecchio scritta da Lorenzo suo figlio*, ed. G. Bini and P. Bigazzi (Florence, 1851), pp. 23–25.

[13] 14 Aug. 1446, excerpted in *Lettere*, pp. 25–27.

and in the company of Florentines, Filippo was perfectly clear that Florence itself held no promise for himself or his brothers. "You see already," he told his mother, "that when you are gone (may God keep you a long time) we will have little to build on there. All our opportunity I feel is outside Florence." Perhaps in the course of time matters in the city might settle themselves in such a way as to make his return possible; "but," he concluded, "I doubt they will so arrange themselves in our day." The tone was sober, but without dismay. He was determined to seize his chances and realistic enough to accept the fact that his own homeland offered none or few.

Strozzi's youthful self-assurance had its unattractive side. Though he expressed a sense of obligation to his cousin and immediate employer, Niccolò Strozzi, Filippo blithely dismissed his mother's fears that he might not be getting along well with the senior partner, his namesake Filippo Strozzi. He was sure that could not be so; in fact, he felt he had good hopes of being named an heir. Besides, he explained with cold self-confidence, when the senior cousins grew old they would want to be well taken care of by their younger kin, so it was in their own interest to show kindness now. With the secret to old men's hearts safely in hand, Filippo urged his mother to be cheerful, because "I still intend to rebuild our house."

Here is the heart of it: Filippo's determination to take on himself the burden of rebuilding his family's fortunes. And though only a young man, he speaks of it as something habitual, as a charge he "still" intended to perform. We have no way of knowing how long he had lived with this responsibility, nor whether the original impulse was his or hers. But whether Alessandra's demands molded her son's self-confident character or his ambition encouraged hers, the result was the same. Filippo had made a compact with his mother; it was the basis of their special closeness, the reason, too, for the severity she used in speaking to him.

As the eldest son in a fatherless household, Filippo had undoubtedly been forced to grow up quickly. (Parenti, as we will see, remarks that perhaps his brother-in-law had never been a child at all.) Filippo was more than willing to play the father, giving his younger brothers the same guidance and chastisement his mother used with him. In this same early letter he informed his mother of his views concerning their futures. "I found Lorenzo here . . . ," he wrote; "I do not know how things will work out, but I cannot think other than well, since I will supervise him and keep him to the mark." Extending his prerogative still further, he turned to the case of Matteo. The boy was only eleven years old and still living at home, but Filippo insisted that the time had come for him to learn his trade, either in the city or, if possible, abroad. Should this leave Alessandra too lonely, he added, she might take "some boy from some poor person" for the sake of company.

This was a provocative suggestion and Alessandra reacted with alarm. The prospect of losing the daily company of her last born was painful even to contemplate. But Filippo was not the only one who felt that the time was coming for Matteo to leave home, and Alessandra's predicament was not made easier by her own realization that, in the end, she owed it as a duty to the family to let the boy follow the path his brothers had already laid out. In the months that followed, the question of Matteo's future became a preoccupation in the family at large—including the new son-in-law, Marco Parenti, who now took his place for the first time as a member of the family circle.

The story of young Matteo's eventual departure from home and its unfortunate consequences is probably the fullest, most revealing of the many family incidents chronicled in the correspondence of these early years. Although only a byway in Marco's biography, it shows as nothing else does the smaller world of Marco Parenti at this time.

★

The boy who was the object of so much of his mother's anxiety is only the dimmest of figures for us. Only a few early letters give a glimpse of Matteo as a child. Nothing else survives that might have preserved something of his own personality, distinct from the pressure of Filippo's ambitions or Alessandra's possessive care.

Alessandra's affection for Matteo called out the softer side of her nature, as we see in the second letter of her correspondence, written in the autumn of 1448. With mixed pride and protectiveness she watched his early efforts at penmanship and called upon the rest of the family to take an interest too. She had not written in some time, she reported to Filippo, partly because she had not been well, but also because she wished to encourage Matteo to have some practice writing for her. "When he writes slowly and puts his mind to what he is doing he writes well," though the opposite was true when he rushed. She had also shown some samples of his efforts to Marco, who "has a fine hand." She was sure that Matteo would benefit from his brother-in-law's instruction, since the boy was more respectful toward Marco than his mother, or so she claimed.[14]

Marco did, indeed, have a fine hand, still legible after five centuries. For men of his class good handwriting was a practical skill as well as an ornament. "The pen is an instrument so noble and excellent," a contemporary merchant's manual advised, "that it is absolutely necessary not only to merchants but also in any art, whether liberal, mercantile, or mechanical. And when you see a merchant to whom the pen is a burden or who is inept with the pen, you may say that he is not a merchant."[15] In fifteenth-century Italy ink-stained fingers were not a sign of clerical bookishness, but of practical energy and patient dedication to trade.

For the young Matteo a good clear hand would be important. Bookkeeping and letter writing would likely be a large part of his apprenticeship and subsequent career, and though we hear nothing specifically about it, we can assume that he was also receiving schooling in other skills needed for business, especially "the abacus" or business arithmetic. Such training would ready Matteo for an apprenticeship—and, sooner or later, the inevitable departure from home. In the meantime, as his mother had instructed him, he wrote Filippo

[14] 4 Nov. 1448; Strozzi, pp. 33–34.

[15] Benedetto Cotrugli, *Della mercatura et del mercante perfetto*, in *Medieval Trade in the Mediterranean World*, ed. R. S. Lopez and I. R. Raymond (New York, 1955), pp. 375–76.

a very grown-up sort of letter that manfully imitated his mother's style.

As his mother's deputy, Matteo reviewed family and business affairs, but he closed the letter with an amusing coda that may have been something of his own. Here he presumed to offer his elder brother a little lesson in the use of ciphers. He was including "a bit of cipher," he wrote, so that if he or his mother wished, they could communicate to Filippo without the danger of others hearing of it. For each letter of the alphabet an arabic numeral would be substituted, beginning with "a" as "7," "b" as "8," and so forth. The device was extremely simple and would have been easy to crack. Matteo, however, was evidently pleased with his brainchild; he encouraged his brother to try it in his next letter, "and I will see if you understand it."[16]

Ciphers were common enough in fifteenth-century Italy, though much more so in diplomatic than in private correspondence, where cryptic or allusive reference served the same purpose. Certainly there were reasons to worry about the security of the post. Personal and business letters were sent in packets with couriers, which meant that they might well travel with others belonging to unfriendly or overly curious parties. The danger of letters going astray was a constant preoccupation, and Marco habitually began his with a summary of those he had received as a check against this possibility. Seventeen years later in a time of urgent political difficulties, he too adopted a cipher and abbreviated the list of letters received to no more than their dates. But this time had not yet arrived, and Matteo's early effort was probably just a boyish game. In any case the code was not adopted and no more is said about ciphers until 1465.

It is doubtful that Filippo alone could have overcome his mother's reluctance to let Matteo go. He was joined, however, by his cousin and employer Niccolò, whose word carried great weight with Alessandra. In the summer of 1449 the visit of another family member with the intriguingly mercantile name of Soldo Strozzi settled the matter. The widow could not

[16] 20 Feb. 1448, *Lettere*, pp. 40–42.

resist the combined voices of the Strozzi menfolk, especially when they spoke in the name of a duty that she understood as well as any man. It was left to her to lament a painful necessity and to remind them all of the price they were exacting. Since they were anxious to do something for Matteo's advancement, she wrote Filippo, she would let him go, "not thinking of my own consolation, but of your benefit, as I have done always and will do until the end." But she took the opportunity to remind him, as she must have done many times, of the pathos of her circumstances, of how his father's death had left her young and alone with five small children to care for: "and this Matteo remained to me in the flesh and I raised him thinking that, other than death, nothing would part him from me. And especially it seemed to me to be enough since of the three, two were away."[17]

How quickly her thoughts narrowed from the five children she had raised to the three sons she could no longer hold on to! Her two daughters, the younger still at home, the elder recently married and already expecting the first grandchild, dropped from her mind; they were not, like Matteo, her "consolation." Nonetheless she dutifully gathered together the new clothes Soldo said Matteo would need for their journey: a new cloak, a sturdy tunic and doublet, sandals, some shirts, and other items.

Everything had been done to prepare for Matteo's trip, but at the last moment it was postponed. According to Alessandra the decision was pressed on her by many relatives and friends. "In sum," she wrote, "everyone shouted at me that I cared little for this boy, and that I am a mad woman to send him in this weather." In the terrible summer heat, with plague everywhere, even a grown man used to travel would suffer, much less a boy "with a weak constitution." Others from outside the family had also joined in dissuading her. Two Observantist friars "who were close friends of your father" had come the previous morning to argue with her, and "no less than Gino di Neri Capponi sent to me to say that I was a fool to send him."

[17] 13 July 1447, *Lettere*, pp. 45–46.

Capponi's name was a trump card. One of the leading men of Florence, he was perhaps the only one who could contend with Cosimo de' Medici on an equal footing. But even with such weighty opinion behind her, Alessandra could not simply rest her case. The decision to postpone the trip had already been taken, yet her letter kept its pleading tone. The delay would only be for a month and a half or two, she urged; in September, when the summer heat had passed, she would certainly send him. Meanwhile they must have patience, "since if he should die, neither you would have him nor would I."

There is no mistaking the tension in Alessandra's voice. Her need to remind her sons (and herself) of all that she had been to them, her anxious elaboration of reasons that seem sufficient, and then this sudden premonition of Matteo's death, all reveal her raw and vulnerable state. Only at the end of the letter did she slip into a more familiar mood, chiding Filippo "that when Matteo comes . . . do not treat him as I heard you treated Lorenzo."

Matteo's planned departure brought comment from Marco as well. His letter is in two parts: the first, written still in expectation of the trip, contains some careful advice to Filippo about his younger brother; the second signals the change in plans. The latter part confirms the details of Alessandra's letter, namely that the boy had, in fact, been on the point of departing when everyone—"even Gino di Neri [Capponi]"—had joined in urging her against it. And Parenti too cites Matteo's "delicate complexion" as a reason for special caution in this season of plague. More interesting, though, is the first part of the letter, because it shows Marco in what would become his customary role as Filippo's counselor and confidant. It demonstrates as well the qualities of tact and intelligence that, over the years, would make Marco's advice something worth having.[18]

The two men were still relative strangers: only two years earlier, at the time of the betrothal, Marco had written Filippo for the first time, addressing him in terms of careful formality and expressing his longing for the time when they might

[18] 11 July 1449, CS ser. 3, 131, fol. 38^{r-v}, and *Lettere*, pp. 50–51.

become acquainted "in person."[19] Marco now took up the subject of Matteo's future with considerable delicacy. It was not his role, he wrote, to recommend Matteo to his own brother, but he would give Filippo his views on Matteo's prospects since by force of circumstances it had been so long since they had seen each other. For Matteo's character Marco had much praise, and he was sure that with the good guidance of Filippo, Matteo would do well. Filippo would understand what was required, "since you know how you would have wished to be looked after by your uncles and masters when in a similar position." This point was subtly made, acknowledging Filippo's rights while urging him to exercise a special and possibly uncharacteristic patience. Do not be "too anxious to make him do more than he can," Marco cautioned, "because nothing is so harmful to a good character as being overburdened."[20]

Marco's first motive may have been his affection and concern for the young Matteo, but he must also have been reflecting Alessandra's anxieties and responding to her wishes. In either case, Filippo's reputation for obduracy was reason enough both for offering the advice and for the gentle manner in which it was framed. While assuring Filippo that he had no fear that the boy would be badly treated, Marco continued to urge him to remember his own early experiences. "But I want to say," he wrote, "that no profession is so light and easy that it does not seem hard and burdensome at the beginning." At first one must go slowly and have the patience to let him learn in several stages, rather than attempting to instruct him in everything at once.

Once again Marco showed how deftly he could put his case in a situation in which to offer advice at all could so easily give offense. Even so he knew that his brother-in-law might bridle at this interference, and he concluded with an apology that nonetheless reconfirmed his concern: "And all that I have said to you above is not said because I do not believe that you do not know what is necessary better than I do, since you

[19] 19 Aug. 1447, A.S.F., CS ser. 3, 131, fol. 33, and *Lettere*, pp. 12–13.
[20] 11 July 1449, CS ser. 3, 131, fol. 38^{r-v}, and *Lettere*, pp. 50–51.

have experienced it and not I. But I say it only because you are young, and it is the nature of youth to be impatient and eager. For this reason I remind you to have tolerance and show discretion in putting up with whatever is needed. Do not think of yourself in this, since perhaps you were never a child, but think of his needs."

This last is an arresting remark and an effective summary of his entire case. In it Marco paid homage to the difficulties of Filippo's early life and the resolution with which he was meeting them. At the same time, it seems an assessment of his brother-in-law's character worth remembering.

Parenti customarily closed his letters to Filippo with the brief and familiar words, "thy Marco." On this occasion, however, he chose a more formal closing, signing "Marcho di Parente Parenti," as if addressing a stranger. Whether he meant in this way to add weight to his advice or merely felt a little stiff in the role of advisor, he must have felt apprehensive about Filippo's response. In the event the reaction proved sharp, and Marco in his turn abandoned the milder sympathies of the first letter. Filippo's letter has disappeared along with the rest of his correspondence, but we can judge its tone from the reply Marco felt obliged to make. Apparently Filippo had declared himself "amazed" at the cancellation of Matteo's trip. In the same letter, though, he let slip that he had tried to dissuade Niccolò Strozzi from traveling to Barcelona, also because of the plague. This gave Marco a ready retort. "I am amazed at you," he returned, echoing Filippo's own words, "that you know how to advise others in a similar case, but do not follow the advice yourself." Surely, he insisted, Niccolò's reasons for risking the trip to Barcelona were more pressing than any Filippo had for wanting Matteo at that moment.[21]

After the restraint of earlier letters we may be surprised by the edge of temper in this exchange. Such irritations were not common, but from time to time there are other hints that Marco's habitual tact and complaisance could give way to exasperated self-assertion. Yet while his relations with Filippo

[21] 19 Sept. 1449, CS ser. 3, 249, fol. 106^{r-v}.

became more normal, Marco still retained an air of awe toward the Strozzi family, especially where the senior members were concerned. Niccolò Strozzi's arrival in Florence, for instance, called forth this respectful sentiment: "It was a great pleasure for me to meet him, and if formerly I loved him by repute, having seen him in person, I love him still more."[22]

It took a long time for Alessandra to trust and confide in Marco. He was still a young man and it was natural for her to look to her late husband's family for help and advice. In the early years she spoke dismissively of his family and kept secret a financial arrangement she had made about Caterina's dowry.[23] And even many years later she was irked when Filippo made a present of linens to Caterina and Marco. He "has the means to pay," she grumbled.[24] But from Marco's side there is no doubt that respect mingled with affection, as is plainly shown when the time finally came for Matteo to depart for Naples. Six months had gone by, not the two or three Alessandra had promised. Though the summer heat and risk of plague had long since passed, Alessandra's sadness was undiminished. "I do not know how I can live without him,"

[22] 6 Feb. 1449, CS ser. 3, 131, fol. 42, and *Lettere*, pp. 76–78.

[23] After the birth of her grandson, Alessandra wrote: "Caterina is well and so is her son. Marco and Parente treat her very well, and she is not lacking any comfort, unless it is that she has a bad mother-in-law. But I tell you truly that they are not relations one can count on for any service at all" (22 Oct. 1450, *Lettere*, p. 89). This was a harsh accusation in a society that assumed that marriage created an alliance between families. With regard to the dowry, the problem was that the part of Caterina's that came from the Dowry Fund would not come due until after the marriage, so long after, in fact, that Caterina's pregnancy would have come to term. There was a danger that she might die in childbirth and the dowry—already paid out to Marco—could not be recouped from the Dowry Fund. Apparently a form of insurance was available, but Marco strongly opposed this, saying that Caterina was healthy and the money would be thrown away. Alessandra nonetheless purchased the insurance, but cautioned Filippo not to reveal this to Marco, who would be displeased, "since the matter is our own concern" (26 Dec. 1449, *Lettere*, pp. 59–60).

[24] Half as much linen would have been more than enough, Alessandra wrote, and went on to say that she had not yet told Parenti that it was intended as a gift and that she would wait for another instruction before saying anything (7 Apr. 1464, *Lettere*, p. 280).

she now wrote, noting as if in explanation that the boy had grown into a fine youth and had become the very image of his father. For his part, despite his liking for Matteo, Marco watched the small party take its leave with eyes for the grieving mother, not the departing son. They left this morning, he wrote, "which I promise you left Mona Alessandra both melancholy and unhappy. To find herself left without a single one of her three sons pains her very much, but she comforts herself, not with the spirit of a woman but a man, with the good she hopes must come of it."[25]

★

The rest of Matteo's brief history is quickly told, though to do so means jumping a little ahead. His departure for Naples came in February 1450. In June of the same year his mother noted to Filippo that she had written to her cousin, the boy's employer, to say that if he was not doing well, he should be sent home. She was praying to God for the right response, she confided; "at times I can't in any way resign myself to having him taken from me."[26] A few months later she was excusing her failure to write to Matteo's absence: "by now it is necessary that one of you return here, since I am already of an age to want to be taken care of, and I am not well, and it seems a labor to write."[27]

Occasionally, there is further mention of Matteo in the sparse correspondence of the 1450s, until at last in the autumn of 1459, Alessandra heard from Naples that Matteo was seriously ill. She waited through long, anxious days while slow and faulty mails brought further word; and when at last her fears were confirmed, she numbly rehearsed the news as it had come to her, recalling her past hopes as well as fears as though somehow they might still be of use:

> My sweet son. On the 11th of last month I had yours of the 29th of July, saying how my dear beloved Matteo had fallen sick; and having nothing from you about the sort of illness, I

[25] 6 Feb. 1449, CS ser. 3, 249, fol. 73, and *Lettere*, pp. 76–78.
[26] 5 June 1456, *Lettere*, p. 81.
[27] 22 Oct. 1450, *Lettere*, p. 85.

> was very worried for him and felt very grieved. I called Francesco and sent for Matteo di Giorgio and I heard from both that his sickness was a tertian fever; this comforted me considerably, since without other complications, one does not die of it. Then I was continually informed by you that his sickness was abating, which relieved my mind a little, though I was still anxious. Then I heard how on the 23rd it pleased Him who gave him to me to take him to Himself.

Knowing that Filippo's first concern would be for her, Alessandra took the measure of her feelings, balancing grief with the consolations of family and religion. "It is a great bitterness," she wrote,

> to be deprived of such a son. Filial love aside, I feel his death is a great loss to me, and likewise to you, my other two sons, now reduced to so few. I praise and thank Our Lord for everything that is His will, since I am sure that God saw that this was the right moment for the salvation of his soul. . . . Though I have felt great heartsickness, more than ever before, two things have comforted me against this pain. The first is that he was with you, so I am certain that the doctors and medicines and everything that was possible to do for his health, with all the remedies that can be applied, were seen to and that nothing was neglected to save his life.
>
> The other thing that gives me peace is that at the moment of death God gave him his grace and help to confess his sins, to request confession and communion and extreme unction, all of which, I understand, he did with great devotion, a sign of hope that God will have prepared a good place for him. Therefore, knowing that we must all make this journey, and that we do not know how it will be, and that we are not sure of making it in the way my gracious son Matteo did—since some die a sudden death, and some are torn to pieces, and thus in many deaths the soul is lost as well as the body—this gives me peace, considering that God might have done worse to me.[28]

Each met the shock of death in his own way. "Though nothing is more certain than death," Marco wrote, "never-

[28] 6 Sept. 1459, *Lettere*, pp. 176–79.

theless I might have feared any other misfortune than this, given your youthfulness; and the less I imagined such a mischance, so much the heavier was the blow I felt. From the time of my father's death until now, I have never experienced such sorrow." Alessandra looked to the consolations of religion; Marco—for once in this correspondence reflecting his humanistic education—offered Roman fortitude. "Worthy men," he urged, "do not allow themselves to be overcome by misfortunes, but when these occur, they grow in perfection and are a refuge and consolation to others."[29]

Filippo, to whom these consolations were addressed, also dwelled on the hostility of Fortune, coupling his brother's death with the family's political troubles. "You see what a blow this is," he wrote Lorenzo, "and how Fortune has not yet done with persecuting us. We must be patient with it all." Less the humanist-stoic than Marco, he was also less the pietist than his mother. "I cannot believe," he wrote, "that this is the result of our sins, but more likely those of our forebears." But Filippo was always a practical man and his first thought was to reunite his diminished family around him. He made plans to bring his mother and brother to Naples and asked Lorenzo to acquire in Bruges a variety of housewares to furnish the larger, more permanent household he envisaged.[30]

The dispersal of her little family was very much on Alessandra's mind as well, and her son's death in a distant city filled her with remorse as well as grief. Filippo's presence at the deathbed was a comfort, but she could not put off the thought that she should have been there too—as she would have been had she given way to Filippo's earlier pleas for her to settle with him in Naples. Now she reproached him for not having let her know from the first day that the illness was grave. But her real regrets were directed at herself: "I wish that I hadn't asked anyone's advice, that indeed I had followed my own opinion and done what I wanted to do, since I would have arrived in time to have seen and touched my sweet son

[29] 1 Sept. 1459, CS ser. 3, 180. fol. 56, and *Lettere*, p. 187.

[30] *Lettere*, pp. 190–91.

still living, and I would have taken comfort and given some to him and you."[31]

This was scarcely practical. Filippo's letter with the first news of the illness had taken thirteen days to reach her, and her own journey south would have been still longer—and this in time of war and threats of war. But without such a trip, it must have been especially hard to come to terms with this intimate but distant tragedy; after all, she had already gone through a kind of mourning years before when Matteo had been taken from her. But Alessandra was a person of practical energies, and Matteo's death made her more solicitous of Filippo than ever. Worried that his health might suffer, she suggested fresh air, some light purging, and a relaxation from the strains of business. "Have more care for yourself than for your possessions," she urged, with a hint at Filippo's frugal temperament, "since you see [in death] one leaves everything behind." At the same time, she now appeared to accept the need for a move to Naples and declared her desire—"with all my heart and soul"—to spend her remaining years with him. "I have no other fear," she wrote, "except that I might die before seeing either one of you."

*

In 1450, when young Matteo left Florence for Naples, the movements of the three brothers were a matter for the family itself to decide. But in 1458, the year before Matteo's death, this situation changed drastically. In a virtual coup d'état, the Medici faction consolidated its power and firmly punished its enemies—including the Strozzi brothers and other descendants of the defeated party of 1434.

Marco Parenti's sudden loss of political favor had come in the wake of the Peace of Lodi; for his brothers-in-law, the blow came a little later, but fell far more heavily. The liberal interlude that followed Lodi lasted only three years. The aftermath of the peace had been greater liberty, signaled by a return to the traditional electoral lottery. But the conflict had put a

[31] 13 Sept. 1459, *Lettere*, pp. 195–200.

heavy strain on the treasury, and an unfavorable economic climate led to strong resistance to tax measures. In 1458 the patricians, burdened by new and heavier assessments and anxious about their authority in the state, began to plot a return to stricter rule.[32] First, however, it was essential to have a Signoria that could be relied on; but, as Parenti commented in his *Memoir*, "the purses were sealed and the lottery did not soon come up with the priors who suited his [i.e. Cosimo's] intentions."

The opportunity the oligarchs needed came at last in the summer of 1458 when Luca Pitti was drawn as Standard Bearer of Justice. Pitti was the first lieutenant of the Medici faction, "a man," in Parenti's unsympathetic view, "entirely devoted to Cosimo, arrogant, and willing to do anything to support Cosimo's power without regard to any other consideration."[33] Pitti's plan was to create a select and powerful council, centralizing authority and reducing the role of the traditional communal assemblies, the Councils of the Commune and of the People. When this "reform" did not seem likely to find enough support, other ways of using the present advantage to control future elections were put forward, but all met strong resistance. Finally, the oligarchy played its most dangerous card, a *parlamento*.

The parlamento or popular assembly was a vestige of the commune's earliest days, when vital decisions could be taken by direct vote of the whole body of the citizens assembled in the cathedral or principal square. In theory, it was an expression of popular will, but in practice it was more often the instrument of faction or tyranny. Whoever controlled the great bells that called the people together, the streets that led to the square, and the chancellor who put forward the resolutions effectively controlled the "voice of the people."

In 1458 the Mediceans took no chances. They arrested their leading critic among the patricians, Girolamo Machiavelli, and

[32] N. Rubinstein, *The Government of Florence under the Medici* (Oxford, 1966), p. 88ff.

[33] *Memorie*, p. 65.

ordered one hundred and fifty others to go to their villas and not to return without permission. Troops under Florence's mercenary captain were brought into the city and the Medici armed their partisans. The others, Marco wrote, "in order not to appear opposed," also obeyed the summons of the bell and assembled in the piazza. The new proposals were read out in a voice so weak that few could actually hear them but under the circumstances it hardly mattered. Their business was accomplished, as one chronicler put it, "without the least commotion."[34] Florence returned to strict Medicean control, and the creation of the powerful new Council of 100 promised to give the regime greater stability and strictness than ever before.

Despite the smoothness of its victory, the regime remained preoccupied with security. Only a handful of men actually suffered banishment, a further indication that the reformist climate of the past three years may have been created by widespread sentiment rather than by any organized plotting. But there remained other, older enemies, the exiles of 1434, and though they could hardly have played a role in the recent troubles, the heaviest blow was aimed at them. Twice before their sentences had been extended; now another twenty-five years was added. Beyond this, the sons and descendants of exiles who had violated the terms of their sentences were also banished for twenty-five years, and the same harsh penalty was attached to the sons and descendants of certain specific families. Among those named were the Strozzi.

By the terms of the decree, the exiles were banned from Florence and its *dominio* and were forbidden to approach closer to the city than one hundred miles. All communication with them was to be subject to the permission and close scrutiny of the magistracy in charge of security, the Eight of Ward. Soon the distance was reduced to fifty miles—providing always that the exiles stayed clear of Florentine territories—and freer correspondence was permitted. "We have been given

[34] See the *priorista* of Agnolo Gaddi, British Library, MS Egerton 3764, fol. 189r, and *Memorie*, p. 66.

license to write without showing the letters to the Eight," Alessandra reported, adding that one can say what one wants, "political matters aside."[35]

For the Strozzi brothers the ban could not have been a complete surprise. A quarter of a century had passed since an earlier parlamento first sent the Albizzi and their allies into exile. Sooner or later the political standing of their sons, now grown men, would have to be settled, and the two renewals of the original exile were a warning not to expect clemency. To Filippo and his brothers Florence must always have seemed an inhospitable place, and the anticipation of eventually falling under the same ban as their late father was surely a large part of their decision to seek careers elsewhere.

Filippo's personal reactions came in a philosophic letter addressed to his "Very beloved and unfortunate Mother":

> These are only the fruits of this world; and for those who, like ourselves, have tasted them often, beginning in boyhood, it doesn't matter so much as for those affected later in life. So for this we must thank God. I remain very patient, since it was done with the consent of those who govern, because I am sure they did it only for the good and peace of the entire city. For this reason I will not diminish the good will I feel for the principal citizens, nor the love I have for my homeland. . . . It is ten years already that you have lived without any one of us and you were prepared to remain so many more. And it could easily have happened that you or we might have died without seeing each other again. Now this accident may be the cause of your leaving and coming together with your sons, to live and die together.[36]

The other shoe had finally dropped, and there was little to do except regroup the family in exile. It was this call to leave Florence—"to live and die together"—that still echoed for Alessandra, embittering her grief, when Matteo died in the following year. She certainly gave thought to the move and Filippo made efforts to prepare his household to receive her.

[35] 19 Feb. 1458, *Lettere*, p. 143 and p. 148ff.

[36] 8 Nov. 1458, CS ser. 3, 180, fol. 60.

Nothing came of it, though, except a temporary reunion with Filippo in Rome in 1460. Meanwhile she offered her household to her second daughter, Lessandra, and her husband, Giovanni Bonsi. There would be some savings for each, she explained, "and also if I stay, I will have company, and the time will pass more easily and with less melancholy."[37]

But Filippo's reactions to the decree of exile can also be seen as hinting—very discreetly—at one other possibility. There is a studied, formal quality to this letter that is unique in the correspondence, a sort of calculated nobility that suggests it was meant for public view; certainly he goes out of his way to express his respect for the Florentine authorities.[38] Filippo already had firmly in mind the necessity of preserving the best possible relations with the regime that had dealt with him so harshly. And in this respect it could be said that his campaign to reinstate himself in Florence had already begun.

[37] 20 July 1459, *Lettere*, p. 153.

[38] See the discussion of H. Gregory, who suggests that the letter was meant to be circulated to prove Filippo's loyalty (Gregory, "A Florentine Family," p. 204).

PART II

POLITICS

Repatriation and Reform

1464–1466

★

DESPITE her emotional promise at the time of Matteo's death to join Filippo in Naples, Alessandra did not leave Florence. Her longing to reunite the family came to focus instead on the possibility of winning permission for her sons to return to the city. This campaign only became intense after Cosimo's death in 1464, and it was both aided and immensely complicated by the reawakening of factional tensions. Behind the repatriation effort was the growing mercantile success of the Strozzi brothers, now trading independently in both Naples and Rome. Large loans to King Ferrante of Naples gave Filippo considerable influence at the court, where he was given the title of counselor of state, and it was an open question how much the king's patronage might accomplish in Florence. Filippo Strozzi had become a man whose favor, even when exercised from exile, was worth having.

For Marco Parenti too the years following Cosimo's death were a critical time. He had become Filippo's confidant and agent at a time when the connection was both more prestigious and more crucial than ever. This involvement with the Strozzi reshaped his own political life, giving him access to the most influential citizens and supplying an opportunity for a limited kind of political action. At the same time, he retained a broader interest in the direction that the regime would take now that Cosimo was gone. Liberalization of the regime might give men like himself new opportunities to participate in the highest offices. Anticipating such changes, Marco conceived the idea of composing a history of Florence in the aftermath of Cosimo's death. From the wider perspectives of such a history, Filippo's hope of repatriation could be seen as a part of the old battle between the regime and its opponents.

Many of the developments of 1464–1466 can be followed in detail. Just at this point, when crucial public events were pressing in on Marco's private world, his correspondence is at its richest—making available, in effect, a second chronicle of 1464–1466 that parallels but is quite distinct from the *Memoir.* A third of his surviving letters date from this time, and they can be supplemented by Alessandra's somewhat smaller correspondence as well as by the wider commentary in his *Memoir.* In the year and a half following Cosimo's death on August 1, 1464, we come as close to Marco Parenti as we ever do, seeing him in many small actions, but even more in his advice and reflections. The focus of activity, as always in this family correspondence, is on the Strozzi, but most often the observing eye is Marco's.

More than most Florentines, the Strozzi were stirred by the rising expectations that followed Cosimo's death. The uncertainty that had entered into Florentine political life presented new opportunities. But with these came choices that were excruciatingly difficult and risky.

The first test of the new situation came when Lorenzo Strozzi made an application to the government of the republic for permission to visit Florence. Clearly, the visit was intended to probe the political support that the exiles could count on in the city. The issue dragged on for some time, revealing that in this small matter, as in much greater ones, the regime was showing unaccustomed divisions. It became apparent that the family's best connections lay among those who were beginning to emerge as leaders of an anti-Medicean faction. Agnolo Acciaiuoli and Dietisalvi Neroni, both senior figures in the oligarchy for many years, had lately become critical of the Medici and were anxious to press their own ambitions against Piero's leadership. Both men were approached about the self-conduct for Lorenzo, and each offered his support.

With Neroni, Marco was chosen as the go-between, a role that would soon become familiar. "And because Dietisalvi is one of your supporters," wrote Alessandra, "it seemed to me and Giovanni [Bonsi] and Marco a good idea to go and ask advice from him too. And because he is close to Marco, he was the one who went." She was convinced that they could count on Acciaiuoli as well, though on another occasion she warned Filippo not to count too heavily on his influence: "your

Messere A. is not as well placed as you think," she said, "and is not *el principale*."[1] The king's patronage counted heavily with Neroni and Acciaiuoli. They too were engaged in a hunt for favor and they were prepared to look as far as Naples to find it. Cosimo's long domination of Florence had effectively turned politics into a system of patrons and clients. It was inevitable that after his death new patrons would seek to establish themselves, in part by promising their favor to new and valued clients.

The terms of this competition for patronage are set out in Parenti's *Memoir* in a description of the rivalry between Piero de' Medici and the third of the opposition leaders, Luca Pitti:

> His [Piero de' Medici's] reputation was much diminished at this time. And M. Luca Pitti held court at his house, where a great part of the citizens went to consult on matters of government. Amongst the other citizens, M. Agnolo Acciaiuoli and M. Dietisalvi di Nerone, were the most outstanding. Though superior to M. Luca in prudence, they consented to his having such prestige, and to increase it they too frequented his house. All this they did to block Piero de' Medici, to whom previously everyone was accustomed to going to consult on public affairs as well as private, and to take away from him the great arrogance which he had put on—something already obnoxious and insupportable to all.[2]

For the Strozzi, Pitti's leadership somewhat disturbed a natural sympathy for the anti-Medicean faction. Pitti had from the first been one of Cosimo's chief supporters. He had figured prominently in the Medici triumphs of 1434 and 1458, and we have already noted Parenti's hostile description of him in the latter year as "a man entirely devoted to Cosimo." For

[1] 13 Dec. 1464, *Lettere*, pp. 332–33; 15 Sept. 1464, *Lettere*, p. 324. Several letters of this period survive from Acciaiuoli to Filippo. In them M. Agnolo speaks of having gone to the *principali* to say that he had heard that the king of Naples wished to send Filippo to Florence on his own business. The suggestion obviously met with hostility and Acciaiuoli excused himself, saying that "these are things that cannot be overcome in regimes of this kind [in simili governi]" (5 Feb. 1465, CS ser. 3, 131, fol. 131).

[2] *Memorie*, p. 75.

her part, Alessandra had never liked Pitti. Earlier, when Pitti was to be knighted, she had commented that the honor would "truly swell his gut."[3] Nor did Pitti—unlike his two partners in opposition—enjoy favor in Naples. Indeed, the prospect of such favor was something Filippo could dangle in front of Pitti's eager eyes.

In the narrow world of Florentine politics personal loyalty or suspicion always counted heavily, but in the end Alessandra's distrust of Pitti was probably not the critical factor, and in the months ahead approaches were made to him with gratifying results. Her natural pessimism and a deep fear of repeating past mistakes made her wary of involving her family too far in the fortunes of an anti-Medicean party. As the factional crisis grew and an outright clash became more and more likely, the parallels with 1434 became oppressive. "May it be God's wish that these things come to a good end," she exclaimed at a moment of high tension, "it makes me remember '34."[4] At the time of the earlier crisis she had been under thirty; now she was almost sixty. Age, conservatism, and an ingrained fatalism inclined her to the belief that the Medici alone held the fate of her sons in their hands. Although both Filippo and Marco at times entertained other hopes, her view prevailed and proved itself correct.

It is not that Alessandra favored the Medici. Aside from her obsessive devotion to her sons' interest, she had few political opinions other than the conviction that the big shots were not to be trusted. "These days," she complained in connection with the delays over Lorenzo's visit, "it is difficult to find a loyal man who will stand by his word."[5] In dishonest times, caution and neutrality were obviously the recommended course. And yet it is in the nature of crises to push people toward difficult choices; nor was it easy to remain inactive when, after years of waiting, affairs at last seemed to be in motion and powerful "friends" appeared willing to help.

[3] 17 Dec. 1463, *Lettere*, p. 267.
[4] 22 Nov. 1465, *Lettere*, p. 520.
[5] 29 Mar. 1465, *Lettere*, p. 386.

To take some initiative, to plan some strategy—if only a hypothetical one—would be a relief from the tension of watching and hoping.

As it happened, an ideal opportunity soon presented itself in the diplomatic arena. Ambassadors to Naples were being commissioned and a Neapolitan prince would be visiting Florence soon after. The occasion was a royal wedding; it seemed the perfect moment to test the good will of their professed friends and to take the measure of Piero de' Medici.

CHAPTER 4

WINTER AND SPRING: DON FEDERIGO'S VISIT

★

EARLY IN HIS *Memoir*, Parenti presents a useful synopsis of the diplomatic exchanges between Florence and Naples in the late winter and spring of 1465:

> On the 4th of February 1465 three ambassadors were elected: for Naples Messer Luigi Guicciardini and Pandolfo di Messer Giannozzo Pandolfini, and one for Milan, Dietisalvi di Nerone. This was done because of current events, both the death of Cosimo and the new marriage alliance made between King Ferdinand of Naples and Duke Francesco of Milan, whose daughter Madonna Ippolita was betrothed to Don Alfonso, duke of Calabria and son of the said king. Therefore it seemed reasonable in every way that our ambassadors should be there.[1]

The commissioning of high-ranking ambassadors to Naples and Milan was a sign that in the aftermath of Cosimo's death the city recognized its need to reaffirm its relations with the major powers. The marriage between the Sforza of Milan and the Aragonese rulers of Naples was a matter of great diplomatic importance. It secured an alliance between two of the chief states of the peninsula and would be a major prop to peace and stability.[2] A secondary effect of the plans for the

[1] *Memorie*, pp. 17–18.

[2] On Neapolitan diplomacy, see E. Pontieri, *Per la storia del Regno di Ferrante I d'Aragone re di Napoli* (Naples, n.d.), esp. ch. 3 for relations with the Medici; and E. Pontieri, *Ferrante d'Aragona re di Napoli: Studi e ricerche* (Naples, 1969).

royal wedding, but one that was of first importance to the Strozzi, was that Don Federigo, the younger Neapolitan prince, would visit Florence on his way to signing the marriage agreement for his brother in Milan:

> Don Federigo was then about thirteen but as handsome and grave in appearance and serious and mature in speech as any prudent man. He was sent by his father to Milan to arrange the betrothal of his brother's wife and accompany her to Naples. . . . He brought with him the prince of Salerno, the duke of Amalfi, and other lords and gentlemen, all well appointed. In total there were four hundred horses and five hundred men in this company.

This party made its ceremonious way up the peninsula. They left Naples on the eighteenth of March. On the twenty-third they arrived in Rome, to be honored by the pope and all his court. Then, on the seventeenth of April, Don Federigo entered Florence,

> dressed in brown with all his companions, because while in Sienese territory the news came of the death of his mother, Queen Elizabeth. With him were our ambassadors who had gone out to meet him at the border in order to do him honor and arrange lodging along the way to Florence. When he was a little way from the city he was greeted by many citizens, well mounted and well dressed. These accompanied him along the direct route to the Piazza of the Signoria.

Having arrived in the main square, Don Federigo, still mounted, visited the priors. To greet him, they came down to the foot of the Ringhiera, the public rostrum. Then the prince was taken to the cathedral, where he offered a prayer, and on to Santa Maria Novella, the great Dominican friary, where he was lodged. He stayed in Florence five days, with much honor, before resuming his journey to Milan, again with appropriate ceremony.

Parenti's account of Florentine-Neapolitan diplomatic exchanges is typical of chronicle literature. His interest in the details of ceremonies, the exact route of a procession, or the niceties of whether a visitor remained mounted or dismounted could be matched many times among the vernacular historians and diarists of fifteenth-century Florence. In this, the first period of regular ambassadorial exchanges, ordinary citizens were fascinated by the ceremonial side of diplomacy. Princely rituals must also have held a special attraction for the Florentines, who lacked a court of their own. But chronicles seldom allow us to see past the bright surface of civic ceremony, and Parenti's *Memoir* proves no exception. Only by turning to more intimate records can we appreciate how these public displays could become the focus of private dreams. In the letters Marco and Alessandra wrote during these months, the departure of the Florentine ambassadors and the expectation of the visit of the younger Neapolitan prince became a continuing preoccupation.

Well before Don Federigo's visit—in fact only the day after the new ambassadors were named—Alessandra first raised the question of the diplomatic situation between Florence and Naples. The selection of sympathetic ambassadors to Naples and Milan and the plans for the prince to visit Florence seemed to present a remarkable opportunity to make use of the king's good will. "Since these things are coming together now," she wrote, "one wants to do whatever is possible, because the city needs these powers." Thus the growing interdependence of the Italian states, which at a distance of centuries we describe in terms of such abstractions as the balance of power, Alessandra seized upon as the key to repatriating her sons.[3]

Even the continuing uncertainties over Lorenzo's safe conduct could not dampen her spirits. In anticipation of receiving official permission, Lorenzo had come as far as San Quirico, on the border of Florentine territory, but a safe passage still remained in doubt. Nevertheless, Alessandra declared herself content: if permission were to be denied, it might be just as well, "because the king will be able to say: the commune does not want to serve me in this little request in order to do me a greater service! And he can ask the ambassadors and press them to write home about it."

Alessandra was so eager for this opportunity that she could

[3] 5 Feb. 1465, *Lettere*, p. 368.

not keep back any part of her advice, even when she knew it to be superfluous. "And also your behavior toward these ambassadors . . . will work in your favor," she wrote, advising that gifts would be useful and would be readily accepted. In fact, Filippo had long been in the habit of cultivating important Florentines visiting Naples, and he had little need of such reminders.[4] But in this moment her only thought was for the prize. "And thus, at this time one wants to do whatever a man can do," she urged, adding, "I know that you understand your own affairs better than I; still I want to remind you and give you the little advice I can."

Two days later Alessandra returned to the same preoccupations. Lorenzo had at last been given permission to enter Florentine territory, though he was still forbidden to enter the city itself, and this partial victory gave his mother grounds for optimism. "If nothing else is gained by this visit," she wrote, "still one sees that you have friends here, and some that would aid and favor you in a matter more important than this." Among those friends, she now felt she could count Pandolfo Pandolfini, who had supported Lorenzo's case "with love and solicitude." Since Pandolfo had just been elected as ambassador to Naples, there was an obvious opportunity to return the favor. "Marco Parenti," she continued, "on his own behalf and mine, has promised them that if there is anything you can do for them over there, they should let you know and you will do it gladly." Could Filippo use his influence at court, they wanted to know, to arrange for their lodgings and expenses?[5]

The choice of Marco as the bearer of this message of good will confirms the impression that the two men were friends. Probably this relationship went back to the days when both were a part of the circle of virtuous young citizens who gathered at Sacchetti's villa. Even Alessandra's description of Pan-

[4] Some years before, Filippo had been obliged to give a formal deposition in response to a royal decree against the corruption of magistrates. In it he recorded gifts to the current Florentine ambassador, Giannozzo Manetti (cf. CS ser. 3, 138, c. 217).

[5] 7 Feb. 1465, *Lettere*, pp. 374–78; postscript (quoted below) is on pp. 378–80.

dolfo as "a worthy and learned young man" recalls Vespasiano's characterization of him as "erudite and a man of the highest virtues."

Alessandra was convinced that the moment was right: "never again would a time come as suited as this. And if the request is made, and made sincerely, as I say, it seems to me certain that one could not deny the wishes of such powers." Even a refusal would have its use, showing that "the others in our situation will not have such Signori [lords] supporting them, nor the virtues and merits you have in regard to your country." For this, she concluded, one must pray to God, "since without Him nothing is possible."

On the ninth of February, Alessandra added a lengthy postscript to her letter to Filippo; that same evening Lorenzo was expected at the gates of the city. Obviously excited, she uttered a prayer that God would deliver him soon and safely. As for herself, "it is certain that the time he is here will be a happy one for me." Even so, her thoughts were not for Lorenzo alone, or at least she did not want Filippo to think so. "Thus, might it have been God's will that I might be with you both," she wrote "although you vex me with saying that he is the one I loved the most."

How characteristic it was of Alessandra to choose this moment, when she was about to embrace one son, to tug at the bonds that tied the other to her. "I shall spoil Lorenzo as much as I can," she wrote; "would that I could do the same to both of you together. But I can do little, since I creak in every joint. And every day I pray God . . . that he give me the grace to spend the little time I have remaining to me together with both of you in peace and consolation in body and soul. Commend yourself to me, as I need to be commended to you!"

Alessandra's emotionalism was readier than ever to flicker up and charge the simplest thing with new intensities. Even a gift of fruit from Filippo could not be acknowledged with easy gratitude; rather it must become an emblem of love and acceptance. "In the past few days I received a barrel of plums," she wrote at the close of the letter, "which cost me thirty *soldi*, between the freight from Pisa and the customs duties, which is more than it's worth. You would have done better to send me something sweet, for which I have a hankering. Still, I am pleased by anything from you; and do not wonder at this letter of mine, since I am dreaming while waiting for Lorenzo."

Lorenzo's reunion with his mother must have been an emotional one; but his temporary return to Florence was as much a political exploration as it was a family occasion. By his own account, Lorenzo was visited by numerous prominent Florentines, from which he gathered that many were moved "to pity toward us; so that I am considerably encouraged and my hopes for our plans have risen."[6] Lorenzo had good reason to feel encouraged, and the readiness he found everywhere to promote good relations with the king of Naples fed his optimism. As his mother had said, the Strozzi were not to be taken for friendless supplicants.

Ultimately the issue of repatriation would be decided by a small circle of men. The first question, therefore, was who held the keys to power. Since the death of Cosimo the answer could not be as clear or automatic as before, but Lorenzo saw no reason yet for redrawing the map. "Piero [de' Medici] and Messer L. [Luca Pitti]," he wrote, "are one and the same. Anything else one might hear is fancy . . . Messer A. [Agnolo Acciaiuoli] and Dietisalvi [Neroni] are in agreement with each other. Messer L. flirts with them, but is tight with Piero. This is the truth." Accordingly, Lorenzo was sure in his own mind that every effort of the king's should be directed at Piero de' Medici, who, in turn, was anxious to have the king's good will. Unless something changed in Florence, he concluded, Piero was the key: "if he is persuaded, everything is won."

★

Only in retrospect is it clear how much Alessandra's hopes had been buoyed by the prospect of Lorenzo's visit. With his departure, she fell into a depression that recalls the time, years before, when Matteo left her. Since Lorenzo left, she wrote,

[6] *Lettere*, pp. 382–84.

"I have not felt well, and I've only eaten some eggs. I haven't any fever, but my head is very weak, and at times I think I am losing my head. Lorenzo's departure has shaken me badly, and just as I felt alive while he was here, so I felt lifeless and dead when he left."[7]

It was a disappointment and a partial defeat that Lorenzo had never been allowed into the city. Lorenzo's letter is dated from Camerata, outside Florence, and though all were hopeful that permission would be granted, it never came. As a result, complained Alessandra, she had not even had a chance to go over her financial affairs with him. Believing that he would be coming to Florence itself, she had not carried her papers with her. "And then," she lamented, "when it became clear, I did not want to come for them, in order not to be parted from him for what little time he had there."

This mood of dejection invaded her thoughts about the future. The plans that she eagerly described a month or two earlier now seemed risky; doubts clouded her trust in the sincerity of their friends. The ambassadors had departed with many reassuring words, she reported. But what the result would be, she could not guess, "since these days it is hard to find a loyal man who stands by his word." In this uncertain and suspicious mood, she advised caution. "Go slowly and carefully in this affair," she instructed Filippo, "since the attempt being made and not succeeding, we will be the talk of the town."

From Marco, Filippo received far more encouragement. In substance, Marco's news was much the same as Alessandra's, but he offered it with a conviction that his mother-in-law no longer possessed. In his first letter of the new year, which in Florence began on the twenty-fifth of March, Marco informed Filippo about the departure of the ambassadors and the beginnings of preparations for the prince's visit. Though the plans were not yet firm, "already one can see that they are planning the visit to be as magnificent as we can manage." The prince will be received not only in the city but throughout

[7] 29 Mar. 1465, *Lettere*, p. 387.

the territory of Florence. "Above all," he wrote, "whatever is done will be done most willingly and ought to be well received."[8]

The prince's visit would take place in a festive spirit, an atmosphere well suited to the granting of favors. Even if the request were refused, Marco speculated, a second opportunity would come when the prince journeyed home again with the bride-to-be, who might add her own voice to their cause. "I do not believe any favor would be denied him" Marco concluded. He urged Filippo to pursue the opportunity and not to turn back. Presumably Marco knew that Alessandra was contemplating just such a retreat, and he was willing to acknowledge the difficulties that stood in the way. For his own part, however, he felt ready to accept the risks: "I am not at all of the opinion of some who think that if one does not succeed, it would have been better not to have tried. It is my opinion that, come what may, you will not be harmed in any respect, because in an enterprise so honorable to you there can be no shame."

Marco contributed more than optimistic advice, however, to the Strozzi cause. In his *Memoir* he described himself proudly as Filippo's most trusted relative in Florence, and though Alessandra's letters show that she had not always taken him into her confidence, his readiness to serve the family was of unquestionable value. In 1465, a year of difficult political and marital bargaining, Marco had an important role to play, as even Alessandra, with a mother-in-law's reluctance, would eventually admit.

On the fifteenth of April, Marco made his way to the house of Luca Pitti, the leading figure in any potential opposition faction. He was bearing a letter from Filippo that he had been asked to present. By his own account, it was the first time that Marco had set foot in Pitti's villa, "though, myself apart, there are few who have not been there a hundred times."[9] This was an admission that he did not belong to the first rank

[8] 30 Mar. 1465, CS ser. 3, 178, fol. 37.

[9] 17 Apr. 1465, CS ser. 3, 131, fol. 136^{r-v}, and *Lettere*, pp. 399–400.

of Florentine society. Implied, too, is the distance that existed between Pitti and the Strozzi, since he seems to have been on friendly terms with Dietisalvi Neroni and Pandolfo Pandolfini, themselves men of high rank.

Pitti's good will at the time of Lorenzo's visit had already shown that he was approachable. Marco's visit and the letter he carried were obviously intended to carry the process a step further. But first Marco had to find a way to speak to Pitti, and this did not prove easy. The house was full of people and he had to wait three hours for it to empty. At last he saw his chance and gave Pitti the letter. Taking it, Pitti said, " 'Oh, from our Filippo.' Then he began to read and it took so long that I could have read it three times." Whatever was implied about the great man's quickness of mind, Marco was pleased by Pitti's air of concentration—or at least expected it to encourage the sender of the letter, now receiving news of its reception. "He put his mind to it," Marco continued, "and I saw that he paid great attention. And after he had read it all, again he cast an eye over the middle of the letter and read a little." His laborious study of Filippo's letter completed, Pitti drew Marco aside, saying: " 'I see that Filippo refers to the words I spoke to Lorenzo. What I told him, I will say again. In any case, I want to do it.' "

With these words, Pitti reassured the Strozzi of his good will. Whatever promise he had made to Lorenzo orally at the time of his visit had been confirmed through Marco, who now became the recognized channel of communication. For this reason, Pitti stressed that he would want to see him often, so that they could examine the best time and method of proceeding. He was all in favor of having the king put forward the demand on behalf of the Strozzi and asked Marco to write on his behalf to Filippo, conveying his assurances.

A letter from Filippo to Pitti dated April 1, 1465, was presumably the one Marco carried with him to Pitti's mansion on the fifteenth. It is a straightforward letter of obligation, neither long nor complex, and one can understand Marco's astonishment at the length of time Pitti spent in reading it.

As Marco reported, Filippo's letter referred to Pitti's actions at the time of Lorenzo's visit, but the formulae of gratitude were general and there was nothing about specific promises of aid. This air of generality was undoubtedly deliberate, since Filippo indicated that he was anxious about writing and asked that Pitti confer with the bearer—not mentioning Marco by name—or any other he chose. In substance, the letter is an appeal from Filippo for advice on how and when to press his cause: "when it seems to you time to move this wagon, either now or to delay." Coupled with this request came the reassurance that no move would be made, either in Naples or Florence, without Pitti's advice. Filippo also wanted to assure the ambitious Florentine politician that his fame had carried as far as Naples and the royal palace, and he concluded his flatteries by offering himself as an intermediary should the need arise.[10]

Marco's reply to Pitti concluding the interview was, by his own admission, brief and apposite, and he left the great house feeling pleased. Even so, the long-standing distrust of Pitti among the Strozzi was not easily erased. There must have been something in Pitti's character that inspired caution—an attitude that later events would more than justify. It was certainly possible, Marco reminded himself, that Pitti's friendliness was all for show, but for his own part he doubted it: "Considering his acts and gestures, to me it seemed that he spoke like one who speaks truly." Proof would come, he added, when plans were put into effect.

Bolstered by this successful interview, Marco was as sure as ever of their plan to swing Neapolitan support into an active campaign for repatriation. Filippo should press ahead, neglecting nothing that had been considered. For his own part, he wrote: "I will take care to keep Messer L. to this path if I see him wandering the least bit: that he should wish P. [Piero] to seem the master and that he will attend to keeping him well disposed and content; but that, in effect, we will recognize

[10] *Lettere*, p. 416.

[Pitti] himself as cause and first principle of all this good etc. I don't know if I speak too obscurely, but I trust you understand me well."

The strategy was a clever one, perhaps too clever. From the letter, it is not possible to be sure how explicitly Pitti had consented to cede to Piero de' Medici whatever public rewards were to be won by repatriating the exiles, while reserving to himself their secret trust and gratitude. The suggestion may, indeed, have come from Pitti himself when he promised Lorenzo Strozzi his support. Equally Marco himself may have plotted this particular "path" and was now attempting to hold Pitti to it—a possibility that is suggested by the conspiratorial tone of his final words. In either case, his remarks indicate once again the central problem of the Strozzi position. Florence was increasingly a divided city. Short of outright partisanship, which the exiles could hardly afford, any approach to one faction or leader would have to be balanced by some compensating gesture toward the other.

Meanwhile the event that had become the focus of so many hopes and stratagems was finally taking place. The same letter from Marco that reported his interview with Pitti also carried the news of Don Federigo's arrival. We have already had the outlines of this ceremonious occasion from Parenti's *Memoir*, but his letters add details that alter the emphasis. The history, though an eye-witness account, smooths away the blemishes revealed by the closer focus of the letter. Here the reception of the prince seems somewhat less magnificent, and the royal person himself is not quite faultless. Few Florentines, it appears, actually rode out to meet the visitors. "Those who were suited to ride out went to meet him," Marco explained, "but, in truth, there are not many at present," partly because of the number of citizens absent on embassies or other duties. No discourtesy was implied, but many were put off by Don Federigo's failure to dismount when visiting the Signoria at the Ringhiera. This was a gesture appropriate to a king and, as it had been allowed to Don Federigo's elder brother on an earlier occasion, so it was allowed to the younger son. "But the former," Parenti complained, "was the firstborn of a king.

The latter is not the firstborn, which makes a considerable difference, since the firstborn by nature will become a king and already partakes of regal honors. The second son does not."[11]

These niceties of protocol aside, the young prince had made a fine impression. "And truly he seems the son of a king," affirmed Marco, "and he displays virtue beyond his years, as is proper to royalty who should surpass everyone else in virtue and appearance." Like many a sober republican, Marco had a soft spot for royalty. All the more reason for a twinge of disappointment that the spectacle had not been more splendid: "His entry did not seem as magnificent as those of many other lords I have seen; and this because they were dressed in mourning in your [i.e. Neapolitan] fashion, and because not a single trumpet sounded."

Surprisingly, the arrangements for the visit seem to have been somewhat less than smooth, for the letters speak of numbers of missed appointments and mislaid plans. For all that, Don Federigo's visit was certainly a royal occasion. In Marco's opinion the outlay could not have been more costly or magnificent, while his brother-in-law, Giovanni Bonsi, estimated it cost 25,000 florins, "between going and coming."[12] Finally, on the twenty-second of April the Neapolitans took their leave. This time, however, the prince dismounted and walked to the door of the Palace. The Gonfaloniere came out and embraced him and together they went to sit at the Ringhiera, where the Gonfaloniere took the place of honor. Florentine pride thus having been satisfied, the prince too was thought to have acquitted himself well. "He makes good replies, for a boy," Marco commented, "and it is clear they are not memorized." With this the visitors departed for the betrothal in Milan, leaving the Florentines reason to hope that they would be back in Florence in time for the festivities of June twenty-fourth—the feast day of John the Baptist, the city's patron saint.[13]

[11] 17 Apr. 1465, CS ser. 3, 131, fol. 136^{r-v}, and *Lettere*, pp. 399–400.

[12] *Lettere*, p. 402.

[13] 27 Apr. 1465, CS ser. 3, 131, fol. 140, and *Lettere*, p. 402.

The public occasions were not, of course, the sole substance of the visit. As in an Elizabethan play, in the intervals between the appearances of the greater men, lesser ones acted out similar dramas on a minor scale. Among those in the prince's party were two confidants of Filippo Strozzi, Carlo Mormino and Messer Rinaldo. Out of friendship to Filippo, these two Neapolitans called on his mother. In return they received the courtesies of Marco Parenti. "On your behalf," wrote Marco, "I went to visit Carlo and Messer Rinaldo. And for that entire day I was a confirmed courtier, such that if it had gone on any longer, I do not know how I would have managed. If this is what it is like to be a courtier, I leave it to you." All day he had stood in Don Federigo's chamber, he reported, even while the prince dined. Nonetheless, since the prince was continually surrounded by so many men, Florentine and Neapolitan, Marco never was able to find an opening to speak with him.

Marco was right to confess that he was no courtier. As on the occasion of his visit to Pitti, he felt out of place. Unable to get to the front of the crowd, he was uneasy and self-deprecating. Still, there were lesser men to talk to, especially Messer Rinaldo. From Marco's report, we gather that Filippo had first given Messer Rinaldo his commission to act for him but then withdrew it, apparently still hesitant about how far he should press his case. For their own part, however, Marco and Rinaldo, the two auxiliaries to the plan, were in full agreement that the return visit of the prince's party should be seized upon. Rinaldo was even more hopeful than Parenti, and he informed Marco confidentially that Piero de' Medici had requested a favor and promised one in return.

There is no knowing how far the visit had provided an opportunity for Filippo's friends to argue his case, or what disappointments and hesitations there might have been. The signs seemed favorable, however, for the second visit and Parenti pressed his brother-in-law for a decision. "Now examine for yourself what seems best to do," he urged, while making his own inclination clear: "I am one of those who is led by his will. Being able, I would do it."

Marco, it seems, was well aware of the optimistic side of his own nature and contrasted it with Filippo's more calculating temper. The long-awaited visit having passed without visible result, he transferred his hopes to the return trip. Though it was not certain yet, he wrote, the return was expected around the festival of Saint John the Baptist, "and when spirits are festive, men are well disposed to do favors, right?"

CHAPTER 5

SPRING: BETWEEN MEDICI AND PITTI

★

FOR ALL HIS natural optimism, Parenti understood that Medici power remained the central fact of Florentine politics. Though the atmosphere of negotiation and intrigue must have been heady, the fortunes of the Strozzi still depended on Piero's benevolence. As one who, by his own admission, was "led by his will," Marco may have found this dependence hard to accept, but as yet there was no alternative. Even Luca Pitti did not have the power to act independently. "And so I have said nothing futher to our friend," wrote Marco with reference to Pitti, "since it does not seem to me to be the time. And also I am rather dubious about the manner, since Piero can still do a lot—almost everything—and to me it does not seem that anything will go forward without him."[1]

Marco's words, written in later April, echo Lorenzo's judgment two months earlier when he stood outside the city. Apparently the royal visit had done little to alter the fundamentals. Like a catalyst, it had certainly quickened the diplomatic process, but the essential formula remained the same. Messages of support from the king of Naples, even when carried by members of his own family and enhanced by civic festivities, would count for little unless Piero de' Medici relaxed his suspicions or found it in his own interest to embrace the exiles. The only alternative was the dangerous road of

[1] 27 Apr. 1465; CS ser. 3, 131, fol. 140, and *Lettere*, p. 402.

opposition and the uncertain hope that, after thirty years, Medici domination would be broken.

If Piero could still do "almost everything," what sort of relationship with his rivals would be worth cultivating? With Acciaiuoli and Neroni there were older and firmer links, but Pitti had been courted for his political influence alone. So far this influence had produced little, and an open alliance with him would not be the best step toward securing Medici favor. On the other hand, Pitti, Neroni, and Acciaiuoli were important men and they had given real encouragement. It would be foolish, if not impossible, to turn a deaf ear. Nor was there any disguising the fact—implied in Marco's words—that Medici power did not sit as securely as it had only a year before.

Much of the practical burden of these uncertainties fell to Marco, who had taken on the duty of dealing with Pitti. In the first week of May he went to see Pitti, whose first suggestion was that they meet again in a few days since the new Signoria had just taken office. "These seemed to me generalities," wrote Marco, "so I entered into particulars with him in order to see whether I was able to put him on that path I described before."[2]

Everything suggests a new mood of self-possession replacing the hesitations of his first interview. "I told him I wished him to understand something of my thoughts," he continued, "since at times occasions arise that do not often recur." The opportunity in question, of course, was the prospect of a second visit from the prince, and Marco sought Pitti's advice on using it to press Filippo's cause. How crucial Pitti's consent to this plan really was might be doubted, but Marco promised once again that "we will understand everything as coming from him." Pitti gave his support without difficulty and pledged to follow the matter as though it were his own.

Thus the return of the noble visitors continued to be the focus of Parenti's hopes and he may have feared some sort of pullback on Filippo's part, as had apparently happened just

[2] 4 May 1465, CS ser. 3, 131, fol. 142.

before the first visit. He knew, however, that large obstacles stood in the way: "Now these things are easily written and said, but I know it is an ambitious thing to execute, involving numbers of important men in various countries who must carry it through. I do not know what you can manage; it is for you to examine."

Marco's tone implied a certain patient acceptance of his role as advisor and go-between; but it is not a long step from stressing one's patience to showing impatience. "About your affairs I have nothing else to tell you," he informed Filippo two weeks later. Lacking instructions or further news, he had not seen fit to pay another visit to "our friend." "I have done what I knew to do," he declared; the rest was up to Strozzi: "But until you decide to get down to business, I don't know what I can tell you more than you already know yourself. Things here remain as they were and I do not see that delay is apt to improve your prospects in these times—more likely the opposite. But enough."[3]

The rest of his news was no comfort to Marco's irritated temper. It was being said in Florence that their ambassadors had been snubbed by the king, who had chosen the day of their arrival to go hunting—a rebuke, it was rumored, for Florence's refusal to admit Lorenzo Strozzi earlier in the year. Any upset in relations with Naples was worrisome, but Marco was especially troubled that the only authority being given for this news was Filippo himself, and he believed he had traced the indiscretion to an employee in their bank—"that Buondelmonti you have there."

Meanwhile the dates of the return visit of the prince and the bride-to-be had been fixed, but even in this Marco was unable to take satisfaction. Preparations were being discussed for a fine celebration, but the Florentines did not seem much disposed to festivity. "What the reason is I don't know," Marco wrote: "I believe it comes from the heavens."

Marco's impatience was the result, no doubt, of the tedium of communication over long distances, as well as the expres-

[3] 18 May 1465, CS ser. 3, 180, fol. 58.

sion of his own sanguine character; on the other hand, Filippo's hesitations may have had another origin than inveterate caution. Just at the moment he had bigger fish to fry. Not long before, he had begun a diplomatic campaign of his own, initiated with a politic gift of linen to Lucrezia Tornabuoni, Piero de' Medici's wife. This opportune present was rewarded with a fine letter from Mona Lucrezia, as Alessandra noted approvingly, while grumbling that "she would do well to pay you back in something that costs nothing more than words: that is, to recommend you to Piero to restore you to your house."[4]

How effective Filippo's closet diplomacy truly was it is hard to say, but soon Piero de' Medici approached him on a more important service. Piero had a galley in Naples, which he proposed to present as a gift to the king; Filippo was to act as intermediary. It was certainly a good sign, as Alessandra noted, that Piero had put his trust in Filippo. In turn, Filippo took the opportunity to express his sense of obligation and loyalty in the fullest possible terms. He declared himself the "good servant" of the memory of Piero's forebears—the very ones, of course, responsible for the Strozzi's exile. Since Piero had begun to employ him, his desire to serve Piero was fully satisfied: "And now it seems to me that, living or dying, I cannot be other than well satisfied. You have bound both Lorenzo and myself to you as slaves for all the length of our lives, and you may dispose of us, high or low, just like the merest youth in your service."[5]

The language of courtly servility was increasingly common in Medici circles, and Filippo must have learned a thing or two in Naples. But one has only to compare this letter to the greeting Marco carried to Luca Pitti to see how dear a prize Medici friendship would be. Even so, Pitti's good will could not be neglected too long, and Marco finally got the answer he had been hoping for: plans to use the opportunity of the prince's return would go ahead and Pitti should be informed.

[4] 20 Apr. 1465, *Lettere*, p. 396.

[5] 12 May 1465, *Lettere*, p. 413.

There is no mistaking Marco's sense of relief. The good news seems to tumble out of the first sentences of his next letter, as though he could not be bothered with preliminaries. He was already able to report another successful interview, at which Pitti, detaching himself from an earlier visitor, called Marco to him "with a pleased look." Mutual compliments were exchanged on behalf of the Strozzi in what Marco, with his new-found confidence, called "the usual manner." Pitti quickly picked up a hint that Strozzi would like a letter from him as a visible token of his support, and he questioned Marco about the frequency of couriers—a further sign that Pitti lacked experience and connections in the south.[6]

Pitti's support was most welcome, but it could also prove problematic. Having won his aid, Marco did not wish to be bound by it, and he preferred at this point to leave matters as general as possible to avoid any disruption. "It seems to me," he confessed, "that I have him in such a good position—that is that others act while he consents—that I would not wish to quarrel with what is already sound." Besides, there was a danger that Pitti might advise something "outside of the plans you have already made," and then be upset if his advice were not followed. "And I know," Marco added, "that he cannot produce better plans than those already made." Thus, returning to the question of the letter that was the ostensible object of his visit, Marco concluded roundly that he really did not care whether Pitti ever sent it!

In this kingdom of subtle maneuver, it is not easy to say who is one-eyed and who is blind. But apart from an unattractive air of self-satisfaction, Marco's position seems reasonably sound. Pitti had no power to bring about the exile's return, but was too important a "friend" to ignore. From the point of view of the Strozzi, it would be a great stroke of fortune if so ambitious a man would content himself with seconding their efforts without demanding the sort of public allegiance that would compromise them with the Medici. If Pitti genuinely followed this course, he would in effect cancel

[6] 24 May 1465, CS ser. 3, 178, fol. 43.

himself out, leaving the Strozzi to pursue their more difficult game with Piero de' Medici.

Despite the apparent ease with which Pitti had consented to their plans, Marco was far from discounting Pitti's power. On the contrary, he ended by stressing Pitti's growing authority. "And I tell you," he wrote, "that it seems to me he grows greater every day. And it does not seem that Piero is aware of it." The worrisome conclusion was that both men would be important, "so that it is necessary to use great skill."

Undoubtedly Marco congratulated himself on having played his part well in his previous meetings with Pitti and looked forward to the next without much fear. The basic question of Pitti's support seemed neatly resolved and the occasion of the visit—to carry a new message from Filippo—gave him no reason to expect an interview as disconcerting as this one proved to be.

His welcome, in fact, was warmer than ever. Both on arrival and departure Pitti took him by the hand, though this had happened before. "But what he had never before done or indicated," Marco wrote, "was that he did not wish to hear me unless I sat down beside him. I resisted strongly and was amazed, but seeing his wish, I did it; and then I began to tell him why I had come to him."[7]

Only a few months earlier, Marco had stood waiting for three hours to present a letter to Pitti, and even now he had no expectation of sitting down with Pitti as an equal. On that first occasion, Marco had noted the painfully slow attention with which the letter was read; this time he chose to read it aloud, and the result was even more remarkable. "As soon as I finished reading and raised my eyes to look him in the face," Marco wrote, "I saw that he was very much enraged and flushed. I was amazed. I stayed silent and waited for a response." Pitti's words gave no clue, however, to his sudden irritation. Having gone over the letter and returned to his normal coloring, he simply repeated to Marco the substance of their earlier conversations and confirmed his support. But

[7] 1 June 1465, CS ser. 3, 131, fol. 151, and *Lettere*, pp. 417–18.

once he had finished speaking, Pitti again became unaccountably flushed, though it quickly passed; and the rest of their talk was about the news from France, a subject not likely to arouse more uncomfortable displays. Shortly afterward Marco took his leave, not without Pitt's warm handshake. In fact, Marco waited until this point in his letter to describe the unexpected warmth of Pitti's greeting, perhaps to indicate his feeling that, despite everything, the powerful man appeared to remain friendly to their cause.

Marco was at a loss to explain what had happened. "I have given you all these details," he wrote, "because I am confused and do not know how to interpret it. I want you at least to know how things stand, so that you can add your own judgment." Perhaps Pitti had not expected the business to come upon him so soon; equally, he may have been dissimulating and now the time had come to throw off the disguise. Then again, it may be that "hearing the name of Piero, he grew distressed, thinking that the honors would go to others." None of these explanations gave much comfort, nor could Marco be sure that any of them really explained Pitti's peculiar behavior, itself a sort of solace. "I don't understand it," he concluded in despair. "Here one can never understand anything from what people say, except after the fact."

Marco's words could well be adopted as the motto of Florentine politics. In a perverse way, Florentines were rather proud of their own cleverness, self-defeating though it often proved to be. Marco himself had been guilty of it in his negotiations with Pitti; at the same time, for all his optimistic temperament and a growing trust in Pitti's intensions, he had never taken Pitti at face value. He had not been content merely to register promises of political support. Instead he always watched for the more subtle indications to be read in the language of gesture. Looking back we can see that from the start Marco had watched Pitti as much as he had listened to him—a habit that gives his reports their vividness.

Despite the setback, Marco apparently expected plans for the forthcoming visit to remain in effect, for he concluded that "everything will become clearer when put to the proof."

About his own role, however, he seemed uncertain, abashed, apologetic. "Your opinion about me," he wrote, "for the present is also my own, that is for me to go slow and wait for your moves, in which I still have great hope, although I remain anxious." Thus, as much as the Strozzi cause itself, the usually strong current of Marco's optimism had suffered a check, and he resigned himself to the undertow of Filippo's caution.

★

In retrospect, Filippo's caution seems well advised. Nevertheless, for all the services tendered and unctuous flattery, Filippo's diplomatic efforts with the Medici had little more success than Marco's negotiations with Pitti. With Filippo's assistance, Piero bestowed his galley on the king as a gift. But despite this evidence of a desire for good relations with Naples, Piero de' Medici was not yet ready to readmit the old enemies of his family; and so he informed the king in the politest possible terms. Replying to the royal expression of thanks, Piero protested his own great pleasure of being able, though only "a little man," to serve His Majesty. His desire was simply to "obey your requests and please you in everything." But when it came to doing the king's bidding in the case of the Strozzi the matter was not so simple. "It pains me that what you request is not in my power," Piero de' Medici wrote, adding that if it were up to him alone, it would certainly be done without delay. "But this, my most excellent Lord, is something which in our city, by the customs and laws we have, is something of the gravest importance." Even so he would take the matter on his own shoulders out of respect for the urgency with which the request was made. Thus, he concluded, there was no reason to trouble Don Federigo with it any further, adding, "I only beg Your Majesty that, given the difficulty of the matter, it should not displease him if it is not done at present."[8]

In effect, Piero de' Medici had declared that this question would have to be handled in Florence. He would deal with it

[8] *Lettere*, p. 414.

in his own way and on his own terms, and there is more than a hint that he would prefer not to be solicited again. The king chose to ignore this, however, and the return visit of the prince provided a natural opportunity to renew the pressure. Nonetheless, prospects that only a month or two earlier had seemed bright and immediate were again dim and uncertain.[9]

[9] Further trouble came in the next few weeks, marked by maneuverings in Florence to have the ambassadors recalled and replaced. Marco was incensed by the slight to Pandolfo Pandolfini's honor and seems to attribute the machinations to Messer Carlo Pandolfini's wish to block Pandolfo from being knighted. "If I were Pandolfo," Marco fumed, "I would get myself knighted before returning. I would do it, if for no other reason than to make him burst [with envy]." Pitti is reported as displeased, but as having acceded to the situation, which prompted Marco to protest, "Now you see how much weight you can give to words and promises" (8 June 1465, CS ser. 3, 178, fol. 41). Fortunately the recall was reversed and in his letter of the following day Parenti claimed to have had "some small part" in the recovery of Pandolfo's honor. The earlier letter also contains the rather mysterious injunction that "if you hear something from here that I did not write to you about, it is not a result of error, but by a certain design [nollo fo per errore ma per certa scienza]."

CHAPTER 6

SUMMER: THE RETURN VISIT

★

ON THE twenty-ninth of May, 1465, Parenti tells us in his *Memoir*, the betrothal of Madonna Ippolita of Milan to Don Alfonso, duke of Calabria, was solemnized in Milan. By special mandate Don Federigo, the second son of the king of Naples, acted in his elder brother's place. Within a few days of the festivities Madonna Ippolita, accompanied by her own party as well as that of Don Federigo, left Milan for Naples where she was to marry Don Alfonso. Six hundred horses accompanied Ippolita; added to those traveling with the prince, there were some two thousand in all. Followed by the sound of trumpets "all along the way," the entire party entered Florence on the twenty-second of June. At the gates they were met by many of Florence's worthies, "mounted and richly dressed," and the populace filled the streets to see their entry. "The head of their train was magnificent to see," Parenti wrote. Wagons were laden with coffers, "richly decorated in various styles and with worthy skill." These contained the gifts making up her dowry and other ornaments:

> Then followed the equerries and young men, and our men, and theirs, according to their rank and dignity, richly dressed on fine, well-equipped horses. Last came the women, seated on horses, dressed in silk and beautiful brocades and adorned with pearls and jewels; then the duchess, more brilliantly

> dressed than all the rest, with Don Federigo and her brothers around her, and the ambassadors and other nobles behind.[1]

Evidently the festivities passed off without any questions of protocol or slighted pride; and since it was also the feast day of Saint John the Baptist, civic games mixed with noble entertainment. "[But] the greatest pleasure that one could give them was to leave them to come together and dance, now in one house and now in another, wherever it suited them, because they were all, young men and young women, in love with each other. And one who is in love wants nothing more than to see his lover and be together."

It was not all courtly romance: once again Marco's letters convey a somewhat less glamorous view of the visit than the *Memoir*. Few of the hosts, it seems, took any part in the magnificence of the procession—"our knights, a few others citizens, and some youths." As for the visitors themselves, their young women could not be compared in beauty to those of Florence. Still, Marco was well pleased by the reception given the bride and her escort. It was a "triumph" for the city, he told Filippo, especially given the large number of foreigners there to see it. Though Alessandra grumbled in anticipation of the expense, to Marco the elaborate welcome seemed a good augury of success.[2]

The king, too, did his part. Setting aside Piero de' Medici's assurances that everything would be done in good time, the king instructed his son by letter to press Piero again and to see the matter concluded "before your departure." Soon word of the progress of their petition got back to the family. Through an acquaintance, Giovanni Bonsi learned of Piero's reaction. "The king wants two things of me," Piero had reportedly told this informant, one of them being the repatriation of the Strozzi. But, despite the pressure, Piero had not changed his mind and was still insisting that he was not in a

[1] *Memorie*, pp. 19–20.

[2] Alessandra's complaint on the cost of the reception comes in her letter of 15 June 1465 (*Lettere*, p. 420). Otherwise, what follows draws on Marco's extraordinarily long and detailed letter of 22 June 1465 (CS ser. 3, 131, fols. 156^{r-v}, 157^{r-v}, and *Lettere*, pp. 423–33.

position to decide the issue. "It is necessary that others take a hand too," Piero had said, "and it will be done when the time comes." Still, concluded Marco, Piero "showed himself to be of good will toward you," and there was some hope in that.

There is no doubt that foreign powers often exaggerated Medici authority. It was convenient as well as natural to see the Medici as princes much like themselves and credit them with comparable freedom of action. For his own part, Piero may genuinely have felt that a consensus was required before any of the exiles could be returned. He was not an indiscreet politician, and he must have known that his conversation regarding the exiles would be repeated. Thus, knowledge of the king's request would be spread about and public opinion might be canvassed.

Whatever reasons Piero de' Medici had for making the affair public, the Strozzi had reasons of their own for wanting to keep it as quiet as possible. On the day after the visitors' arrival, Marco went to visit Messer Rinaldo, the Neapolitan courtier with whom he had discussed Filippo's affairs during the first visit. Rinaldo was once again busying himself on behalf of the Strozzi and showed Marco a letter, intended apparently for Piero. So far all was as it should be; but the Neapolitan let slip something that disturbed Marco considerably. Rinaldo, it seems, had already conferred with Agnolo Acciaiuoli and had informed him of the king's instructions regarding the Strozzi. "It displeased me a good deal," Marco wrote, "but because I saw that he was fond of Messer Agnolo I stayed silent."

Marco had found his Neapolitan friends just as they were about to present themselves to Piero de' Medici, and he was obliged to return after dinner to hear the results of the interview. As planned, Don Federigo had presented his letter to Piero, urging him "long and hard" to grant the king's request. Predictably, Piero's reply was along familiar lines and, for the moment, Marco was more concerned with the possible complications that could arise from Acciaiuoli's knowledge of the affair. "I told Messer Rinaldo," he wrote, "that your intention was that no one should be told anything before we had an answer from Piero."

The Neapolitan might well have wondered at the fuss: among all the Florentines, who was more respected than Agnolo Acciaiuoli? A powerful, if restless, figure in Florence, he was well known in the court of Milan, the king's chief ally, as well as Naples.[3] But Acciaiuoli himself was not Marco's real worry; his thoughts were as usual occupied by Luca Pitti. "I remained much concerned about how I should manage things with Messer Luca," he wrote, "thinking that Messer Agnolo might confer with him about it." Should this happen before either Marco or Filippo had themselves consulted with Pitti there might well be trouble. Having assured Pitti so many times that nothing would be done without his approval, Marco now faced the uncomfortable thought that Pitti would have heard all about their negotiations through a third party. There was every chance that all his cleverness had only succeeded in losing Pitti without gaining Piero.

Caught in this already tangled web, Marco began to spin the tale he would take to Pitti. His *fantasia* was to tell Pitti that the king had given his people a commission to make the petition "in general and to whomever they saw fit," but to take counsel whether, on account of the festivities, this was the right moment. And, on the other hand, he would say that Filippo had written to say that Pitti was the person to consult and that his opinion should then be referred to Rinaldo. Unfortunately, his imaginary dialogue continued, "they [i.e. the Neapolitans] had received their letters before I did mine, and they already asked Messer Agnolo for his advice." This advice being negative, they had dropped the idea and had said nothing to Piero. "And that I had not been able to have his opinion earlier because of not getting my letters in time," he continued, still addressing an imaginary Pitti in his mind, "but now I was telling him all this to inform him of everything and to ask his advice about doing anything further, things having turned out the way they have."

[3] In her letter of 15 Sept. 1464, Alessandra reported that Acciaiuoli had been given a fiefdom in the kingdom of Naples (*Lettere*, p. 325).

Faulty mails, it seems, have always been a ready excuse—though a convenient apology is not necessarily a convincing one. But in the absence of anything better, Marco was prepared to try his story and even managed to conclude it on a hopeful note. Not only was his stratagem designed to escape the present embarrassment, he explained (addressing now a real Filippo rather than an imaginary Pitti), but to demonstrate to Pitti, "that the king wishes to act and has already begun." Even so, with the uncomfortable memory of his last meeting with Pitti still with him, Marco could not have arrived on Pitti's doorstep a happy man. What a relief, then, it must have been to discover that Pitti was away! "But Fortune served me better," he wrote, "since when I went to him, I found that he had gone to his villa—and there he stayed until this morning."

Pitti's absence from Florence afforded Marco a brief respite, and he used the opportunity to pay a more ceremonious call. On Rinaldo's advice, Marco presented himself to Don Federigo. While conveying the thanks of the Strozzi, Marco also won from the prince the promise that he would raise the whole matter one more time with Piero on their departure. The prince was very obliging and Marco was obviously much impressed by this private audience with youthful royalty: "And if until now I have commended his presence to you, I must praise even more his prudence, which he showed clearly in his conversation. His replies could not have been more gracious. With the highest praise for you, he related how much obliged he and his father are to you." As a courtier, Marco was evidently making some progress.

Pitti returned the following morning, and Marco, armed with his excuses, hurried to see him. The story he told was the one he had been rehearsing, with Pitti's unfortunate absence as an added point in its favor. There was no predicting, of course, Pitti's reaction, and Marco was again in the position of searching Pitti's face for clues. Having said his piece, Marco reported, "I stopped speaking to see how he would react." This time, however, he was not disappointed: "Quickly—and with good countenance—he asked me, 'So, did he [the prince] say nothing to Piero?' I said no. He replied, almost consoling with me a little, 'still, it would have been better if he had said something to him about it, so that when the times comes, he would be better disposed.' "

Reassured of Pitti's continued support, Marco plunged on. "Having heard this," he wrote, "I went on and said, 'Wait and hear what happened.' " At this point he introduced the question of Rinaldo's recent discussion with Acciaiuoli, adding strictly for Pitti's benefit that he himself had stipulated that nothing at all be done without Pitti's advice. Sure now that he had it, Marco respectfully paused for Pitti's approval, and the great man assured him that the opportunity should certainly be taken. Not content with words alone, however, Marco again scanned Pitti's features for reassurance. "And in my opinion he said it to me with a very happy face," Marco observed, adding that on his arrival at the house Pitti had called him over immediately, though many others were present, and made him welcome.

At a distance of five hundred years it is difficult to know whether the situation truly required such subtle practices, and there is a hint that Marco anticipated some doubts even at a distance of five hundred miles. "I have done all this," he wrote, "judging it to be the timbre of this instrument, which, as they say, is very hard to tune—and much more so than you can see from down there." There is an unmistakable note of pride in this image of himself as a musician, but just as evident is the sheer relief he felt at having made it safely through a difficult solo. "I stand in great torments of fear," Marco continued, "because he is more delicate than a harpsichord. May God grant us his help."

There is more than a hint of strain, in the anxious, almost obsessive detail with which Marco reported the intricacies of his conversations and maneuvers. Marco himself partly acknowledged that this was so, but he preferred to attribute it to Filippo's anxiety to know rather than his own impulse to tell: "And if I have written to you in a style perhaps contrary to your own ('I said,' 'he replied to me' etc.) I have done it to give you the sense of it, because one who is much involved desires much, even the most minute details." Even so, Marco admitted, there was a good deal more he would have liked to have written, "but this must suffice to calm your spirits."

For all his habitual optimism, Marco's spirits were as much threatened as Filippo's. "I am always in fear," he conceded, "that those who are willing are not able," the implication being that those who were able, namely the Medici, had not yet shown themselves to be willing. After the exhilaration of his escape from multiple disasters, real or imaginary, this admission represented a return to the sober realities of the situation. Even Marco had to admit that "in truth, now is not the right time." For the moment the Colleges were not passing anything, and even if they were, their terms were coming to an end and there would not be time to get anything through. He was unhappy with "the delay"—an optimistic way of putting it—but the new members would take their places on the "calends" of July. And it was now Marco's opinion that things would go more smoothly once the visitors had departed.

Apparently, most of the luster had gone out of the royal visit, even for Marco. An endless round of dances occupied the visitors' time—though Piero had forbidden such levities in his own house out of respect for the memory of his father's death—and they seemed aloof and unappreciative of the festivities arranged in their honor. In return, the Florentines no longer flocked around. "I see our humor," Marco wrote; "no one visits any of their courts other than themselves." It seems a far cry from the tolerant commentary of the *Memoir*, where the same situation is smilingly accepted as the natural self-absorption of young lovers.

For some of this, the Florentines themselves may have been responsible. The lion hunt they arranged miscarried when "a bull chased the lions back in their stalls like sheep." The feast of the Carmine—the church that houses Masaccio's extraordinary fresco, the "Tribute Money"—was much admired, far more so than the celebration of the city's patron saint. "Indeed," grumbled Marco, "we are of the opinion that they tasted little and appreciated even less of any of our festivities and doings." That morning, he added, setting the final seal on the visit, they had departed almost entirely unattended by the Florentines.

The duchess and Don Federigo departed on the twenty-seventh at the tenth hour, Marco reported, "and before they left I was anxious to see Messer Rinaldo and remind him that his lord recall your affair with Piero before departing." Despite waning confidence and enthusiasm, Marco made one last effort, though the opportunity was very nearly passed over: "And I went with them right to Piero's chambers; and because he was sleeping, they were on the point of leaving him, since no one dared to disturb him. But I was so insistent that in the end the servant was sent back in and woke him." Piero listened patiently once again to Don Federigo's petition, but the answer, of course, was unchanged. Only someone as devoted to the Strozzi as Marco Parenti would have begged to have Piero de' Medici awakened in his own bedchamber for such a purpose.

★

Don Federigo's parting request to Piero de' Medici was hardly a masterpiece of tact, but considering the events that followed, perhaps it was just as well that one final effort was made. The prince and the duchess had barely left Florence before disturbing news arrived from Naples. For a time, the Strozzi's royal patron was embroiled in troubles of his own and relations between the Italian powers in general were upset. The Strozzi themselves were not directly involved, but their affair was eclipsed and the atmosphere of reconciliation on which they depended evaporated. For his own part, Marco eagerly followed the news and chronicled these new difficulties both in his correspondence and his *Memoir*.

"On the 27th of the said month [of June]," Parenti later recounted, "they all left on their way to Siena, having first made a proper leave taking. . . . They were strongly urged by the king to leave here quickly and to ride fast because he knew what he had in mind to do . . . and he could not hold out any longer. Because of this, he wanted to have these people as close to him as possible and, most of all, to have them out of our jurisdiction."[4] The cause of the king's anxiety and the focus of the events that followed was Count Iacopo Piccinino, one of the leading condottieri of Italy. Piccinino had once been the mainstay of the Angevin attempt to win back their lost kingdom in Naples from Ferrante of Aragon. At a decisive moment, however, the soldier switched sides and accepted the joint commission of his former enemies in Naples, Milan, and Rome—a bargain that was sealed with the hand of Sforza's illegitimate daughter. But although the new alliance was made, Sforza continued to mistrust his former rival. He knew, Parenti commented, "the ambition of great men, the variety of Fortune, and the opportunities time offers, and how these have the power to change men's minds." As Marco noted, Sforza himself had been such a son-in-law to Duke Filippo Maria Visconti and had made himself ruler of Milan. Learning the lesson of his own victories, Sforza persuaded his ally King Ferrante to invite Piccinino to Naples.

The count and his son set out from Milan for Naples, where they arrived on the fourth of June, only a few weeks ahead of Don Federigo and his party. They were greeted with the fullest ceremony, which began to trouble Piccinino, since for all his hospitality the king showed no signs of releasing his guest so that he could take up his promised lordships. The truth was that the king had no more intention than his ally in Milan of harboring so dangerous a subject—a man who would not only be "an intolerable expense," as the *Memoir* puts it, but "almost a court of appeals" inside his realm. Only the unexpected tardiness of Don Federigo's return delayed Ferrante's plans; but Piccinino seemed restive and the king feared he might escape. At last, on the same day that the prince was celebrating the feast of Saint John the Baptist with his Florentine hosts, his father ordered Piccinino to be seized. Soon after the count was killed, strangled in his prison cell by a Moorish slave.

Official murder of this sort was hardly unprecedented. In

[4] *Memorie*, pp. 21–27. On Piccinino's death, see A. Portioli, "La morte di Jacopo Piccinino," *Archivio storico italiano* 5 (1878); C. Canetta, "La morte del Conte Iacopo Piccinino," *Archivio storico lombardo* 9 (1882): 252–88.

1441, for example, the Gonfaloniere of Florence caught the city's mercenary captain by surprise, killed him, and tossed the body from the palace window.[5] Even so, Piccinino's surprising fate was certainly a major piece of news. The count was a leading figure in his own right and the apparent complicity of both the duke of Milan and king of Naples—one his father-in-law, the other his lord—added both seriousness and spice to the story.

On the twenty-seventh of June, Marco was thanking Filippo for news of the count's arrival in Naples and his elaborate welcome; by the fourth of July he had received news of the imprisonment, which had happened only ten days earlier. The strange turn of events "amazes everyone," he wrote, and he was anxious to know the reasons for it. "One wishes to understand it for everyone," he stated, indicating that he was willing to spread the king's side of the story, if only he knew what it was. Meanwhile, "the friends of the duke are saying that they believe that he knew nothing about it. It seems difficult to believe."[6]

In a postscript, written two days later, there was fresh news. The duke had written with the greatest urgency to his daughter ordering her to go no further toward Naples. For the moment, at least, the whole marriage alliance was in jeopardy. But Sforza's show of anger over his son-in-law's imprisonment does not appear to have made Marco reconsider the duke's supposed complicity; neither did the news later in the month "of the death of the Count I. and the rupture of his

[5] This was the fate of Baldaccio d'Anghiari. On this and other instances of misunderstanding between condottieri and their employers, see M. Mallett, *Mercenaries and Their Masters* (London, 1974), esp. pp. 97ff.

[6] 27 June 1465, postscript to letter of 22 June (cited in note 2 above); 4 July 1465, CS ser. 3, 178, fol. 22. On July 3 Agnolo Acciaiuoli wrote in similar terms to Filippo Strozzi: "ma il Duca sa bene che il Re non potrebbe fare cosa che fussi o in danno o in dispiacere della Signore sua, che non fussi comune alla Maestà sua." He was sure that the "recent errors" of the count were not minor. In Florence, he concluded, some were pleased and others displeased, "ma ogni savio et buono huomo loderà il consiglio del Re, sappiendo maximamente la Maestà sua essesi mossa con grande ragione, come mi pare essere vero" (A.S.F., CS ser. 3, 249, fol. 194).

thigh" provoke any comment on the suspicious circumstances of Piccinino's death.[7] Obviously, Marco was more than willing to accept the official Neapolitan version of events. The count, it was alleged, was plotting treason, and this was the reason for his arrest. Unfortunately, the accident that took his life also prevented a proper confession. Hearing a noise outside his prison, the count had hoisted himself up on a desk to look through the high window. He overbalanced and fell, and despite medical help, the injury to his thigh brought death within five days.[8]

It is unlikely that Marco was so naive as to mistake the signs pointing to murder. As much as possible, it appears, he wanted to regard the whole incident as a purely diplomatic crisis, which the friends of Naples would naturally wish to see settled in the king's favor. By early August, certainly, Marco had lost whatever interest he might have had in the details of the Neapolitan case. When he heard from Filippo that an ambassador was being dispatched with justificatory letters, Marco promised to pay an honorific visit, but greeted the mission itself with a sort of languid carelessness: "The justification you say he will bring with him is already here, and I have read it. It is very long, but there is little substance to it." Only the effectiveness of the excuses now interested him. "And if it satisfies the duke," he wrote, "it's enough."[9]

In Florence itself reactions were mixed. Some had accepted the king's explanation, others had not, but there was little excitement over the issue and Marco was sure that the affair would blow over. His only real concern was the indirect effect on the Strozzi's prospects, which had been damaged by the scandal in Naples and the interruption of the wedding. As always, he was inclined to optimism. "The longer matters drag on," he wrote, "the older it will grow and the more it will be accepted. If it was done with the consent of the duke, so much the better."

In the short run, Marco's cynical and partisan observations

[7] 20 July 1465, CS ser. 3, 249, fol. 169.

[8] *Memorie*, p. 28.

[9] 9 Aug. 1465, CS ser. 3, 180, fol. 64.

were certainly borne out. In a last effort to clear himself, the duke insisted that the corpse be disinterred, but it proved too decayed to reveal the cause of death. Sforza accepted the *fait accompli* and yielded to the Florentines and other friends who wished to see good relations reestablished between Milan and Naples. After nearly a month's delay, Madonna Ippolita was again instructed to proceed to Naples, where the marriage took place on the fifteenth of September.

Thus the immediate crisis passed. Yet for Marco himself the bizarre incident remained intriguing. By the time he composed his *Memoir* he had acquired new information from highly placed people—including Filippo Strozzi himself—and he made a point of exonerating the duke of Milan.[10] At last he could separate great and public events from his own devotion to the Strozzi cause. No longer bound to simplistic views by his loyalty to Naples, he could understand events more clearly and more broadly. In his history the moral blankness of his letters gave way to a livelier curiosity about men's motives and a stricter regard for truth.

[10] Filippo's testimony has the added importance that it provides the grounds for attributing the *Memoir* to Parenti (see Appendix). In addition to his *cognato*, Parenti cites the testimony of the Neapolitan ambassador to Florence, Antonio Cincinello: "I marveled," Parenti writes in the *Memoir*, "that such a man would excuse the duke, whom everyone accuses, and inculpate the king, when it seemed that even if the king were guilty he should absolve him. Messer Antonio was known to be a man of conscience, and from this I conclude that, constrained by the truth, he did not wish to excuse one who was guilty since it meant incriminating one who was innocent" (p. 27). Armed with such good authorities, Marco could take a certain smug satisfaction in going contrary to the "common opinion," and he concludes that "*ragione* requires everything be considered with good care."

CHAPTER 7

AUTUMN: UNCERTAINTY AND THE STIRRINGS OF REFORM

★

IN THE months of autumn, Marco continued his worried attention to the Strozzi cause. The departure of Don Federigo and Madonna Ippolita, however, left him without an immediate focus and no new opportunity came along on which to build new hopes. He wrote to Naples as frequently as ever, but without a central thread of expectation, his letters seem a confusion of detail. Yet as the chances for repatriation faded, the prospect of another and wider opportunity began to unfold. Rumors of political reform began to be heard, encouraging the expectations that had already led him to take the first steps toward his *Memoir*. In this atmosphere, dense with mistrust, the family protected its maneuvers behind a blanket of code, and it is amusing to see even routine messages guarded by ciphers. We must pick our way with care through this welter of coded numbers and deliberately laconic, allusive language. Though desirable details are lost, this numerological enigma expresses better than anything else the new political mood in Florence.

The code Marco used—like the one use by his mother-in-law and studied by her modern editor, Cesare Guasti—was extremely simple in conception, but not for that reason any easier to unravel. Marco substituted a long list of numbers (unfortunately not the same list as Alessandra's) for key individuals, places, groups, institutions, and even concepts. These numbers were arbitrarily assigned and no internal logic will clarify their sense. The only key is an intimate knowledge of the context of the correspondence—a knowledge which is not easily won since the writers did their best to veil their messages behind hints and private allusions. Fortunately, the more often a cipher is used, the more information can be gathered. By correlating references we can reconstruct perhaps half of all the ciphers, but it is easily the more important half.[1]

From the perspective of the late summer and early fall, the cycle of hopes and disappointments that had dominated the spring and summer stands out more clearly. Now that the illusions surrounding the princely visit had disappeared it is apparent how much the Strozzi had fallen under its spell. Filippo's financial services to King Ferrante had given him a claim on Aragonese patronage. At the same time, the visit underlined the necessity of paying court to the unofficial rulers of Florence.[2] In this way, led by opportunity and necessity, the family came to see their own problems as an item in a diplomatic exchange between the two powers.

Broader circumstances, too, had brought Florence and Naples closer together at this time and so favored this diplomatic strategy. In the reign of King Ferrante's father, Alfonso, Florence had warred with Naples and given sympathy to the rival

[1] It was common practice for the recipient to decode such letters between the lines. One partially deciphered letter has survived; it is Marco's letter of December 9, 1469, which is also interesting for its description of the death of Piero de' Medici; cf. CS ser. 3, 247, c. 130. There are occasional explicit references to the code and its inconveniences. On August 20, 1465 Parenti wrote to Naples concerning the selection of new Accoppiatori, but his code only permitted him to name two. For the others, he wrote, Filippo would have to ask "4" to whom he had already written, "since here I don't have the names by number and I don't want to mention them otherwise" (CS ser. 3, 249, fol. 200^{r-v}). Obviously Marco was more careful in his use of ciphers than the anarchist Bakunin, who, according to his biographer, sent out coded letters with the code sheets enclosed.

[2] For the way in which their diplomatic role enhanced Medici prestige, see J. Hale, *Florence and the Medici: The Pattern of Control* (London, 1977), pp. 62–63.

pretensions of the house of Anjou. Ferrante had ended this belligerence toward Florence, and recent decisive victories over the Angevins gave him added prestige and security. At the same time, he created a strong link with Milan, which swung Naples and Florence into the same diplomatic orbit. A change in direction in Rome also added impetus to this reconciliation. Pius II had generally been a compliant partner to Naples, but King Ferrante's relations with Paul II, who succeeded in 1465, were strained, and it was feared that the new pope might align Rome with his native Venice. All this helped bring Florence and Naples together, and to symbolize this realignment plans were made for the young Lorenzo de' Medici to visit Naples.[3]

In the long run, Filippo Strozzi's cautious reliance on Neapolitan patronage did not prove wrong, but in the late summer it appeared that pro-Neapolitan feeling in Florence had suddenly evaporated. Many Florentines, Marco included, had been alienated by the aloofness of their aristocratic guests, and the sparse escort mustered for their departure contrasted poorly with the elaborate welcome prepared for their arrival. But it was the Piccinino affair that wrecked the Strozzi's hopes. The death of the famous captain was a diplomatic shock, if not a moral one, and relations between the powers were badly jarred. These upsets also came at a difficult time. Many citizens had grown restive with the alliance with Sforza, so clearly a buttress to Medici power, and some were plotting a return to the old friendship with Venice.[4] No wonder, then, that the regime urgently dispatched embassies to Milan and Naples to urge that the marriage be allowed to go ahead; no wonder, too, that many citizens looked warily for a time at entanglements with either power.

[3] See E. Pontieri, *Per la storia del Regno di Ferrante I d'Aragone re di Napoli* (Naples, n.d.), ch. 3.

[4] N. Rubinstein, *The Government of Florence under the Medici* (Oxford, 1966), p. 154. In January, Parenti would write of a plot by the opposition leaders to swing Florence into an alliance with Venice. The plot was said to be highly secret, but defensive in nature—in case Piero should use Milan against them. See below, ch. 9, p. 185.

Marco's hope was that the Piccinino affair would gradually be accepted and forgotten and relations would return to normal. Meanwhile, he focused his attention on the impending arrival of a new ambassador from Naples. On the eighth of August he wrote that he was expecting the envoy and would visit him soon. A week later he was still awaiting the arrival "from day to day," but he had apparently been warned by Filippo not to expect too much. "I am discouraged," he wrote, "that you say that he is not the one you would want. You have done well to say so, because I will go more carefully." But Marco's curiosity was aroused as well. What, he asked, was the reason for this hesitation? Was the ambassador lacking in good will, or just in effectiveness?[5]

Before Marco had completed his letter, the new envoy at last arrived, and the manner of his welcome brought more disturbing thoughts. Marco wrote that he had visited the ambassador—Messer Tommaso Vassallo—and found him "a pleasant person." They talked for a long time and Vassallo promised to take the Strozzi's case to Piero once again. Marco, of course, was not the only one who wanted to pay his respects or had a favor to ask. During the course of their conversations, a number of prominent Florentines paid visits: Luigi Guicciardini, Carlo Pandolfini, Francesco di Nerone, Pierfilippo Pandolfini, Giovanozzo Pitti, Agnolo Acciaiuoli, and Vespasiano da Bisticci. The delegation sounds impressive, but we should not be misled. All these men had connections with Naples and strong reasons for paying court to its ambassador. Even the bookseller and biographer Vespasiano da Bisticci, though no match for the others in rank or influence, was later commended by the king as "our devoted friend."[6]

[5] 8 Aug. 1465, CS ser. 3, 180, fol. 64; 14 Aug. 1465, CS ser. 3, 180, fol. 66^{r-v}.

[6] Luigi Guicciardini, having only recently returned from an embassy in Naples, was about to set out again. Pierfilippo Pandolfini's brother, Pandolfo, was currently the Florentine representative in Naples, and Ferrante had honored him by standing as godfather to one of his children. As we have seen, Marco was also hoping to see Pandolfo knighted. Nor was Pandolfo the first of his family to win Neapolitan favor, since his father had been knighted there two decades earlier. The Acciaiuoli had ties in Naples going back to

The men that Marco mentions as visiting the ambassador that day constituted a circle of Neapolitan clients, and his own presence among them is significant. Like his friend Vespasiano, Marco was not their equal in rank, but as a representative of the Strozzi he had become one of their number. A decent welcome from men such as these would be taken for granted, but the general picture was quite the opposite. The ambassador had arrived, wrote Marco, to be met by no one except his Milanese counterpart, the omnipresent Nicodemo Tranchedini, Sforza's agent in Florence. The snub was obviously deliberate. "You can believe," he wrote employing the number of ciphers that now become the secret second lexicon of the correspondence, "that (the ambassador) of (Milan) who stays here—you know who—asked a number of (principali) to go to meet the (ambassador) of (Naples). No one wanted to do it, so he went alone." Even one of the close associates of the Strozzi, a man frequently mentioned under the cipher 15 and intimate enough with Alessandra to have been drawn by her into a discussion of a possible bride for Filippo, had declined to appear. He "will not risk being seen with him," Marco wrote.

The extraordinary importance of face-to-face encounters—visiting, meeting, greeting, dining—comes through again and again in these letters. In a political society built on so small a scale such gestures were bound to be central, and the traditional ban on political activity and organization outside of the public councils added to their significance. Visiting was the first means of declaring allegiance, as in the case of a wavering ex-Medicean who, Marco reported later in the autumn, had gone to see Pitti "where there were many others, to show himself among them." Obviously, the symbolic meaning of paying a courtesy call was not lost on the cautious "15" or others like him, and their action—or inaction—spoke plainly to Marco. "Now you see," he wrote, "how likely it is in the

---

the fourteenth century, and Agnolo's son Iacopo had recently joined the camp of the Aragonese forces fighting the Angevin pretender. On Vespasiano as a Neapolitan partisan, see G. Cagni, *Vespasiano da Bisticci ed il suo epistolario* (Rome, 1969).

matter of (Filippo) to obtain anything by means of (Naples)."

Despite this discouraging start, Marco followed in detail the doings of the Neapolitan ambassador over the next few weeks: his presentation to the Signoria and to Piero de' Medici, his warm reception from Pitti, his search for a suitable but inexpensive house—in which he was assisted by Nicodemo Tranchedini who, in addition to reporting to Sforza, ran a sideline in real estate. In time Parenti's initial fears about the ambassador, prompted by Filippo's warning, seem to have disappeared. He visited the envoy often, and even the cautious "15" followed suit. Meanwhile, Marco was as committed as ever to playing the role of a partisan of Naples. "Advise me," he asked, "how our meddling has pleased the king. I believe it will please him more every day, because we are on a good path."[7]

As always Marco was inclined to look for bright spots and he would certainly have liked to find some encouragement for Filippo. Still, the sum of it was simply that "15" had told the envoy that "at the moment nothing will move."[8] It is evident that the recent diplomatic crisis was not the only factor contributing to an uncertain or even gloomy prospect. Sforza's reluctant decision to permit his daughter's marriage to go ahead had averted the threat to the stability of the Italian alliance, but this had made no apparent difference to the feeling that the moment to press for repatriation had passed. As Marco's letters soon made clear, the pressure for reform was building in the city and the Medici regime, for the first time since 1458, was facing a serious challenge. It would not be long before Agnolo Acciaiuoli would be writing to Filippo that Florence was "a paradise inhabited by devils." More ominous, though less flamboyant, was the report of Agnolo's son: "I want especially to tell you this: I do not see that our friends and our cause are inferior to anyone else—neither in council nor in backing."[9]

[7] 20 Aug. 1465, CS ser. 3, 249, fol. 200^{r-v}.

[8] 13 Sept. 1465, CS ser. 3, 131, fol. 166^{r-v}.

[9] Agnolo Acciaiuoli to Filippo Strozzi, 9 Nov. 1465, CS ser. 3, 178, c. 14; Iacopo Acciaiuoli to Filippo Strozzi, 8 Nov. 1465, CS ser, 3, 178, c. 24.

Once again the *Memoir* provides a convenient introduction to the reformist pressures that began to shake the regime in the late summer and autumn of 1465:

> From 1458 until now the purses in which the name slips for the Signoria of Florence are kept had stood open, and the slips were drawn by hand by a few men called the *accoppiatori*. And before that it had been the same for most of the time since 1434. Now it was decided on the 16th, 17th, and 18th of August, and ratified by the councils of the People and the Commune and the Hundred that they should be closed. This was done to reduce the power of Piero di Cosimo, which everyday became irksome to men's minds, in order that he would not be able to choose the priors according to his own wish, as was done at his orders by the accoppiatori, his partisans elected from time to time. The leading citizens [huomini dello stato] were roused to follow this path, led chiefly by Messer Luca Pitti and other knights already mentioned who were Piero's adversaries. The latter, seeing this coming full upon him so that it could not be resisted and counseled by his friends, thought to take the goodwill upon himself, and began as much as the others to speak out, saying that since the city was peaceful and prosperous, it was better to seal the purses. It was done, then, as mentioned, but this gave him no more favor since the good of it was attributed to others. . . .
>
> The first priors that were drawn by lot from closed purses entered office on the 1st of November, 1465, and the Gonfaloniere of Justice was Niccolò Soderini.[10]

In the pages of Parenti's narrative this general description leads directly into a discussion of the turmoil of Soderini's two-month term, a dramatic historical moment that gave clear warning of the crisis to come. But in the more detailed chronicle of the correspondence another pace prevails; there, as so often, we find a somewhat different sense of events.

On September 13, Marco wrote two strongly contrasting letters. One was his customary report to Filippo and, as had become usual, it was heavily marked with ciphers. The other was to Marco's friend Pandolfo Pandolfini, currently the re-

[10] *Memorie*, pp. 33–34.

public's ambassador in Naples. It is the only surviving letter of his not addressed to his brothers-in-law—though its preservation among the Strozzi papers suggests that Pandolfo shared it with Filippo. This letter, blessedly clear of code, is a straightforward summary of recent proposals for reform.

The main item was the proposal to return to the traditional blind electoral lottery: "Let me tell you that in the last few days it was decided by the entire Consiglio de' richiesti—who numbered more than 150 and I myself was among them—and then by the entire Pratica [consultative council], and especially by Messer Luca and Piero di Cosimo that the purses should be closed."[11] A second petition struck at the arbitrary authority of the regime in another way. It proposed that the Eight of Ward—the magistracy in charge of security—should lose its special powers, which it had exercised since 1458. The Eight would reacquire their "former authority," Parenti reported, "with the understanding that this in no way means having extraordinary powers (*balìa*)."

Marco also reported on three other petitions. One dealt with the reform of some minor offices—and here too the call was for a return to the "old way"; the other two dealt with taxes. All this Marco summarized clearly and methodically for his friend the ambassador, but his only comment before passing on to other news was a general one, reflecting the broad climate of opinion as much as his own. "All [of the petitions] are held to be a good thing," he wrote, "and every day it is expected that still better things will be thought of and accomplished."

In this way Marco glossed over the factional pressures that had led directly to the five petitions, as though such matters were not proper to be discussed with the envoy of the republic. But he left it to the pages of his *Memoir* to draw the widest conclusions: "Thus the city came to be cured of its ills in the distribution of taxes, just as by the closing of the purses it was reformed in the distribution of its honors; two fundamental matters in which consists all the entire good of the

[11] 13 Sept. 1465, CS ser. 3, 178, fol. 26.

city, that is the distribution of its honors and its taxes according to justice, the life of cities."[12]

Ambassadors were always hungry for news from home, and Marco—ever a dutiful correspondent—had done his best to provide it. To the Strozzi, on the other hand, he addressed a very different sort of letter, bearing little relation to either the straightforward summary of news sent to Pandolfini or the larger issues discussed in the *Memoir*. Filippo would probably get the general news from Pandolofo, and if the letter Marco sent him is less informative on recent political developments, it reveals much that the other letter concealed: the atmosphere of deep distrust, the sharp divisions in the city, and the opening stages of a dangerous contest for power.

Included in the same mail packet, Marco informed his brother-in-law, there was also a letter from "15" addressed to "4," a Florentine resident in Naples—probably Pandolfo Pandolfini himself. The address on the letter, however, was a subterfuge and it was really intended for Filippo, "so it is not meant to be handed on, but kept by (Filippo). He does this for greater safety since they [i.e. the letters] are not prohibited to "4" (Pandolfo?) as they are to (Filippo) and (Lorenzo)."[13] Marco expressed some skepticism that such a ruse would succeed, but there is no hint that he thought it unwarranted, and he was also concerned that two letters—one his, one Filippos'—had gone astray.

These opening lines already indicate that Marco reported from a place of mistrust and maneuver. But behind the tangled messages that followed, he communicated an essentially simple warning: that the unity of the regime was now so badly shaken that no course of action could be followed beyond watching events from day to day:

> Nonetheless, (the Gonfaloniere) now follows (Piero de' Medici), but the larger part of (the priors) follow (Pitti) and they are one with (Acciaiuoli). And yesterday they sent to (Milan) for (Acciaiuoli) to be in (Florence) quickly. . . .

[12] *Memorie*, p. 34.

[13] 13 Sept. 1465, CS ser. 3, 131, fol. 166^{r-v}.

> The matter of (closed electoral purses) is accepted by (Pitti), (Dietisalvi), and (Acciaiuoli) so that the larger part of (the principali) go along with them and are of good cheer. (Piero de' Medici) with some of the (principali) at the last moment made a great show of wishing (closed purses) but secretly it is thought they lamented it. But they could not resist it. Now, after the fact they made a show of great unity.

This false unity was a characteristic feature of communal politics, which left no place—short of exile—for formal opposition. Opposition meant faction, which by definition represented putting special interests ahead of the common good. However, the reality of the situation can be gauged by the fact that even the cautious "15" was allowing himself to be drawn into the factional game, both in his own behalf and for the Strozzi:

> "15" said to the (ambassador) of (Naples) that nothing will move for the moment. And every day "15" moves closer to (Pitti) and they are agreed that for now it should not be spoken of, and especially with this (Gonfaloniere). Two days ago they spoke of it with great intimacy, and "15" thought it best to reveal to (Pitti) that the (ambassador) was authorized to attempt it with whomever and whenever it seemed best to him, as advised by "15" and "15" by (Pitti).

To the Strozzi, the rules and limits of factional maneuver were by now second nature. For months they had worked on the assumption that there indeed were two parties—two centers of power—in the city. Yet all their persistence and skill seemed only to bring out more clearly the irony of their position. As much as anything, it had been the fragmentation of the oligarchy after Cosimo's death that had allowed the exiles to press their case among the inner circles of Florence. At the same time, this fragmentation was destroying the effectiveness of the regime and none of the competing leaders now felt secure enough to give the Strozzi what they so desperately wanted.

In this sense, medieval political theory had proven itself in practice: the politics of faction were indeed sterile. Marco put the truth plainly to Filippo: "And do not expect that the affair of (Filippo) and (Lorenzo) can be managed any longer by (Medici) nor (Pitti) nor (Acciaiuoli) nor (Francesco Neroni) nor (Dietisalvi Neroni)." All of them, warned Marco, had other things to put right first.

CHAPTER 8

MATCHMAKING AND OTHER TROUBLES

★

WHILE they waited for the political turbulence to die down, the Strozzi had an important family matter of their own to see to. This was the question of finding a suitable wife for Filippo. The idea appealed strongly to Alessandra's heart and, as political prospects faded, she gave more and more of her attention to this alternate goal. Filippo himself was less keen, and Marco found himself once again playing the part of advisor and chief negotiator. His letters began to report the unfolding of this new campaign of domestic maneuver with much the same seriousness—and often the same secretiveness—as marked the other.

At the best of times, marriage among the propertied class was rarely a matter of simple personal choice. Too serious a business to be left to lovers, marriage was a matter of deliberate policy: a compound of financial arrangements, family prestige, and social and political loyalties. But these were only the normal complications of matchmaking; for the Strozzi, the added disabilities of exile cut across them all. An exile could not be considered the best of prospects, even if he was wealthy and had a good name. Political suspicion clung to such families and could be the hidden cost of an alliance, as Marco himself had discovered. From Filippo's standpoint, too, there were obvious problems in negotiating so important a question at a distance. He had to depend on his mother and Marco for personal impressions, and the exchange of news was slow and fitful—the same practical difficulties that dogged his political negotiations. The way around these problems would have been to marry outside of Florence, most likely to other expatriate Florentines drawn by politics or business to Naples, but the family never seems to have considered this option; marriage away from Florence would have meant accepting the permanence of exile. The other alternative was to wait in the hope of repatriation—and this Alessandra was no longer prepared to do.

For her, marriage and repatriation were two parts of the same ambition. In practice, though, the two plans ran counter to each other—at least in the short run. A marriage struck in exile would not be the brilliant match Filippo might make once the ban was lifted. As long as the promise of political success drew her on, Alessandra was content to leave her sons to their bachelorhood. But this could not go on forever. Filippo was already in his later thirties and she herself was probably close to sixty. Having held the family together for so long, she claimed the "consolation" of seeing it reestablish itself in a new generation.

When the royal visit had passed without any visible benefit, Alessandra was left fretful and pessimistic. Piero de' Medici's bland reassurances that everything would be worked out in due time gave her no confidence. Men who are "good and whole and stand by their word" she would trust, she said, but she had no faith in those "who say yes and no to the same thing." She was pleased to hear that a gift of 450 oranges was on its way to sweeten Piero's good will, but in general Alessandra fell back into the mood of pious fatalism that marked her response to adversity. When Piccinino's murder shattered her last hopes, it was left to her only to declare her irritated indifference. "These things would hardly bother me," she wrote "if our own affairs weren't involved."[1]

Against this background, the marriage plan began to develop. At first she raised the subject tentatively: she had spoken

[1] The oranges are mentioned in her letter of 5 July 1465 (*Lettere*, p. 435). Her comments on the Piccinino affair come the letter of 26 July 1465 (*Lettere*, pp. 442–43).

with Marco about it, but his advice was to wait a little until they knew Filippo's wishes. Content with having raised the question, she also made it clear that she had no intention of letting it drop. "Let it be soon," she urged, "the longer one delays, the more time is lost."[2]

Very soon she had something more concrete to offer. Marco had come to see her with the prospect of a match with the daughter of Francesco Tanagli. Until now, she informed Filippo, they had done little about finding him a wife, though they had looked quietly about. What they had determined was that anyone who was willing to marry his daughter to an exile had some deficiency, either of money or something else: "Now of such defects, the least is lack of money, and when the other necessary parts are present, one should not care about the money, as you have told me many times."[3]

This, of course, was prelude to a proposal whose advantages would be social rather than financial. Tanagli, it seems, was a great friend of Marco, whom he had approached "in a fine manner and with wise words." Blessed with six sons and six daughters, Tanagli was not able to offer a large dowry, she explained sympathetically, and he would "rather send her outside of Florence to people of worth" than lower himself by making a poorer match at home.

Pride and need seeming to be well matched on both sides, Marco was invited to his friend's house. Tanagli "called down the girl in her gown" for Marco to see and he issued a similar invitation to Alessandra and Caterina whenever they chose to take it up. In the meantime they had Marco's observations to go on, and his report was that "she has a good figure, and that she seemed to him an acceptable girl." She was also, according to their information, "a girl who is capable and has good sense." With twelve children in the house, she had had a lot of responsibility: "and from what I hear she runs everything, since the mother is always pregnant and isn't up to much." With more charity, Alessandra added that those who

[2] 5 July 1465, *Lettere*, p. 436.

[3] 26 July 1465 (continued on the 27th), *Lettere*, pp. 443–44.

were often at the house said that the girl managed the household, "since that is how her father raised her." And as for the prudent father himself, "he is well thought of and was one of the fine young men of Florence."

A mother's eagerness shines through this discussion of the worthy Tanagli and his industrious daughter, and Alessandra pressed for a quick decision. "It does not seem to me time to put off taking this step," she wrote, evidently fearing that Filippo would look for a postponement, and for the same reason she took pains to underline the cautiousness of her preparations. She also suggested that Filippo sound out Pandolfo Pandolfini, evidently a friend of Tanagli as well as Marco. Pandolfo being "the closest person we know to this girl, he should know all about her and also about her father's standing." But, sure as she was that Pandolfini's word would be favorable, Alessandra was already celebrating in her mind. Her words ring with jubilation: "Get the jewels ready, and beautiful ones, for a wife is found! Being beautiful and Filippo Strozzi's wife, she needs to have fine jewels—since, just as you are honored in everything else, you should not be lacking in this."

Alessandra was undoubtedly the moving force behind this campaign, but the practicalities had to be left to others. The business of marriage had its formalities and professional brokers were widely used. Alessandra, however, chose to employ Marco, a sign of her trust as well as a convenience in view of his friendship with Tanagli. "I believe," she wrote, "that Marco will give you more details than I have, because he arranged it and understands it better than I do."

In a lengthy letter of the same day (the twenty-seventh of July) Marco covered much the same ground but in quite a different spirit. As the one delegated to negotiate the business, he must have felt more keenly than she did how much work remained to be done before the bells could be set ringing. And, lacking a mother's emotional hold over her son, he was obliged to suit his remarks to Filippo's cautious temper. Marco was inclined to feel neither as hopeless about politics nor as enthusiastic about an early marriage, and he scrutinized the prospects in both arenas with a spirit of pragmatism and patience.

Though he had initially advised delay, Marco now joined in urging Filippo to make up his mind and choose a wife. The choice, however, he left entirely to Filippo and in the lengthy report that followed, Marco performed the service of an agent whose job it is to gather and arrange information, not to make decisions. Accordingly, he presented a much more detailed picture than the impatient Alessandra. "We have examined all Florence," he stated, "and have done your account in two ways: the one, if you were here; the other, being still as you are [i.e. in exile]." Starting with the first hypothesis, Marco assured his brother-in-law that "being here" he would be able to "go right to the top" and then named four girls who inhabited that high region.[4] The leading two, in fact, came from families so powerful that Marco spoke of them only in ciphers—though we can only guess whether he was truly concerned to protect the information or simply enjoyed practicing the new code. (They were, in fact, the daughters of two of the chiefs of the opposition faction, Francesco and Dietisalvi Neroni.) The whole exercise has about it an air of unreality: after all, the marriage scheme was only being considered because repatriation looked so remote.

When Filippo's "account" was redone on a more realistic basis, all higher ambitions were quickly dropped, and Marco dismissed the available girls bringing large dowries as "rustic and common." It came down to a choice between two families: the Adimari and the Tanagli. Both would be desirable connections, though each presented its own difficulties. The Adimari were offering 1,500 florins and he was sure the figure was firm. The reason—a revealing one—was that there were no sons. It was a good dowry and Marco's real worry was that it might be too high—high enough to attract other suitors not suffering Filippo's special disabilities. Nor did he know yet whether they had their eye on Filippo. In the case of Tanagli, the situation was reversed, since he had six sons and

[4] 27 July 1465, CS ser. 3, 131, fol. 161^{r-v}, and *Lettere*, pp. 447–51.

"wants to spend little." But, he said, "in this case we know you figure in their plans."

Having examined the case many times, Marco concluded, he and Alessandra had found nothing to choose between the two girls, assuming "both were equal in price and you were suited to them." In figure, they were equal. As for birth, there would be advantages either way:

> The Adimari are more noble than the Tanagli, but they have no family at all—no father, no brothers. Cousins and uncles enough, but they are unpleasant men; and all their relations are men of this sort. But with this loss, there is also this advantage, which is that there is no bother or responsibility at all.
>
> The other [i.e. Tanagli] is just the reverse. If they are not from a great family, nonetheless they are old and worthy, and this line is even descended from knights.

"The father of the girl," Marco continued, recommending his friend, "is a man of my age, a man of substance, courteous, eloquent, and sociable. And he is well liked, has some political standing [*un poco di stato*] and has many relations, all good." Marco went on to list the family connections of the man's wife, sister, brother, and even his wife's sister—each, apparently, an item to be entered in the full accounting of the girl's status. Nor should the eleven siblings be forgotten. Marriage into such a family would have to be a mixed blessing: "with this honey," he wrote, "there will also be a few flies, and sometimes it will bring some bother as well as aid."

How neatly balanced, as Marco himself remarked, the choice was between these two girls: the one an orphan blessed with everything but family, the other almost a mother to her many brothers and sisters. The decision rested entirely on Filippo, though it would be surprising if Marco himself did not lean a little to the daughter of his friend. As he was quick to acknowledge, their friendship permitted him to give more details, including an explanation of Tanagli's eagerness for the match. Tanagli felt himself to be "in a poor position, and saw himself slipping below his rank and ambition; and by this means he feels he will gain." This confession of need seems to have raised no obstacles for Marco; since it could be assumed that marriage was an alliance of interests, there was no reason for him to scruple about revealing how his friend hoped to benefit.

On Tanagli's invitation, Marco had gone to visit the family and examine the girl. He had seen her up close—from no more than four braccie—and could give a good report. "The girl is as large as our Caterina," he wrote, using his own wife as a handy, if possibly risky, standard of comparison: "but she is better built; good skin and good flesh. The face is not up to that of the Ardinghelli girl, or Messer Palla's daughter, but she is in no way unattractive, is dignified, and has a good manner. And I promise you that she can be compared to Madonna Ippolita, or better." In this second comparison Marco was on safer ground, but whether the girl was as beautiful (or as plain) as Sforza's daughter was unlikely to be the sticking point. Even duchesses came with dowries, and to marry a girl with too mean a price would not only be a bad bargain, it could be a kind of dishonor. As yet, unfortunately, Tanagli would not name his price. He wanted to know if the rest of the arrangement was appealing, and "as for dowry, he says he wishes to have the benefit of my judgment and discretion."

This appeal to his friendship could have put Marco in an awkward spot, but he gave his assurance that the business would be safe in his hands. "And if it pleases you," he wrote, "give me your commission and say how low you are prepared to go." But there was no reason to worry that the bargaining would immediately descend to this minimum: "we will begin at the top, and if we can stop at the ceiling we will never go down to the ground, even if we had your permission to do it."

Marco could not resist adding a word of advice. Though he had promised to bargain like the best of merchants, he wanted Filippo to remember that more was at stake than money. He had in mind, said Marco, "a certain saying of yours," namely that he would spend what he had but no more.

This was obviously sound practice for a merchant, but Marco was worried that Filippo would apply it to the business of marriage: "To save yourself from error, you must not base yourself on this, since it would not be to your honor nor ours. I am not telling you that you must prepare a hundred gowns, but what you do should correspond to your reputation; it should be honorable and complete."

This recalls a similar conclusion to Alessandra's letter and probably reflects her concern. For all their differences, Filippo's two advisors shared a common anxiety. Success in business had won Filippo the protection of a king and the friendship of important men. Nonetheless, his cautious frugality might yet stand in the way. Family and honor were no less important than mere wealth if Alessandra's dream was to come true.

Though Marco had fully accepted Alessandra's plan for the marriage, the contrast between their letters is as marked as their common purpose. Careful to keep to the role of agent rather than principal, he supplied Naples with businesslike reports, while sharing with Filippo an implicit assumption that these domestic matters would always be subordinate to public and political ones. Alessandra, on the other hand, had little to do with these reticences and preoccupations of the male world. She could not afford simply to inform and advise. Her feelings were neither simple nor insincere, but—like an actor performing in a large hall—she needed to make her gestures strong and expressive so that they could be read at a distance. Above all, she wanted reassurance that her love was reciprocated, and she would caress, cajole, bully, and beg to have it.

This emotionalism is one of the delights of her letters. When, for instance, her complaints about the lack of mail apparently brought a nettled reply, she was quick to take up the attack. Certainly, she began, she had not meant to say that they had forgotten her, "since it is natural that a son remember his mother, especially when he had not been abandoned by her when he was needy." How ready she was to reach for her strongest weapons! But having made her point, Alessandra dropped back to sketch instead a picture of her own patient vigil that in the end is even more effective. When their letters are infrequent, she wrote, she knew this meant they were busy with important business and knowing this gave her patience to wait. Still, she looked for a letter, so that, "I wait with pleasure Wednesday or Thursday when the courier should come, believing I will have two lines from your hand." And if nothing came, she would set her mind to waiting for the next; and if nothing comes still, "I send to the bank to inquire, and if I find they have something from you, I take comfort that you are both healthy and well. And so I carry on, passing the time."[5]

This mixture of emotional suppleness and tenacity kept the marriage issue alive. Evidently Filippo was hesitant about coming to a decision and others had advised him to put it off. Alessandra felt that she had no choice but to accept her son's decision, though it was an acceptance not far removed from protest: "As for a wife, if others urge you to hold off a bit, I don't know what I can say, since I understand little and know less. And I am sure that you and the others understand this and every other thing better than me."[6] Ten days later she gave Filippo a lengthy description of one of the girls that she at least continued to regard as his prospective bride. On Sunday she had gone to early mass at the cathedral, as she had done on several other feast days, in order to get a look at the Adimari girl. Unfortunately the girl was not there, and Alessandra fell to scrutinizing a stranger in her place. "And not knowing who she was," she wrote, "I placed myself beside her and gave thought to this girl."[7]

She found the stranger possessed of "a fine figure and well made," as large as Caterina or larger and with good skin—"not one of those that is white, but it is healthy." Her figure was obviously the girl's best feature, however: "she has a long face, and she does not have very delicate features, but not like a peasant either." Neither her face nor her manner showed

[5] 16 July 1465, *Lettere*, pp. 441–42.

[6] 9 Aug. 1465, *Lettere*, pp. 453–54.

[7] 17 Aug. 1465, *Lettere*, pp. 458–60.

any signs of sluggishness, and—given her other pleasing features—Alessandra felt sure that her face would not "spoil her price."

This stranger, so frankly examined, was Francesco Tanagli's capable daughter, as Alessandra only discovered when she followed the girl out. To the eager mother, the coincidence seemed "a remarkable thing," since the Tanagli did not make a habit of attending that mass: "I believe that God set her in front of me in order that I might see her."

Since Alessandra already had Tanagli's cordial invitation to come and see his daughter, Providence would seem to have gone to unnecessary lengths, but Alessandra herself was prepared to carry her own quest still further. At the end of August she wrote to say that by talking to several friends and neighbors of the Tanagli she now had "very good information . . . and all are agreed in saying the same thing: that whoever had her will be well pleased." They also confirmed her impression of the girl's good figure. As for her face, Alessandra—varying her story a little—now admitted that she had never gotten a very good look,

> because it seemed that she realized that I was looking at her; then she took herself off like the wind. But I can put together what little I saw with what I was told. Her face is not the prettiest, but it will not detract from her figure; she will be handsome, and more so when she is dressed as a young woman rather than a child. As for her skin, it is not very white, but it is not brown either—olive rather.[8]

And, stressed Alessandra, she had seen her plain, without adornments.

With this confirmation, Alessandra now felt sure that she was not mistaken. Her friends had been able to tell her about qualities less easily discerned in church. From Gostanza Pandolfini—who had stayed in Florence while Pandolfo carried out his embassy to Naples—she learned that the girl could read very well: "And when I asked whether there was anything uncouth about her, she answered me no, that she is quick and

[8] 31 Aug. 1465, *Lettere*, pp. 463–68.

knows how to dance and sing." But to Alessandra this welcome news was no surprise in view of the gentility of the father. "He gives all his affection to this girl," she wrote. "It is easy to believe that he raised her to have good manners."

Having brushed aside any lingering doubts of her own, Alessandra was more than ready to dispose of any other rival. The Adimari girl with her large dowry was surely out of reach, and as for other girls whose names had been mentioned, their families were inflexible and haughty: "You cannot find any that have those things a man would want; and if there are any who have some good qualities, they are not pretty. For myself, I would not want to see these sorry things in front of me." None but "the dregs" were prepared to marry outside of Florence.

From such a conclusion there was really only one way forward, and Alessandra had already taken it. On the previous day she had sent for Marco and they had agreed that Tanagli should be given some words of encouragement—though nothing, she reassured Filippo, that they could not get out of if they wanted. Alessandra suspected that her difficulties would not be with the girl's father but with her own son, and she was pleased to have his word that he had no inclination "to perform such marvels as Ardinghelli did." This unfortunate young man, we gather, so delayed his nuptial arrangements that it was thirty months before his bride saw her husband, and then to make up for his follies he had redoubled them by spending lavishly to entertain and adorn her.

Meanwhile Alessandra's thoughts were racing ahead to entertainments and ornaments of her own. Filippo's wife would need to have jewels and they should not be any less fine than the others. She had the "vainglory," as she put it, to want to see the girl beautifully dressed: "and if her clothes are not ornamented with pearls, it is necessary to decorate them with some other trifles, so that you will spend a lot and it will be thrown away." Beyond urging this "useful expense," she also wanted his advice on other matters of dress: in making up silks or linens, should they follow the style of Florence or that of Naples—whose fashion in women's dress, she admitted, did not please her. "Give me a little of your thoughts," she urged her son in concluding, "although it is not yet time."

There is a touch of the pathetic in this last request, a momentary recognition that her hopes could not feed on themselves forever. Only a glimpse of Filippo's intentions comes to us reflected in his mother's replies, but it is enough to tell us that he was still far from thoughts of pearls and silks. Two weeks later (September 13) we find her writing: "I do not marvel that you go slowly in this matter of a wife, since as you say it is a thing of great importance, and of all the things one can do the most serious, since having a good companion consoles a man in both soul and body. And just the same when it is the other way round, since when they are snivellers, or pea-brained, or like the one Filippo had, you live a life of tribulation."[9]

Despite Filippo's cautiousness Alessandra lavished him with advice on how to treat the still hypothetical bride. "A man, when he is a man, makes the woman a woman," she wrote. For this reason, men should not be too enamored of their wives, so that when at the beginning the wife commits some small faults, she will be admonished and prevented from falling into larger ones. "And good company avoids a bad outcome," she added. "There are many who do wrong for the lack of having someone watching over them."

For all this stern advice—and the lack of solid evidence that it was yet needed—Alessandra was happy and optimistic. From everything that she had been able to find out she was convinced that "this one is no silly." Growing almost silly herself in her eagerness, she had even taken to walking by the Tanagli house and staring up at its windows: "I have walked by there many times and sent others, and she is not to be seen hanging out the windows all day, which seems to me a good sign." Alessandra now knew all she could think to know about the girl, and she was sure that "you will find consolation together."

Once again she could hardly hold herself back from pleasant

[9] 13 Sept. 1465, *Lettere*, pp. 469–73.

thoughts about the bustle of preparations soon to be needed. "You say that I should put the household linens in order," she wrote, gladly accepting the responsibility along with the measure of encouragement it implied. "It will be ready in good time," she joked, "perhaps sooner than the bride. And if you don't have twice as many things, you will have to excuse me, since one cannot provide both here and there without a full purse."

This may have been meant as a rebuke to her thrifty son, but thoughts about the lack of linens also led Alessandra—rather oddly—to reflect on other drawbacks to his sober character. "And if," she went on "in order to be reputed a good Christian, you have not taken one of those you might have [i.e. a woman, a slave girl] who could have done it for you. . . ." It was a ticklish thought but the drift is clear. Had Filippo taken a concubine, she might have done him the office of wife in more than one respect, and his domestic arrangements, if not his Christian conscience, would have improved. On the other hand, it was also possible that this sort of person might have ruined such goods as he already had. Consoled by this thought, she shook off her wayward notions with perhaps only a lingering hint of regret for the fine linens that might have been: "One cannot but praise the desire to be a good Christian, both for the soul and the body, and it is to the honor and good fame of all men in this world."

Having put these curious temptations behind her, Alessandra brought her anticipations of the forthcoming marriage to an end in a mood of thorough satisfaction. After all, with Filippo's prosperity there was no need to worry about the preparations: "You have so much in this world that it can be done quickly. The jewels being in order and I myself providing the linens, it seems to me we need not wait any longer to see it brought to a conclusion."

⋆

In a work of fiction such untroubled, complacent thoughts would instantly be recognized as a sign of a coming setback. But even real and ordinary lives contain moments of disillusionment that fall so precisely it seems they must have been plotted. She had not yet sealed her letter before Marco arrived to give her the bad news that all her plans had collapsed, and the postscript was as grim as the letter was hopeful: "I had written the letter and Marco came to me. He said he had approached Francesco Tanagli and that Francesco had spoken of it very coldly, in a manner indicating that he had given up the idea. . . . And he said that it was a serious matter to send a daughter so far off and to a house one could call an inn." For this change of heart she blamed both Filippo and Marco. It was the result, she told her son, of "your delay and then Marco's, since fifteen days ago he could have given [Tanagli] a little hope." Her bitterness overflowed. She could not, she declared, remember even having felt its equal. With the earlier pages of her letter still lying open in front of her, she recalled the preparations she had planned: "So, then, I shall not have to find the linens, nor you the jewels, as when I thought we were on our way I still needed to do. Let it all be in God's name. Marco will have to advise you of the rest; I have no spirit left, having endured so much effort and lost everything."

For his part, Marco ruefully admitted that, with the bad news he had brought, he had given his mother-in-law "a bad morning," and he must have approached his meeting with her with as much trepidation as in some of his interviews with the unpredictable Pitti. As usual, his report to Filippo was considerably less charged than Alessandra's, but there is no doubt that he too felt ill used. Disinclined to bear the blame that he knew she would heap upon him, he stiffly reviewed the history of their negotiations. "This morning I met the father and spoke with him," he wrote. "But first I want to tell you that even up until the end of the past month he hung around me every day and passed the time with my friends more than he was accustomed in order to be familiar with me. And when I was with them, he made much of me, and I did the same with him."[10]

According to the customs of the times, this was true court-

[10] 13 Sept. 1465, CS ser. 3, 131, fol. 166^{r-v}, and *Lettere*, pp. 477–78.

ship. But even such devotion could not go on forever without encouragement. Eventually Tanagli decided that his proposal had not been favorably received and he began to look elsewhere. Having waited from the twenty-seventh of July to the middle of August, Tanagli felt that he should have had a reply, "and for another 15 days he still remained in suspense day by day; and I, having nothing from you, had nothing to tell him. Since I had nothing to say, I never had the courage to see him again."

Then, at the beginning of September both men had left for their villas, further delaying any contact, and now he found Tanagli aloof and unwilling to treat. The situation was thoroughly uncomfortable, and Marco could do nothing beyond taking Filippo to task for his delay. Nor did it make it easier for Marco that he sympathized with Tanagli's position. "In my judgment he was right," Marco wrote, "and time is pressing for him because although he says the girl is 16, she has completed 18 years."

There was nothing else for it but a show of resignation—"they say these things are made in heaven"—and a hint of pique. Should the negotiations be resumed, he warned, it must be with the sort of commission that would allow him to carry through, "so that the conclusion is not lost by delay, since in these matters if one does not respond in time, the other side believes itself rejected."

In the collapse of the negotiations with Tanagli Marco had not only wasted much time and energy but stood to lose a friend. Yet the whole matter remained for him a secondary pursuit, and this perhaps saved his temper. It is indicative of the real focus of Marco's attention at this time that his account of the embarrassing setback with Tanagli forms just a part of a lengthy political report—that long, coded letter of September thirteenth we have already examined.

For Marco it had been a day of difficult interviews followed by lengthy communications, the culmination of several weeks of watching and waiting. Along with the general hopes of reform, his letters to Naples brought together news of the two campaigns the family had been pursuing, neither of which, for the moment, seemed to offer much encouragement. But as Marco thought over what he had written, it is doubtful that he would have drawn any real distinction between the efforts invested in each. Both campaigns were part of the patient loyalty he owed his wife's family and he pursued each as the occasion arose. In a society that tied family and politics so closely together, it was perhaps inevitable that politics should resemble a dance of courtship while marriage was planned as a political strategy.

★

On the heels of the rupture with Tanagli, new troubles arose. First came the sudden death in Naples of Pandolfo Pandolfini. On the nineteenth of October, Parenti wrote to Naples acknowledging the unexpected news. It had left him "so overcome that I do not think I have it in me to reply to you or to do anything. The loss is too great, both to our entire city, since among our young men (let it be said with due respect to all) there are very few his equal, to his own family, and to our cause. May God grant him mercy."[11] Since Pandolfo had died in public office, he was entitled to public honors. It was feared, however, that any lavish ceremony, even though at public expense, would carry great cost to the family. For this reason, "out of respect for the eleven children he leaves," it was thought best to moderate the honors. Nonetheless, Marco was sure that the mourning would be worthy of Pandolfo. "I cannot describe to you," he concluded, "the sorrow shown by Pierfilippo [his brother], his family, and the entire city, because he had in him two qualities that rarely come together, knowledge and goodness, from which universal *grazia* is born."

The generous spirit in which Pandolfo was mourned is clear testimony to the character of the man himself, as is confirmed by Vespasiano's laudatory *vita*. Marco's grief is unquestionable, yet even in a private letter he lamented first of all the loss to the commonwealth. Not that he neglected the private

[11] 19 Oct. 1465, CS ser. 3, 131, fol. 170^{r-v}.

consequences of this unexpectedly early death—for the many children, the loss of a father; for the Strozzi, the loss of a well-placed sympathizer—but Marco put these in a framework dominated by the public concern. Here we feel the echoes of the classical world, and the praise for Pandolfini's rare combination of "knowledge" and "goodness" recalls that earlier time when both young men had taken part in the discussions of politics and literature at Sacchetti villa. No doubt Parenti was right in feeling that in quattrocento Florence the possession of such virtues would bring a man "grazia universale."

The news from Naples affected Alessandra too, but she took the death more personally. With a widow's memories she felt the tragedy of the young wife and children; with a mother's partiality, she worried over the consequences for her own sons; and with a fine sympathy, she pictured a man dying away from the consolations of his family. She was sure that God had called Pandolfo to himself for the good of his soul: "And if he had patience in his illness, away from home and the care of his wife and without being able to see his family around him—which I am sure grieved him—I believe he will have merited a great deal, because he was very loving with his family and will have felt great pain in leaving it."[12]

But Pandolfini's death was only the first of several worries. "Marco has had three troubles in two days concerning your affairs," Alessandra noted with sympathy.[13] Her words are a near copy of his own in a letter of the same date, an indication of their close communication in this period. The second of these "troubles" concerned another setback to Filippo's marriage prospects. After the Tanagli proposal collapsed, the Strozzi had turned to her rival in the Adimari family. But, though Marco had thought he had her "in his hand," as Alessandra put it, another suitor had been accepted, leading Alessandra to cry out that perhaps it was not fated that she should live to have this "consolation." The third setback was political rather than matrimonial, and though it was a relatively minor

[12] 19 Oct. 1465, *Lettere*, pp. 491–92.

[13] 19 Oct. 1465, *Lettere*, pp. 494–95.

matter, it is interesting for the fierceness of the reaction it provoked in Parenti.

Through their wealth and court connections the Strozzi brothers had earned considerable standing in Naples. Now the news came that the Florentine merchant colony there had elected Lorenzo Strozzi as its consul, and Marco, backed by Alessandra, reacted sharply. "It displeases me greatly," he wrote, ". . . and in my view he must renounce it immediately in order that it does not seem that you are snatching at trifles." Under normal circumstances, of course, this dignity would have been taken as an honor. Marco was sure, however, that it would simply serve the purposes of their enemies. It would be said, he warned, that "it is most unworthy that exiles should have any office or jurisdiction over any Florentine; and let us not delude ourselves, this is the truth."[14]

For once Marco was entirely out of sympathy with his brothers-in-law. His own patient negotiations on their behalf stood to be upset, but his reaction went well beyond chagrin. It was not simply that he thought Lorenzo's position impolitic. He thought it wrong. Something in the situation touched him as a Florentine and as a man of basically conservative instincts. "It is far more honest," he avowed, "to seek your restitution than to uphold this. Indeed, the first moves one to pity, while the second excites indignation."

The flap over the consulship became one more thing to be negotiated, and Marco recorded conversations with various of the leading citizens. He even checked the communal statutes to find out the legalities of the case. Fortunately for the Strozzi, Lorenzo's withdrawal coupled with Parenti's assurances that his brother-in-law had never sought the honor smoothed the matter over, and the question soon disappeared from the correspondence.

It is remarkable how seldom tensions of this sort arose, but it is hard to believe that misunderstandings did not interrupt the relationship from time to time. Filippo was far removed from Florence, yet desperately interested in its doings. He

[14] 19 Oct. 1465, CS ser. 3, 131, fol. 170^{r-v}.

must often have felt irritation at being so dependent on others. Under the circumstances few men could entirely escape a sense of frustration that at times may have been tinged with fear of betrayal. To Marco, on the other hand, it must have seemed that those in Naples could not appreciate the realities of the Florentine situation or the obstacles he had to cope with on their behalf.

Although the two men had written to each other steadily over twenty years, it was still possible for Filippo to accuse his brother-in-law of neglecting the correspondence. "And when I do not write to you," Marco wrote—obviously in response to a complaint—"it should be assumed that I have nothing important to say, rather than anything else."[15] Whatever reasons lay behind Filippo's impatience, Marco made it clear that he had his own reasons for feeling frustrated. "I will keep you well informed as much as I can," he protested, "as long as I know something. In truth it is difficult for me to know about things that are hidden—and I don't want to make myself out to be better than I am." Nor, he added, was it always easy to send news quickly, since "my occupation is little suited to such things." Filippo would have to have patience if his letters were not as full or as quickly sent as might be wished. Nonetheless, Marco promised, "I will exert myself as much as I can."

[15] 7 Oct. 1465, CS ser. 3, 131, fol. 169^{r-v}.

CHAPTER 9

FALL AND WINTER: NICCOLÒ SODERINI AND THE SCRUTINY CRISIS

★

PERSONAL disappointments were soon overshadowed by signs of a general crisis in Florence. The beginning of November brought a new priorate to office and a Gonfaloniere prepared to challenge the Medici hegemony. The mood of excitement deeply affected Marco. His correspondence for these months did not neglect the family concerns of the Strozzi, but more and more his reports were bracketed by a reluctant admission that little was possible as long as the city remained in such a state of unrest. To Alessandra this was the greatest frustration, but for her son-in-law the strained situation held a deeper fascination.

The Signoria that began its term on the first of November, 1465, was led by Niccolò Soderini. The new Gonfaloniere was a prominent, forceful, and independent-minded patrician, a man unlikely to be subservient to Medici interests. His was the first magistracy—as Parenti later wrote in his *Memoir*—to be selected since the electoral reforms of the late summer, in which the electors (accoppiatori) had been stripped of their special powers and the traditional method of selection from "sealed" purses reinstituted. More than a year had passed since the death of Cosimo. At last the succession crisis had begun in earnest.

The events of November and December of 1465 are murky

and difficult to follow. The balance of political favor shifts again and again, and the issues underlying (or excusing) the contest for power are hard to pin down. The sources hint that Soderini may have tried to bring in considerable changes in the traditional electoral system through the establishment of a group of citizens with permanent eligibility for office, somewhat in the style of Venice. This reform would have hit hard at Medici manipulations of elections. At the same time it would have represented a large departure from communal tradition in which eligibility for office was decided by quinquennial "scrutiny councils." Historians have even seen Soderini's term as a brief foreshadowing of the democratic constitutional changes of Savonarola's era a half-century later.[1] These remain speculations, but it is clear that Piero de' Medici found himself faced with a general expectation of reform and a Signoria led by an independent and potentially dangerous Gonfaloniere. Over the next several months Piero's authority was challenged by a tide of opposition more powerful and widespread than any the regime had seen since its inception in 1434; arguably it was also a more dangerous moment for Medici power than any to come until the regime collapsed in the French invasion at the end of the century.

Though historians have given little time to Piero, his durability in the teeth of this crisis proved to be enormously important to the development of Florentine politics in the fifteenth century. In the short term, his triumph simply meant the continuation of his father's system of informal oligarchy. But Piero's victory of 1466 also moved the Medici, now in their second generation of domination, a crucial step closer to the dynastic power they would eventually possess. For Piero's patrician opponents on the other hand—Dietisalvi and Francesco Neroni, Agnolo Acciaiuoli, and Niccolò Soderini—the months of crisis now beginning would end only in betrayal and defeat, followed by the bitter recriminations of exile.[2]

[1] See G. Pampaloni, "Fermenti di riforme democratiche nella Firenze medicea del Quattrocento," *Archivio storico italiano* 119 (1961): 11–62.

[2] On these factional struggles, in addition to N. Rubinstein, *The Government of Florence under the Medici* (Oxford, 1966), see the rare monograph by

Marco Parenti kept close watch on the events of the winter and he reported to Naples in abundant detail. At no other time do we have as many letters as for these crowded and confusing months from November to February—when suddenly the correspondence falls silent. But the extraordinary tensions disturbing the city also required the utmost effort to protect the family from potential spies and enemies. More than ever, to read Marco's letters is to thread a maze, guided only by a general knowledge of the direction of events and a sense of his twin loyalties to the Strozzi and to civic reform.

As before, we can take the broad narrative of events from the *Memoir*:

"The first Signoria drawn by lot from the sealed purses took office on the first day of November, 1465, and the Gonfaloniere of Justice as Niccolò Soderini. He was a proud and fearless man, forceful in his speech. In private affairs he was opposed to his brother, Messer Tommaso, and so also in public matters, because Messer Tommaso was the brother-in-law of Piero di Cosimo [de' Medici] and in every respect one of the first men of his party. Because of this conflict between them, Niccolò Soderini joined together with Messer Luca, Messer Dietisalvi, and Messer Agnolo, who were opposed, as we said, to the regime of Piero di Cosimo. Thus these men drew close to the Gonfaloniere and gave it out to everyone that he shared their views. But in truth Niccolò kept his own counsel, wishing to lead the regime in a manner that

---

A. Municchi, *La fazione antimedicea detta del Poggio* (Florence, 1911). The role of Agnolo Acciaiuoli is discussed by M. Ganz: "Donato Acciaiuoli and the Medici: A Strategy for Survival in Quattrocento Florence," *Rinascimento*, 2d ser., 22 (1982): 33–73. On Niccolò Soderini the best guide is the forthcoming monograph of P. Clarke on Tommaso and Niccolò Soderini. I am grateful to Dr. Clarke for permission to consult her manuscript in advance of publication. On Francesco Neroni, see N. Rubinstein, "La confessione di Francesco Neroni e la congiura antimedicea del 1466," *Archivio storico italiano* (1968): 373–85. Municchi's monograph reprints valuable documents relating to these events, as does Pampaloni's study of the *consulte*. Useful material is also to be found in B. Buser, *Die Beziehungen der Mediceer zu Frankreich wahrend der Jahre 1434–1494* (Leipzig, 1879).

was different from the views of either party. But he was in total disagreement with Piero's party, while with the opposing side he was in some agreement because each sought to emerge from tyranny and to come to a kind of rule that would be more free, in which the authority of government would be extended to more men and would not be held by one alone.

"But Niccolò was deeply involved in his own interests and his finances were in disorder because he had involved himself too boldly in various ways, in wanting possessions and pasture lands in the district of Pisa, cattle, money on the Monte with various merchants, and other things. Because of these affairs he had for a long time been in great anxiety and involved in disputes with many, especially Giovanni de' Medici, the brother of Piero. All of these troubles he hoped to set right while in office, almost grafting his own affairs onto those of the commune. Saying that he wished to do things that would be very beneficial to the people where he himself was involved, he wished to regulate matters so that he could pursue his own needs to his own advantage. So he brought forward some regulations concerning the Tower Officials, the government of the district of Pisa, and the regulations of the Monte.

"At the beginning of Soderini's term, Piero di Cosimo feared him and followed along, because never had there been a Gonfaloniere who took office with such a spirited welcome from the people and with such expectation of good. But when these things did not follow, it was the origin of much evil, as we will say below. The supporters of Piero saw him lose courage, and already for some time he had been lacking the customary crowd of those who came to visit him at his house, where because of his gout he spent most of his time in bed. His supporters began to consider their own affairs and to realize that if Piero were pushed out, they were finished as well. And for this reason they gathered together to urge each other to counter the actions of this Gonfaloniere. Many of them, including the most respected, drew up a document. It was subscribed to by those who were entirely in favor of Piero and his and their regime. And, with great craft, they showed it to those they thought most likely to go along with them, and they had them subscribe to the document. And as the petition grew, so did their support and, little by little, they showed it to those who would not have been so prompt to subscribe at the beginning. To such as these—seeing such a noble company, and one finding there a relative and another a friend—it seemed a fine thing to join together with them; and judging they were doing it for them [i.e. their friends and relatives], they subscribed their names. In this way having gathered together a number equal to or stronger than their adversaries, they came out openly in the Councils of the People and the Commune against the Gonfaloniere, blocking his petitions and his ideas. Among other things, he wanted to have himself made a knight in order to win a greater reputation, something the *popolo* was accustomed to granting to men of substance like himself. But they did not let it succeed in the Council.

"The Gonfaloniere, seeing himself defeated in all his plans by the others, changed his mind and, in order to accomplish something, he turned his attention to a scrutiny something to which everyone gladly concurred; and on the 27th of the said month [of November] it was carried in the councils. In this action also he was led by a private interest. He had a bastard son, a doctor called Messer Geri, whom he loved immoderately and not less than his legitimate sons, who were young boys, and to whom he wished to make Geri equal with regard to every honor. But in this too he failed, because he was not able to win the votes that he needed.

"To carry out this scrutiny more than five hundred men were elected by such broad criteria as he established for membership in order to bring in those he wanted; and these men [of the Scrutiny Council] carried out the scrutiny for the priorate with the notary of the priors. It was decided that each be given two ballot slips, and not more; and in this way he used up the remainder of his time. Then on the first day of January, the new Priors took office, and the Gonfaloniere of Justice was Francesco Bagnesi, the reverse in every way of Niccolò

Soderini, a man of little weight and without eloquence who never spoke in public. He was directed by Piero di Cosimo."[3]

These were Marco's afterthoughts as a historian on Soderini's troubled days in power. By then, time enough had passed—though we don't know how much time that was—for Marco to clarify the lines of his own disappointment: an opportunity for change wasted because of excessive ambition, a well-intentioned and vigorous leader who lacked steadfastness and allowed the public good to be distracted by private interest, a deepening split in the city while the Medici party cleverly regrouped for eventual victory. But in Marco's correspondence for these months, we can trace a path that is remarkably unlike the one he later recollected. Here we read a chronicle of another sort—one that offers an opportunity to measure the gap separating the writing of history from the unfolding experience of events.

On the second of November, the second day of Soderini's term, Marco wrote to Naples: "You see the (priors) and (Gonfaloniere). All (Florence) is in an uproar over it and I cannot tell you how much for the supporters of (Pitti) it seems to their (good) and for those of (Medici) (bad). Still, for the moment little is known, but much (good) is expected."[4] But for the Strozzi themselves there was one catch. Niccolò Soderini and Alessandra Strozzi were related, but an old quarrel stood between them. And there was further worry in the fact that Soderini had no love of Naples, the real basis of the family's support.[5] For once, however, Marco was prepared to distance himself a little from the *spezialtà* or "interest" of the Strozzi:

[3] *Memorie*, pp. 35–38.

[4] 2 Nov 1465, CS ser. 3, 180, fol. 70.

[5] The letter ends with a report of a visit with "Priore"—presumably Priore Pandolfini—who expressed his good wishes to the Strozzi and wanted to pursue their cause with Soderini, "considering the kinship [parentado]." Marco continues, "and I did not wish to reveal to him the problem [la macchia], but I told him it did not seem to me yet to be time. We are in full agreement that the help of (the King of Naples) no longer is much good." Alessandra too reports Soderini's coldness toward herself and toward Naples in her letters of 2 Nov. and 22 Nov. 1465. (*Lettere*, pp. 503, 519).

> and so for this reason I am sorry. But for all the others, it could not please me more to see where (Florence) is going. . . . And I cannot tell you what a great spirit he shows, and he has the (favor) of all (Florence). Everyone visits him at his house. And so . . . he has ordered a large (Council) where the (priors) can seek (counsel). And then one will begin to know something more about where this path leads—may God make it good.

The setback to the Strozzi's hopes could not be denied, but their particular troubles seem to be swept away in the general mood of excited expectation reflected in Marco's letter. Above all Soderini himself was stirred with great ambitions, a glimmer of which we can still catch in the notary's transcription of his speech to the Pratica, or consultative assembly. This was that "large 52 where the (priors) can seek 52"—to use the clumsy circumlocution enforced on Marco by his code—and to it the Gonfaloniere addressed a lengthy discourse on the classical and Christian virtues that strikes our ears more like a sermon than a political program.[6] But when Soderini's eloquence passed beyond this vague plea for a resuscitation of lost virtues and began to take on some substance, Marco grew worried, and the tone of his letters became flat, negative, and depressed.

The reversal was not long in coming. On the twelfth of November Marco wrote again to Naples:

> As for the affairs of (Florence) there is no more to be said. (The Gonfaloniere) and others have the notion [fantasia] of creating a new form of (good state). . . . They have grand ideas and it seems to me that no one knows clearly where this (Gonfaloniere) stands. "15" doesn't understand it. He [i.e. Soderini] has led (Florence) into confusion. . . . I don't know whether I would call it a new (good state) or (bad state). To me it seems a (bad state). And it seems to me he has fallen into (disfavor) with all of (Florence), except for those who were drawn as (Gonfaloniere) during the time of 56 (the closed electoral purses?). It was hoped that the opposite would be done and [he would] dismantle the (Council of 100), but he

[6] Soderini's speech and the subsequent debates in the *consulte* are printed by Pampaloni, "Fermenti di riforme."

> has established it that these [i.e. the former Gonfalonieri] will always take part in every (Council of 100, Council of the People, and Council of the Commune).[7]

Marco was not alone in being upset by Soderini's proposals: they were opposed by a majority of the Pratica. In these consultative sessions, one speaker attacked the Gonfaloniere for wishing to introduce an oligarchical government in imitation of Venice. Without invoking the Venetian comparison, Marco's reaction was essentially the same: "And then he has confirmed in perpetuity anyone who has been (prior), as well as many other things, in such a way that whoever was not himself one of these [i.e. priors or Gonfalonieri] over the last 20 years, or descended from one who was, can be dismissed." In short, Marco had expected that the reforms would broaden the base of the regime and return it to its communal traditions—eliminating, for instance, the Council of 100, a major and still recent Medici addition. Instead, the proposals were proving unexpectedly restrictive and seemed designed to produce a privileged group within the citizenry, who alone would have access to office. Lesser men, like Marco Parenti, could find themselves permanently excluded from the major offices.

Meanwhile, on the thirteenth of November, Soderini proposed a new scrutiny. A temporary council would be created to review the qualifications of all Florentine citizens and to establish a new roster of names to be entered into the electoral purses. This was a controversial and divisive step that, as Parenti later wrote in the *Memoir*, consumed the rest of his time in office. But Soderini was obviously not the type to step aside from difficulties, nor is it easy to judge whether the risks could really have been avoided. The return to a blind electoral lottery, which had brought Soderini and his fellow priors to office, was only partial measure. The composition of future priorates still depended on the names that had been placed in the bags—a process that the Medici had tightly controlled for many years by avoiding the traditional scrutiny councils in favor of a narrower special commission, or Balìa. To carry the drive against Medici hegemony still futher, a

[7] 12 Nov. 1465, CS ser. 3, 249, fol. 177^{r-v}.

broader group of citizens would have to be made eligible. The unfortunate thing—from Marco's point of view—was that in attacking a key element of Medici power, Soderini seemed to want to rigidify rather than liberalize access to office.

The scrutiny dominates Marco's letters to Naples for the next two months, as it must have dominated all political conversation in Florence. It is first mentioned in a postscript on the sixteenth, but by the twenty-first matters were becoming clearer. Reminding Filippo of Soderini's continued personal antagonism, he cautioned against any approach to the Gonfaloniere. One of their friends had foolishly taken it upon himself to bring up their case with Soderini and had been rebuffed: "It seems to me like going to wake a sleeping dog." But above all, it was the scrutiny that stood in the way of any other concern. Even talk of marriage was hopeless for the moment, since "here no one is interested in anything except the scrutiny, and so for a while do not expect any other sort of news."[8]

If Marco meant to suggest that he himself was free of this obsession of the scrutiny, the implication was false, as we learn from Alessandra. "All the men are preoccupied with what is to be done in the Palazzo about governing the city and deciding how we will live," she wrote. "Every day they are in consultation and those who were removed from the bags in 1458 stand in hope of being reentered; and Marco is much taken up in it." This is Marco's biggest concern at the moment, she added, and since she herself had not been well enough to go out, she had not seen him in two weeks.[9]

Already, Marco reported, the scrutiny measure had passed in the Council of 100. But in the Council of the People it was meeting strong resistance because of Piero de' Medici's opposition. "So I am doubtful it will pass," he wrote, "and I see (Florence) in great chaos whether it passes or not; and the division [of the city] is fully revealed."[10]

This issue overshadowed any earlier proposals for reform.

[8] 16 Nov. 1465, postcript to letter of the 12th (CS, ser. 3, 249, fol. 177^{r-v}); 21 Nov. 1465, CS ser. 3, 131, fol. 176.

[9] 2 Nov. 1465, *Lettere*, pp. 512–13.

[10] 21 Nov. 1465, CS ser. 3, 131, fol. 176.

"The party to establish a new (good state) or (bad state) is quiet for the moment," writes Marco, throwing out another muffled clue that larger changes had once been entertained. Soderini himself was lobbying furiously. He had gone to see Pitti, but at the same time he had also arranged that Lorenzo de' Medici—who was only sixteen years old—would participate. A special exception was being made for the under-aged Lorenzo, but Marco thought the whole idea of a hereditary qualification a gross mistake. The inclusion of "all those who have been (Gonfalonieri) in the past and their (descendants)" would bring in many undesirable people—men "vile, foolish, and bad, both young and old." In all there would be more than 450, perhaps 500 men, an unusually large number for a scrutiny council. "Already," he wrote, "secret parties are forming, so you can see how (well) it goes. And this is the (good state) the (Gonfaloniere) would create for us."

By the twenty-ninth Marco could report that the scrutiny measure had been passed and that they were trying to bring in "certain good petitions concerning the Monte, taxes, and the contado."[11] But the real burden of the letter was the threat of open and bitter divisions among the leading citizens. Piero was making a "great (war) of words with Acciaiuoli and Neroni," and vice versa, so that "all (Florence) boiled over again, and some run to (Pitti) and some to (Medici)." Later, calm was reestablished and visits of reconciliation were paid to Piero by many of the principal citizens—including "6 and 11 and 10 and 59 and 60 and 54 and others."[12] But more outbursts could be expected.

[11] Regarding these "good petitions," we should remember Parenti's later judgment in the *Memoir* that these were areas in which Soderini acted out of a personal financial involvement. Parenti also notes another reform in this letter that would have a special interest to the exiles, namely the abolition of the bounty offered for killing a rebel. This was a sign of some thawing in the relationship between the regime and its former enemies. It did not directly affect the Strozzi themselves who were not *ribelli* but *confinati*; that is, they retained certain rights as long as they adhered to the conditions of their "confinement." Only if they broke these terms—as some of the exiles of 1466 later did—would confinati become outright enemies of the republic, or "rebels."

[12] 29 Nov. 1465, CS ser. 3, 180, fol. 73. The guest list, when partially

A week later came another letter, and once again the scrutiny was Marco's chief concern. But now a new tone makes itself felt: "You have never seen a stranger business than this. The (Gonfaloniere) who entered with so much (favor) will leave with more (disfavor) than any one ever has before, if something new does not occur."[13] Soderini's term was little more than half over, but already Marco was looking toward its end. In his mind, the time had arrived to sum up and explain the odd turn of events:

> The reason is that the (Gonfaloniere) and (Acciaiuoli) and (Pitti) and (Dietisalvi Neroni) were not 41 (prudent?). By wanting to make for themselves too much of a (good state) and for (Piero de' Medici) a (bad state), they lost their way. They proposed to the (Councils) a new (good state). It displeased many (principali); then they turned to this thing [i.e. the scrutiny council] in which (Bonsi) as I say is taking part, whose form was displeasing to many. . . . All these things coming together, turned a large part of (Florence) to (Piero de' Medici) and they are so tightknit now as you can't believe.

Marco was obviously in a mood to summarize and explain, but his desire for secrecy could also lead to some rather odd circumlocutions.[14] A long discourse on the sweetness of the oranges sent to Alessandra from Naples is clearly an elaborate, if crude, allegory in which the combination of cipher and pseudo-agricultural almanac is quite bizarre. It seems that (Piero de' Medici) is recovered, having surrounded himself with much "straw" of (principali), and being covered over by the (Priors) has nothing to fear in the present cold spell. The "vigorous blooms" of the "oranges" of "(Accciaiuoli), (Pitti), and (Neroni)," on the other hand, are "drooping a little because of this cold fog and frost" that has lasted several days, and they have lost many leaves.

---

deciphered, reads: "Agnolo Acciaioli, Dietisalvi Neroni, Francesco Neroni, 59?, Tommaso Soderini, 54?, and others."

[13] 7 Dec. 1465; CS ser. 3, 180, fol. 74.

[14] This elaborate circumlocution for "scrutiny council" indicates that the scrutiny had not been anticipated at the time the cipher list was made up and illustrates the restrictive effect the code exercised on Parenti's correspondence.

The scrutiny might have had more direct consequences for Marco and the Strozzi, and early in his letter he reported that his brother-in-law, Giovanni Bonsi, had qualified because he was consul of his guild. For himself, Marco confessed that he had no more hope of succeeding in this scrutiny than in previous ones. But this personal note is fleeting, and the letter mainly conveys a sense of general failure rather than personal loss. Most of all, Marco was clear that the real legacy of Soderini's term would be a bitterly divided city. "If he has done anything (good), which he has, it is lost because of the very great (evil) of the division of (Florence), which is now openly revealed and—one might say—stamped and sealed, so that now it can never be undone." If only the city had been left in peace with the purses sealed, the differences between Pitti and Medici would have "resolved themselves into smoke." Instead "because of their needs regarding (the scrutiny)," the barriers between Medici and Pitti had gone up and Florence had returned to the state it was in before the electoral reform; "and this is the consequence of having lost their way."

This is the second time that Marco had written that the opposition had "lost its way," and it is worth lingering over the phrase a moment. His view seems to have been that the anti-Mediceans had been too ambitious. They had attempted too much and worked in too partisan a spirit. This had alienated moderate citizens, with the unintended consequence that Medici power was reinforced even while factional tensions rose dangerously. But whatever else losing one's way signifies, it does not indicate that the "way" was false from the start. Only so much remained of Marco's initial enthusiasm for Soderini and his reforms.

⋆

By mid-December, to judge by Marco's letters, Florence was settling in for a period of troubled waiting. The first wave of Soderini's reform energies, from which so much had been expected, had played itself out and the regime appeared to be on its way to reconsolidating its authority. This, on the fourteenth of December, was Marco's rather weary summary of the situation:

> (Medici) moves ahead and (Pitti) falls back, and every day it is said that they have made (peace) again. (The Gonfaloniere) pursues the enterprise he began [i.e. the scrutiny] . . . and bears with his (disfavor). The rest of (Florence) remains unsettled waiting to see the new (priors). And so we go on, one step at a time. And so in the matter of (marriage) there is nothing doing, since everything is frozen up in the great cold we have, and today it is snowing here.[15]

This air of wintry resignation promises an end to the crisis; and, as if in confirmation, the opening sentences of Marco's next letter, written on the twenty-third, are free from ciphers. For the first time in many weeks Marco refers simply to the "scrutiny" and the "Gonfaloniere" without the usual double cover of code and circumlocution, as though these subjects had suddenly lost their menace: the scrutiny for the priorate was almost complete and the rest would be done by the new Signoria taking office in January—if they so chose. Also, Marco reported, the Gonfaloniere was petitioning to have himself knighted by the commune (a considerable honor, but not one normally beyond the expectation of a leading citizen like Soderini) but the move had failed in the councils. But in the middle of the same letter, having made his report, Marco suddenly doubles back on the subject, this time under protection of code. The failure of Soderini's petition for knighthood is "entirely the doing of (Piero de' Medici)," he writes; "otherwise it would have passed." Opinion is divided, "but in truth whoever is not for (Piero) is displeased, and his (favor) is turned to (disfavor)." Evidently, the time of tension was not over yet, and while certain matters of public fact could be spoken of more openly, the fuller implications of events retained their edge of partisanship and danger.[16]

Public opinion had not entirely deserted Soderini, since he retained enough general respect to make his claim on the knighthood plausible. But in general the opposition had been thrown on the defensive, and Marco even reported rumors of dissension between Pitti, Neroni, and Acciaiuoli. For the moment their strategy was necessarily a cautious one. They were

[15] 14 Dec. 1465, CS ser. 3, 180, fol. 77.
[16] 23 Dec. 1465, CS ser. 3, 178, fol. 90.

attempting to keep to the middle ground because the Mediceans would only draw together still more if faced with a challenge. "But," said Marco of the opposition leaders, "they do not abandon the (Gonfaloniere)."[17]

In Marco's eyes as well Soderini had regained some of the reputation he seemed to have squandered. This reversal takes us back to the expectation of a broader regime that had been raised at the beginning of November. There are many men, Marco wrote, as the magistrates' term entered its final week, who never before had enough votes to win, men who were always disregarded or suspect, and now they have succeeded in the scrutiny: "And never before was [the scrutiny] so broad as it is now, though at the beginning the opposite was thought true, because of which much (disfavor) fell on the (Gonfaloniere); and now it brings (favor). And this thing is reputed holy and just." Nevertheless, he concluded, it was thought that Piero would block the scrutiny if he could, just to oppose Soderini.

These comments confirm the consistency of Parenti's political stance. His early enthusiasm for Soderini had been built on an expectation of reform. When these hopes were disappointed by the apparently restrictive character of the Gonfaloniere's proposals, Marco became critical and bitter. And now, either because he had misread the signs or because Soderini had changed tack—and it is a puzzle to know which—Marco was again showing signs of his old enthusiasm.

How far others in Marco's circle shared in this revival of sympathy is hard to know. Certainly Alessandra did not. Consistent in her own way, she greeted the news that Soderini was hoping to be knighted with a sort of dyspeptic grumble. "And this is the benefit we get," she wrote, "that we will pay some florins toward the ceremonies." She was pleased when his petition failed and saw it as a judgment of God: "I am prepared to believe that if he had restored the innocents it

[17] Parenti's statement is worth noting in view of Pampaloni's rather dramatic contention—drawn perhaps from Machiavelli—that Soderini was betrayed by the other leaders of the anti-Medici faction, who did not want to see him get the credit for breaking the Medici domination.

would have been such a charity that God would have aided him, and he would not have been so disliked as he is now."[18]

Given her feelings, it is no surprise that Alessandra tells us more than Marco of Soderini's humiliating retirement from office. Bonfires were lit in the piazza, and someone had written: "Nine fools have departed." And since then, she reported, Soderini had gone about with five or six armed men for his protection—though the physical threat apparently came from a dispute with the counts of the Maremma, not civic partisanship. When called upon by Filippo to confirm these facts, Marco gave much the same picture, though with less relish, and he added that "Niccolò di Lorenzo seems a sick man. No one comes near him and the Signoria never calls for him." By the end of January, the former Gonfaloniere's enemies had even succeeded in having his name removed from the scrutiny, a bitterly ironic conclusion to these many weeks of reform agitation.[19]

★

Soderini's term was over, but the scrutiny he had begun continued to agitate the city, helping to keep the tensions alive that would soon lead to the final clash between Piero and his enemies.

On the thirtieth of December Marco reported that the name-tickets for those eligible for the priorate were complete, and a new Signoria was preparing to take office, led by Francesco Bagnesi as Gonfaloniere. Marco thought them about equally divided between the two rival parties, though "the best of them are for (Pitti) and also the (Gonfaloniere)"—a

[18] 21 Dec. 1465, *Lettere*, p. 531; 28 Dec. 1465, *Lettere*, pp. 536–37. Though Alessandra was well informed on public matters, largely, it seems, through Parenti in this period, her tendency was to look at events primarily in their relation to her own family concerns. Commenting on Soderini's humiliating departure from office, she wrote, "There is no need to speak further of this since it does not concern us." (4 Jan. 1466, *Lettere*, p. 540).

[19] Alessandra's comments come in her letter of January 4 cited above. Parenti discusses the former Gonfaloniere in his letters of 25 Jan. 1466 (CS ser. 3, 178, fol. 39) and 1 Feb. 1466 (CS ser. 3, 180, fol. 76).

judgment that would be sharply reversed in the *Memoir.*[20] But there was no doubt who had the upper hand. Pitti, Neroni, and Acciaiuoli were standing back, "thinking more or less to let him [i.e. Piero de' Medici] run until he tires himself." Whether Marco could put any faith in so optimistic a formula we cannot say, but by the eleventh of January he was gloomily predicting that Florence would suffer "if the winds do not change." The Mediceans were pressing the new Signoria very hard to annul the results of the scrutiny and redo the name-tickets. Their measure had passed through the Colleges with great effort, but it was now held up in the Council of 100, thanks to Luca Pitti.[21] And even a week later Marco was still quite unsure of how matters would turn out: "they would like to change the (name-tickets) either in whole or in part, opinions varying with each type of person; each one gives his (favor) or (opposition) according to how it affects his own interest."[22]

Obviously the scrutiny had become the focus of a considerable struggle. The pressure to revise it, coming largely from Piero and his allies, had run up against a stubborn defense. Most of January had gone by before Marco could pass on more definite information. The result of the previous scrutiny for the priorate had at last been accepted, but the successful nominees would receive only one name-ticket instead of two as previously decided. Their chances of being drawn in subsequent elections were, therefore, cut in half. The remainder of the scrutiny, which concerned lesser offices that were often financially rewarding, if politically less significant, would be carried out by a new council. It has also been decided, he added, that the current accoppiatori would have to be reaffirmed or removed. More menacingly, they were to be given

[20] 30 Dec. 1465, CS ser. 3, 131, fol. 179. As we have already seen, the *Memoir* describes Bagnesi as a Medici pawn: "costui guidò Piero di Cosimo e suoi ordinatori." Alessandra's opinion was entirely favorable. She thought him "un buonuomo e buono" (4 Jan. 1466, *Lettere*, p. 540).

[21] 11 Jan. 1466, CS ser. 3, 180, fol. 78.

[22] 18 Jan, 1466, CS ser. 3, 178, fol. 13.

new powers to strike out any name. "This is what (Piero) wants," he wrote.[23]

We might judge this settlement of the scrutiny debate to be a compromise, and Pitti himself made a belated demonstration of support.[24] But for Marco the uneasy truce patched up between the principali seemed simply a reflection of Piero de' Medici's recaptured dominance. The rival leaders were sometimes friendly, sometimes not, he wrote, but "(Piero) seems in more (favor) and in better 82 (?), and the (opponents) stand back and watch, almost fearing the (displeasure) of (Piero), and they make a show of following him."[25]

Florence's internal battles were never fully separate from its ties to other powers, and the present crisis would prove again how interconnected the politics of Italy had become. The Medici had long derived crucial support from Milan—a steady dividend paid on Cosimo's support of Francesco Sforza in his struggle for power—and both Acciaiuoli and Neroni had ties of their own to the Sforza court. Now, as it appears from Marco's cryptic remarks, Milan was putting pressure on the Florentines to settle their differences. Behind this interference lay the worry that Florence—unsettled in its diplomacy as well as its politics—might swing away from Milan toward an alliance with Venice. There was a real cause for alarm, as Marco's letter demonstrates: "As for what (Milan) wrote about the turning of (Florence) toward 29 (presumably Venice), '15' already knew it all, not, that is, about the writing, but about the business itself, which was most secret on the part of (Pitti), (Acciaiuoli) and (Neroni) with the assistance of the factor [i.e. agent or ambassador] of 81 (Ferrara?)."[26] But, Marco went on to insist, this was not a "turning," but rather "a plan for defense against (Piero) if he had wanted to

[23] 25 Jan. 1466, CS ser. 3, 178, fol. 39.

[24] "A questo 8 da 92 e 9 93, dipoi 9 monstra di dare anche lui 92" (25 Jan. 1466, CS ser. 3, 178, fol. 39).

[25] 25 Jan. 1466, CS ser. 3, 178, fol. 39.

[26] Ibid. The possibility of a "plot" to swing Florence back into an alliance with Venice against Milan is discussed briefly above: cf. ch. 7.

employ (Milan) in his (favor) against themselves, of which they had some suspicions because of words spoken by the 'factor' of (Milan) to certain (principali)." These suspicions were to prove entirely and (for those involved) tragically correct.

On the surface there was a reduction of tension, and dinners of reconciliation were the order of the day. Rather incongruously, Marco wrote, "Tomorrow morning we go to dine with Mona Alessandra, and similarly (Pitti) with (Medici) and a few days ago (Tommaso Soderini) and (Francesco Neroni) did the same."[27] Alessandra found these maneuverings laughable. "One day they seem to want to exile each other, the next they have made peace, just like little children."[28] But at least the public peace making had cleared the way for carrying out the rest of the scrutiny—not without further discussions and confusions due to the new mode of selection.[29] Again the city was thrown into an election fever. It was hopeless to pursue marriage negotiations, complained Alessandra, since no one would pay attention to anything except securing enough support in the scrutiny: "they go to fantastic lengths and neglect to eat and sleep, according to what I hear from Marco and Giovanni, who themselves are among those tiring themselves out."[30]

It does not seem likely that Parenti could have been opti-

[27] 8 Feb. 1466, CS ser. 3, 180, fol. 79.

[28] 30 Jan. 1466, *Lettere*, p. 568.

[29] The passage is worth quoting for the picture it gives of the complexities of the Florentine electoral procedures as well as the added difficulties imposed by the cipher: "Col nome di Dio. Istamani si fanno pure gl' uomini di 83 (name-tickets) ch' è durata la pratica 8 dì colla maggiore confusione che mai si facessi, e questo perchè va a modo novo. Interviene a fare questo 83 (name-ticket, i.e. scrutiny) tutti suti 13 (Gonfalonieri) con gl' ufici consueti, e tutti e' 12 (priors) hanno a nominare 6 per uno i quali s' anno a cimentare per 49 (Council of 100) e tutti e' suti 13 (Gonfalonieri); e la metà di quegli che aranno più 19 (white beans?) s' intendono essere approvati e avere a fare 83 (name-tickets). Onde è nato grande tresche. 6 (Agnolo Acciaiuoli) che sarà costì t' el dirà più a punto."

[30] 7 Feb. 1466, *Lettere*, p. 570.

mistic for himself in this second and less numerous council, so his efforts may have been on behalf of Giovanni Bonsi, who as consul of his guild had been a member of the earlier council. As he started a letter on the eighth of February he spoke hopefully of Bonsi's chances, saying, "I believe that by the grace of God we will entirely recover our lost place." But by the time Marco closed the letter he knew that Bonsi had been eliminated. "And I cannot tell you," he writes, "how disappointed I am."[31]

*

With the completion of the scrutiny—so long delayed—we come to the abrupt end of the spate of letters from Florence to Naples that has carried us through almost twenty months following the death of Cosimo. Neither Marco's nor Alessandra's extant correspondence resumes for several years, by which time Piero de' Medici had defeated his opponents and the family's situation had entirely changed. In taking leave of this rich correspondence, it seems appropriate to record two last comments that summarize the mood of these winter days, an atmosphere of tension and uncertainty that surely continued into the unchronicled months to follow. After an account of further maneuvers in the battle to win a place in the scrutiny, Marco gave his brother-in-law this rather despairing summary: "And in truth, if there is nothing else to be done, (Filippo) and (Lorenzo) should willingly remain in (Naples) since in (Florence) everyone is (discontented). Those who are accustomed to governing either cannot do what they want or act with excessive contempt, while those who never had any power think they should still expect something better, but cannot do anything. And so matters go on."[32]

Marco's summary was typically rational and deliberate, one of a long series of balance sheets that he, like a good political factor, had drawn up for his distant associates. A few days

[31] 8 Feb. 1466, CS ser. 3, 180, fol. 79.
[32] 25 Jan. 1466, CS ser. 3, 178, fol. 39.

later, Alessandra added an assessment of her own, no more hopeful than Marco's, but spoken with her characteristic directness:

> You can well believe that here the *popolo* is very discontented, but there is nobody that is worth a fig. . . . (Antonio Pucci) is much occupied in rushing here and there. The brother of (Niccolò Soderini) [i.e. Tommaso Soderini, a leading Medicean] is bigger than ever, and he has honey in his mouth, but a razor in his belt. And things go along in such a way that—though I may have only a weak understanding—while these things are developing, it seems to me I would not want to open up a shop or anything else in this city until it can be seen where things end up.[33]

As it happened, it took nine more months before the crisis reached its conclusion and it became possible once again for the Strozzi to think seriously of setting up shop in Florence.

[33] 30 Jan. 1466, *Lettere*, pp. 566–67.

CHAPTER 10

THE CLIMAX OF THE STRUGGLE

★

An early Scottish novelist left deliberate lacunae in his fictitious journal, claiming that the previous owner of the manuscript used to tear out pages as wadding for his gun.[1] Historians, unlike the author of this ingenious parody, cannot be so artful in arranging the gaps in their narratives. The disappearance of Marco's and Alessandra's letters in the very months when their family drama reached its climax means that there is no way to continue an intimate chronicle of their lives in this decisive moment. But Marco's life as a writer had another dimension, and as a diarist he devoted his energies to constructing a historical account of these same events. The *Memoir* cannot transmit the sense of intricacy or uncertainty that makes the correspondence so intriguing, but it provides something just as valuable: a sustained attempt to see the meaning of events, not just as an individual of family is affected, but as they form a chapter in the life of the Florentine republic.

The time has come to let the *Memoir* speak for itself:

[1] " 'I should be glad to see this medley,' said I. 'You shall see it now,' answered the curate, 'for I always take it along with me a-shooting.' 'How came it so torn?' 'Tis excellent wadding,' said the curate. This was a plea of expediency I was not in a condition to answer; for I had actually in my pocket great part of an edition of one of the German Illustrissimi, for the very same purpose. We exchanged books, and by that means (for the curate is a strenuous logician), we probably saved both." Henry Mackenzie, *The Man of Feeling* (New York, 1958), p. 2.

"In these times a large part of Italy was in a sense renewed by the succession of new princes after the deaths of their predecessors: in Rome, Pope Paul II succeeded Pope Pius II at the end of August 1464; in Florence because of the death of Cosimo on the first day of the said month; in Milan because of the succession of Duke Galeazzo on the death of his father on the 8th day of March 1465; Cesena because of the death of Signor Domenico Malatesti. . . . And other things occurred likely to create apprehensions about the disruption of the peace and league of Italy, which was still in force. Thus each ruler considered his own affairs and how he might best strengthen his government in the face of whatever disturbances might arise in Italy and made whatever provision seemed to him to be suited to his needs. . . .

"Piero de Medici, who no less than the princes of Italy needed to consider his affairs if he wished to maintain himself in the authority his father had left him, decide to take action against the city and its citizens. His reputation was much diminished at this time, and M. Luca Pitti held court at his house, where a large part of the citizens went to consult on matters of government. Amongst the other citizens M. Agnolo Acciaiuoli and M. Dietisalvi di Nerone were the most outstanding. Though superior to M. Luca in prudence, they consented to his having such prestige, and to increase it they too frequented his house. All this they did to block Piero de' Medici, whom previously everyone was accustomed to consult on public affairs as well as private, and to take away from him the overbearing position that he had assumed—something already obnoxious and insupportable to all. In this manner they had brought him down to such a degree that few frequented his house and they were men of little consequence; and thus they thought that in a short time they might wear him down entirely.

"Piero, seeing himself in a situation in which he recognized his own manifest ruin, took counsel with a few friends who remained obligated and tied to him so that for various reasons they were not able to do otherwise. For a long time the ambassador here of the duke of Milan (both past and present) was Nicodemo, an astute man and one with great experience in matters of government and with men-of-arms. Both by inclination and by office he was most devoted to the house of Cosimo, a house tied, one might say, to the duke of Milan for the reasons given. This man was so favored by Cosimo and Piero that he had only to give the appearance of asking, and nothing was too difficult (whether just or unjust) either for himself or for his friends. And the more he gave his favor to these friends the more the Medici supported him, which was so profitable that without any salary from the duke he was pleased to remain here, and he bought a house and farms.

"Piero was advised by Nicodemo and by M. Tommaso Soderini and a few others of his closest, most faithful partisans that he should wait no longer since his reputation and authority and that of his followers was being destroyed. They saw no other way to defend his government from those attacking it, but with arms. And it should be at the first opportunity, before his adversaries—not expecting such resolution in his humiliation, but relying on time to bring their designs slowly into effect—would take note of it. This counsel pleased Piero greatly, and it was most fitting to his own nature, as long as he could find a way to carry out so great a business. He set out, therefore, to have at hand sufficient men-at-arms and soldiers.

"The arrangement was as follows. In the territory of Bologna there were 2,000 horse of the duke of Milan. Secretly it was ordered that these troops be made ready for Piero's use. And the Signori Ristori, who had a great following in the Val d'Arno, arranged a great fish hunt in the Arno and many festivities for Lorenzo, Piero's son. To this would come a great gathering of peasants and especially their leaders. Everyone desired to show himself a follower and well-wisher of Piero, and in speaking together they made many offers to Lorenzo. These were accepted with words cunningly suited to the plans they were arranging—which the others knew nothing of—to bring them in a few days to Florence under arms in support of Piero. In other places, similarly, it was arranged under various pretexts that peasants and gentry would quickly appear in arms when requested. Having established these plans, Piero, in order to justify his maneuvers, enacted the following deceit.

"On the morning of 27th of August, 1466, Piero had himself carried in a litter—racked by gout he could not travel any other way—to his villa at Careggi, three miles from Florence. And on the same day around the 22nd hour he returned in great fear to Florence, with many armed men, giving out that they were for his defense against those who plotted to have him torn to pieces. He claimed that at Sto. Antonio del Vescovo, where he had to pass, there were armed men ready to assault him, stationed there by M. Dietisalvi, the brother of M. Giovanni, the archbishop of Florence, to whom Sto. Antonio belonged. But this was not true. And further, he said that he had heard that at our border at the river Albo 800 horse and 6,000 infantry of the duke of Modena were drawn up against himself at the instance of M. Luca Pitti, M. Agnolo Acciaiuoli, and M. Dietisalvi, and their followers.

"With this explanation, a tumult broke out in Florence and arms were taken up. Couriers were hurriedly dispatched to the 2,000 cavalry of the duke of Milan in the territory of Bologna, ordering them to come into our territory around Pigliano, toward Bruscoli. All across the contado men were assembled, who, by marching all night, were at the gates of Florence by morning. In the meantime, those citizens who were his partisans and those who wished to renew their support armed themselves and from all parts rushed to defend his house.

"At this time Piero found himself in financial disorder. He sent for his cousin, Pier Francesco de' Medici, a very rich man, and asked him for a loan of 10,000 florins. Seeing such an upheaval, Pier Francesco did not know how to refuse, though in other times he would not have helped out, and quickly he brought it to the house. With this money, Piero demonstrated great liberality, spending freely for all their needs. First of all, he emptied all the bakeries there were in Florence of all of their bread and sent it to his house. This was a double blow: he supplied himself and deprived his adversaries of the opportunity. He emptied the shops of their arms and the piazza of wine; from these places they rushed through the streets to his house. With great speed the shops were shut up and the men withdrew to their own houses, marveling at this unexpected tumult. Nicodemo, skilled in these arts, set about defending Piero's house with planked scaffolding up high above the windows to be used as battlements, furnished with many stones and other stores for battle. And with armed soldiers he [Piero] seized the streets around the house, and he took the gate of S. Gallo in order to be able to bring in his own men, whom he was expecting, while the other gates that had been shut were guarded so as not to allow opposing forces to enter.

"M. Luca, M. Dietisalvi, and M. Agnolo, seeing so great a commotion suddenly fall upon them, stupefied and unprovided, remained almost bewildered. Nonetheless some of their warmest supporters quickly armed themselves and hurried to the house of M. Luca. And thus there came into existence two strongholds, more or less, each guarded by its own men. M. Dietisalvi and M. Agnolo consulted with M. Luca at his house about what to do. They recognized that they needed—and soon—men, a quantity of arms, and money. Immediately they sent for the troops of the duke of Modena, spoken of above, and had them halt at the river Albo. M. Luca had a great throng of men in the countryside and he sent to many places for a large number of infantry. But Piero had already occupied the gates so that they were not allowed to come in. And already it seemed that the prestige of Piero was winning out over that of M. Luca.

"There remained the question of the provision of money, the lack of which was the thing that made them lose. There were three leaders and each one waited for the others to act. Each kept his hand in his own pockets. But these affairs cannot be managed without funds—and they must be quick and plentiful. This lack of money meant a lack of provisions for the foot soldiers called from the countryside, of arms for their unarmed friends, and of many other things required in unexpected incidents of this sort. These deficiencies were known by many who desired their victory as the party of liberty against tyranny and it made them hesitate to come out in their favor. These people were doubtful about joining up with those who they could see were in manifest danger because of their stinginess; so, keeping to their houses, they held off to see what would follow in these commotions.

"On the contrary, others quickly came out in favor of Piero for two diverse reasons. One part because in their minds they favored a rapacious and unrestrained tyranny. Others, more moderate but eager for reward, did not want to risk losing the reputation of being his supporters by hesitating too long. In this way they might lose the favor of his regime, which they judged would be victorious because they saw it was better provisioned and because in past disturbances his house had always won out since their affairs were well considered and arranged, while their opponents were unprovided and without leadership. Thus such people consulted their own private advantage and chose to follow it, forgetting the city and its civil regime, public honor, and the dignity of a free republic.

"While matters stood in this fashion, Niccolò Soderini, a bold man as we have said, arrived at the house of M. Luca armed and on horseback and with many companions. There already were M. Dietisalvi, M. Agnolo, and many other honorable citizens. Finding them engaged in many discussions, but few provisions suited to their need, he told them that actions were needed here, not words—and quickly too before Piero's situation would be further strengthened. Thus he asked that all the armed men gathered there along with his own people should follow him right then; and he wanted to go to the houses of their friends who—out of doubt and fear—were staying hidden, and bring them out to follow him like the others. And whoever would not show himself should be treated as an enemy. And having gathered together many men in this way, as seemed probable, he would ride through the city, shouting "Liberty!" and rouse the whole city to arms. And with this support he wished to ride to Piero's house and attack him and with every available means overcome him, capture him, put him to flight, and rout him entirely.

"This seemed to everyone a plan that was likely to succeed, but one doubt held them back. This was the fear of the lower classes roused up in arms. After Piero was defeated and his house and goods put to sack, having once tasted the delights of this vandalism, they might be excited to such a fury that the desire would come over them to turn upon the rest of the well-to-do, thinking in this way to be able to throw off their misery, to become well-off instead of needy. And then perhaps, with growing boldness, they might rise against the government and take it for themselves, as they did in 1378.

"This was a highly prudent consideration, so Soderini's proposal was set aside. But in their need it was very cowardly since matters had come to such a state that they had no other possible way of providing for their safety.

"The greater part of the Signoria and the Gonfaloniere, Bernardo Lotti, were favorable to these men [i.e. the opposition] and to a considerable extent they rested their hopes on this support. But the next morning on the 28th the new Signoria was to be drawn—and by lot since the electoral purses were closed. It seemed to each side that victory would largely depend on the outcome. Thus the preceding night, each of the parties kept to its own house, well guarded and with many armed men. They awaited the morning with many foot soldiers from the countryside for their defense, while in the city they hoped for good fortune in the drawing of the new priors.

"During this same night a small incident occurred that showed quite clearly how important to their safety was the plan Niccolò Soderini wanted to follow of assaulting Piero's house—of which he stood in fear.

"M. Antonio Ridolfi, who was one of Piero's supporters, wishing to go at night to speak to him about what was going on, reached the door of his house accompanied by some armed men. When they knocked, the armed men inside demanded to know who it was and why they came, as was reasonable. A minor disturbance broke out, with both arms and voices raised. From this a false rumor spread to those deeper in the house that their adversaries had come to assault them. Almost all of them became so fearful that in bewilderment they rushed about the house looking for any place to hide themselves, and some, wanting to flee, disarmed themselves. Later, the error being understood, they settled themselves again as before. From this event, one can judge what defenses Piero would have had if he had been assaulted then.

"In the morning the soldiers arrived from every direction. They were kept outside of the gates; those of Piero at San Gallo were more numerous and were well stocked with food, those of M. Luca on the other side of the Arno were meagerly provided. That same morning at the usual hour and with great expectation from all sides, the new Signoria was drawn. The lottery fell to the friends of Piero, proving in him that verse of Virgil that says: Audaces fortuna iuvat, timidosque repellit—Fortune helps the bold and repels the timid. Roberto Lioni was drawn as Gonfaloniere of Justice, a judicious man and a good *popolano* who by his nature should have followed the common good and liberty. Nonetheless, ambition led him to uphold Piero, believing that he would be advanced by Piero to a place amongst the first citizens and be rewarded with considerable honors and profit. According to custom the priors were accompanied to the palace by many citizens and both there and at home they were visited by many friends and relations. They were urged in various ways according to their views toward one side or the other, but nothing made an impression on them except Piero's wishes. Thus fortune seemed to have turned.

"In the evening when the members of the new Signoria customarily returned to their own houses, the new Gonfaloniere tried to remain in the Palazzo in order to guard it and to give security to his party—to which (though he spoke favorably to everyone) he had revealed his allegiance. He suspected that his return might be blocked by the old Signoria, reputed to be favorable to the opposing party. He was not permitted to stay and, though resisting strongly, he was shown forcefully that he must leave—which at last he did. After this incident, the old Signoria was tempted not to let the new one enter. It seemed an extreme measure, and attempting it would clearly bring on a clash of arms. In this they had little confidence because of their lack of men, of money, and of reputation—since already it seemed that everyone thought they had lost and Piero won. And so they stood confused.

"In these four days during which the new Signoria stood alongside the old, various negotiations and attempts at agreement were undertaken both in their houses and in the Palazzo. Many good citizens took part, hoping for a happy result. Piero's supporters were free with their promises until the new Signoria had taken its place, when they thought they would not have to live up to anything they had promised. The adversaries listened to these agreements willingly and, in their great necessity, easily believed them. Finally they come to an agreement that they would put down their arms—which the party opposed to Piero observed, but that following Piero did not entirely. And in this way they would await the entry of the new Signoria and the establishment of a new regime with good government and security for all.

"One of those also urging this agreement was M. Marino Tomacelli, longtime ambassador here of the king of Naples, with whom I was very friendly. For this reason he was anxious that I should go with him to the house of M. Luca and the house of Piero in order to see the state of affairs in each and hear what they were saying. He thought that I, as a citizen knowing the citizens perhaps better than he, could help him to arrive at a truer sense of what he saw and heard in order to better advise the king. And I did it willingly so as to have this means of seeing and understanding for myself as well the direction things were taking without risking blame from either party.

"Up until this time, the king of Naples had always been very friendly to M. Dietisalvi; and with M. Agnolo he had become favorable after the war which he had fought with Duke Jean, the son of King Renée, whose strong supporter he [Agnolo] had been at that time. Out of love for the others, M. Luca was also taken as a friend, though he and his father had long been devoted to the king of France. The good will of the king bolstered their strength, just as the duke of Milan's did Piero's. But at the moment, because of being far off, they were not able to draw on the help of the king or his men, as Piero profited from the duke's men by having them close by. King Ferdinand, having been advised by M. Marino, stood in suspense, and, thinking more of himself than of his friends, judged that he would have to deal with whoever won out.

"At the same time it was suggested to Piero that it would be very useful to attempt to divide the three men we have named, and that if this were done, they would be much weakened. And it was thought possible to detach M. Luca from the others as a man easily swayed and open to corruption. The man deputed for this task was Francesco Sassetti, Piero's partner in business and much involved in all his affairs. He went to M. Luca's house and, meeting with him in secret, began to speak to him to this effect—namely that he had been sent there for Luca's own safety. First of all, he should remember the good friendship that he had always enjoyed with Cosimo and that Piero had not forgotten the favor done him in 1434 when Luca had been one of the priors who restored his father from his exile in Venice. Now he should consider the condition in which he found himself and in what poor company. He should not fool himself: things going on in the way they had begun, their ruin was certain. And if M. Luca would stand with them, he would see his own ruin as well—something that Piero would not in any way want, for the reasons given. Therefore Piero would wish to be reunited, not to abandon old friendships for new ones, but to overcome the resentments that between lovers bring a renewal of love. If he would like anything from Piero, he should ask freely, since he was ready and able to do it, sure in the knowledge of his wisdom—and other promises that it is not necessary to relate in detail.

"M. Luca was convinced the offer was made sincerely, and he accepted Francesco's invitation. If they had any disputes or arguments in speaking together it is not known to me, but I do know the conclusion that they reached. M. Luca asked three things. The first was that he wished to be made accoppiatore. The next was that Luigi, his brother, should be one of the Eight of Balìa. The third was a marriage alliance with Piero. M. Luca had a girl of a tender age to marry off. And Piero had Lorenzo, his son, who was eighteen. This was the intention of M. Luca, but out of delicacy he did not specify further. With these agreements he thought he would be able to remain secure and important in the regime as before. The accoppiatori choose the priors, which confers considerable authority. Since the Eight have the power of exile his brother's membership would give him security. And the match with Piero would give both the first and the second.

"Francesco departed from M. Luca, assuring him that he believed that Piero would do everything being asked of him, and returned to Piero. The discussions being related to Piero, he consented to the requests, moderating the third with ambiguous words, namely that he would marry the girl to someone he held most dear. When Francesco returned to M. Luca, he freely and happily made these promises. M. Luca relied on the generalities regarding the marriage, believing that Lorenzo was that dear one he spoke of, but in this he was mistaken.

"M. Dietisalvi and M. Agnolo, seeing these proceedings of M. Luca, began to be suspicious of being duped, and they did not find M. Luca as firm as he had been in considering and organizing matters needed for their safety. Thus they carried on as best they could.

"On the first day of September 1466, the time came for the new priors to enter, and in the customary manner they took office and the old ones departed. Rid of his fear of the latter and leaving his adversaries to fear instead, Piero felt secure because the new priors were men of his stripe, and he began to show his vigor. He placed in arms the foot soldiers brought by his order from the countryside to Florence, around 6,000 men, and kept them in Florence for several days. And quickly he began to arrange for a parlamento. M. Luca, M. Dietisalvi, and M. Agnolo had already agreed to this step as a matter of form, but it did them little good.

"On the 2nd of September, being called to a parlamento, the priors came out on the rostrum [ringhiera] around the

20th hour. A petition was put forward by Bernardo di Francesco Paganelli. Read out, it was confirmed by shouts from the great multitude of the people, armed and unarmed, who were in the piazza. It was accepted by the two-thirds of the people needed to give the petition the force of law. In effect, its content was that from then on until the end of December 1466 the authority [balìa] of the entire *popolo* of Florence should be given to the present priors and to all those from the year 1434 to the present picked [veduto] as Gonfaloniere of Justice, leaving one-third of this number to the minor guilds in order that the artisans would have one-fourth [of the total]. Beyond these, they elected 25 men per quarter of the city, giving 1/4 to the artisans. In conducting a scrutiny the priors and Colleges then in office would join with the above-mentioned men of the Balìa to carry it out. And they confirmed the Council of 100, over whose termination there had been such a battle between the two parties, a large part of the reason for this parlamento.

"On the 4th of the said month, the said *arroti* [i.e. elected members of the Balìa] were chosen and on the same day the complete Balìa met together. And the following petitions were carried. That when the time came for a scrutiny, 80 arroti would be chosen [in addition to] the above. That the electoral purses containing the name-tickets for the priors should be done by hand for ten years, and that 10 accoppiatori be appointed with all their past authority: and these would hold office for one year; afterward for up to ten years there should be five per year. That every year for ten years the Eight of Balìa should be established. That special powers [balìa] be given to a rector from time to time for 5 years and this was assigned to the Captain of the People. That up to 1,000 foot soldiers be hired to guard the piazza, and afterward 400. That 5 Officials of the Abbondanza be established. But the first decision taken was that the following Sunday, the 7th, a solemn procession should be held, with all the orders, signori and magistrates of the city to thank God that the danger of a clash between the parties had been removed.

"On the 6th day of September the said balìa established the

Eight of Balìa and the Officials of the Abbondanza. As a result, that night M. Dietisalvi and M. Agnolo—considering the character of the Eight as men completely in Piero's lap, willing to do anything for him without scruple—fled the city in fear. M. Dietisalvi went toward Modena, and M. Agnolo toward Siena. Niccolò Soderini had recognized before the others Piero's ill will against himself and others like him, and he saw that Piero would not have to keep faith with earlier agreements. Even though by the new law he would be included in the Balìa, nonetheless a few days before the others, he left and went toward Fucechio; from there passing through the territory of Lucca, he went to Seravezza. In Genoa he had some standing because of having been ambassador there earlier.

"On the Sunday morning following, which was the 7th, the procession that had been decided upon earlier was organized. It was done as much as a net in which to trap men as for devotion. Francesco di Nerone, understanding these snares, decided to flee but was not in time. On this morning he was already on the Via di S. Gallo mounted on horseback when the Eight, anticipating his flight, ordered him taken; and it was there that they found him and led him off to the captain. Next Nigi, Filippo, and Antonio, his brothers, were taken. Agnolo, their brother, hid himself, and was not found for the moment. Such things—searches and arrests of various others—were being done even while the procession was going on. During it, while the priors and the other magistrates were listening to a solemn mass near the high altar in Santa Maria del Fiore, it was decided to capture Salvestro Nardi there in the church. But he, quickly recognizing what was happening, fled to the altar, staying at the feet of the Gonfaloniere of Justice, who was his relation. In this way he was saved from being taken, and all along the way right up to the Palazzo, Salvestro never left his side. And as the Signoria was returning to the Palazzo, and they were already in the piazza—the captains of the Parte Guelfa (among whom was Guido Bonciani) being present along with the other magistrates in their ranks—the servants of the Eight dragged Salvestro from the company and led him away a captive. It seemed to those nearby who saw it an abominable act that a high magistrate should be so cruelly humiliated in the company of the Signoria.

"The same thing happened to others, and they arrested Carlo Gondi, Piero Giacomini, Amerigo Benci, Antonio di Fronte, Tomaso Redditi, and Simone Beccannugi, who was at his villa. Roaming through the city, searching for others in this way, they produced great fear in those who saw them, so that each asked himself whether in the past by words or by deeds he might have made himself suspect to Piero—or to whoever was leading this dance for him. As a result, a number fled Florence in their anxiety: Ruberto Altoviti, Giovanni di Brunetto, his brother, Giovanni Macinghi, Giovanni de Guarente hid himself, Rafaello di M. Agnolo, and some others. And when they were not able to find those they wanted, the Eight published a ban naming those they sought who had absented themselves, declaring that within three days they must appear at their office under pain of their authority.

"And when they did not appear on the 11th as set by the Balìa, M. Dietisalvi and Francesco and Agnolo di Nerone were confined to Sicily for 20 years with all the penalties imposed on the exiles of the year 1434. And they decreed that within 10 days they must be gone from the contado and district of Florence, and within two months they must present themselves at the place of exile. Agnolo, who subsequently came out of hiding and complained a good deal of the wrong done him, was condemned to pay one thousand florins larghi, and within three hours was sent out of Florence—and thus the wrong done him was righted.

"Messere Agnolo and Neri, his third son, were confined to Barletta, or wherever they wished in the kingdom below that point and he and M. Dietisalvi were condemned to have their grain confiscated.

"Niccolò Soderini and M. Geri, a doctor, his bastard son, were confined in Provence, and his two legitimate sons, age 12 and 14, were admonished ["warned" of disqualification]; and when they had reached the age of 18 they were required to present themselves at the place of confinement, 100 miles away or further.

"On the 12th day of the said September, the Eight of Balìa confined the following men for 20 years to remain not less than 3 miles from Florence and not more than 20:

Nigi di Nerone and sons, and they were fined 2,000 florins larghi and their goods confiscated; but if within 10 days of the giving of the sentence they paid 1,000 florins larghi they would be free of the larger sum and confiscation of goods

Filippo di Nerone was condemned to pay 2,000 florini larghi, commuted to 1,000 as above

Antonio di Nerone was confined, as specified above

The sons of M. Dietisalvi and of Agnolo di Nerone, as specified

Iacopo di M. Agnolo Acciaiuoli was confined to the same place as his father and in the said manner

Rafaello di M. Agnolo was confined 3 miles outside the city as above

Piero di Tomaso Giacomini and brothers and sons were confined as above and condemned to pay 3,000 florins larghi, commuted to 2,000, as specified if paid within 10 days

Ruberto Altoviti with his sons was confined in the Vicariate of Valdarno, five miles or more outside of Florence, and condemned to pay 2,000 florins, commuted to 1,000 as above

Guido Bonciani and sons were admonished for 20 years, and condemned to pay 2,000 florins, commuted to 1,000, etc.

Carlo Gondi and his brothers and sons were admonished for 20 years and condemned to pay 5,000 florins larghi, commuted to 2,500 if paid within 10 days, as specified above

Niccolaio Bartholini, admonished for 20 years and condemned to pay 2,000 florins, commuted to 1,000 etc.

Gherardo Davizi and sons, admonished and condemned, as above, for 20 years and 1,000 florins etc.

Iacopo di M. Poggio, admonished and condemned for 20 years and [ ] thousand florins, commuted to 1,000, etc.

Antonio di Fronte and sons, admonished for 20 years and confined for 10 outside of Florence
Simone di M. Piero Beccanugi and sons, admonished for 20 years
Tomaso Redditi and sons, admonished for 20 years
Francesco Riccialbani and sons, admonished for 20 years
Marco di Salvadore del Cassia and sons were admonished for 5 years
Giovanni de Ser Pagolo of the Wool Guild and his sons and descendents were admonished for 20 years

Later, on the 22nd, Giovanni Macinghi was confined beyond the walls for 10 years.

"A few of these men were quickly restored to their prior state.

"The leaders of these [new] exiles, had they been able to maintain themselves in government against Piero, had wanted to restore those exiled from 1434 on—men expelled from the city at that time because of the return of Cosimo from Venice where they had exiled him. The chief of these were M. Rinaldo degli Albizzi, M. Palla and Matteo degli Strozzi, Ridolfo Peruzzi, Bernardo Guadagni, and others. Most of these men were now dead, but there remained their sons and descendents. Piero di Cosimo, in order not to appear worse than his adversaries and in order to replenish the city a little after having so much diminished its citizenry, decided to do the same thing himself. He did not recall all of them since he did not wish to bring back the sons of M. Palla and some others, but only a part, and with the exception of a few, they were not men of great worth.

"Filippo and Lorenzo di Matteo degli Strozzi were in exile on account of their father and they resided in Naples at this time. They were rich merchants, highly reputed by merchants of all kinds and much favored by King Ferrante of Naples. They were well esteemed by all his court and by the nobles of the kingdom, as well as by many others in Italy. At this time, these men had acquired such standing that—whoever might win in Florence—they could not lose. The first who wanted to restore them were M. Dietisalvi and M. Agnolo and the other adversaries of Piero. And so that nothing should be wanting for their needs, it seemed that fortune exerted itself to favor them.

"The king of Naples at first was very friendly to Piero's adversaries, but seeing their defeat, he made up his mind to draw closer to Piero. And to give him a token of his confidence, he began to ask favors of Piero. And the first was this: that it might please him for his sake to restore Filippo, and to this effect he sent Piero a letter, as did the Signor Federigo, Count of Urbino. These were despatched and came to me, his brother-in-law, as his most trusted relation, so that I might give them to Piero. And as soon as they were handed on and read, Piero replied to me that it was a great pleasure to have done for himself something that was pleasing to two such signori. And at the moment the bell of the Palace began to ring for the Balìa. And Piero said to me, "Listen to the bell which rings for them." It rang to call together the Balìa to restore the exiles and admonished ones listed below, as I will say.

"And so on the 20th day of September, the above-mentioned Balìa met in the Palazzo and restored some of the exiles to the city and its honors [i.e. office] and some to the city alone. And the admonished were free of their penalties and were made eligible for office.

Filippo and Lorenzo di Matteo degli Strozzi, restored to the city and to office
Niccolò di Piero de Neri Ardinghelli, restored to the city only
Piero di Iacopo Ardinghelli who was admonished was restored
Francesco Castellani, one of the admonished, was restored
Piero di Donato Peruzzi, one of the admonished, was restored
the family of the Serragli
Stoldo Frescobaldi

the sons of Bernardo di Giorgio Canigiani
the sons of Iacopo Baroncelli
the sons of Battista di Francesco Baroncelli
the sons of Bindaccio da Ricasoli
the sons of Matteo da Panzano
the sons of Francesco della Luna
the sons of Francesco Caccini
Matteo Caccini
Tadeo di Duccio Mancini
Niccolò di M. Zanobi Guasconi
Giovanni and Piero Borghini
Giovanni di Doffo Arnolfi
Bartolomeo and Benedetto Fortini
Iacapone Gherardini
Bono Ristori
Domenico Ginori
Lorenzo di Giovanni della Stufa
Nicolaio Viviani
Daniello di Nofri d'Azo
Lorenzo di Francesco Michi
Giovanni Benizi
the sons of Alesso Doni
the sons of Ser Martino di Ser Giovanni Martini
Giovanni di Stefano di Salvi
Giuliano Delbesso

"All of their descendants are understood to be restored.

"After so great an upheaval in Florence it seemed fitting and useful to those remaining in power to give some justification of these events to the ruling powers of Italy, both to reconfirm friendships with those rulers and to condemn their adversaries and undermine their credit, should they go searching for favor in order to return to Florence. Accordingly, on the 23rd of September in a single action they chose 6 ambassadors. Two went to Rome and Naples, who were M. Antonio Ridolfi and Giovanni Canigiani; and two to Venice and Milan, who were M. Tomaso Soderini and Iacopo Guicciardini. Matteo Palmieri went to Bologna and M. Bernardo da

Boggio, doctor, to the marchese of Ferrara, duke of Modena. The latter departed from Florence on the 30th, returning on the 26th, and Matteo [Palmieri] on the 4th of October, returning on the 14th. M. Tomaso and Iacopo left here on the 6th of October and returned on the 13th of December. M. Antonio and Giovanni left on the 7th of October. M. Antonio returned here and left again for Naples. Giovanni Canigiani returned from Naples to Rome, and stayed there for some time. Later he was made a knight by Pope Paul, and he returned to Florence on the 3rd of July 1467. He was received with great honor and accompanied by many citizens, relations, and friends, who went to meet him at the Palace of the Signoria and at the Parte Guelfa, where he was given the banners it was customary to give to returned knights.

"External matters having been arranged in this way, internal arrangements followed. On the 14th of October, 1466, 10 accoppiatori were elected by the Council of 100. For the quarter of Sto. Spirito M. Luca Pitti was chosen, as he had requested, and M. Antonio Ridolfi. For the quarter of Sta. Croce, Ruberto Lioni, then Gonfaloniere of Justice, and Francesco Sachetti were chosen; for the quarter of Sta. Maria Novella, Giovanni Ventura and Andrea di Niccolò Carducci, with Niccolò di Michele di Feodini for the minor guilds; for the quarter of San Giovanni, M. Domenico Martelli and Giovanni Lorini, with Romolo d'Andrea di Nofri for the minor guilds. They were empowered for a year to draw the priors by hand.

"In this way the promise made to M. Luca that he would be made an accoppiatore was observed and before this the promise to place his brother Luigi on the Eight of Balìa was also made good. There remained the third request: to make a marriage alliance with Piero. This was carried out according to the letter but not in the sense that M. Luca understood. It was promised to him that he could marry his daughter to one of those whom Piero held most dear. M. Luca understood by this Lorenzo, his son, but Piero had in mind another relation, who was very close and dear to him, a young man of good presence, a pleasing manner, able, very noble, and very rich as a result of his favor. And with this it seemed to him that he had sufficiently satisfied what he had pledged. This was his brother-in-law Giovanni di Francesco Tornabuoni, the brother of Madonna Lucretia his wife, his partner in the Florentine bank and in the Roman branch, where he was the manager—earning a great reputation and being much esteemed by the pope, the cardinals and all the Roman court. Therefore M. Luca could not complain of having such a son-in-law with such excellent qualities, even though he was not the one he had in mind. Piero wished to reserve Lorenzo for a marriage with nobility [signori] since he already felt himself to be more than a mere citizen; and this he later did, giving him one of the Orsini, old and important lords in Italy and noble captains at arms.

"Having had all his requests satisfied, M. Luca nonetheless was not left in the position he had thought. He was an accoppiatore but no one went to him to be chosen as one of the priors. Luigi was one of the Eight, but his colleagues held him in no esteem. He was allied to Piero in marriage, but this had not in the least cheered him. He remained cold and alone at home, and no one visited him to talk about political affairs—he who was used to have his house full of every kind of person. Occasionally he ventured out and he would hardly find anyone on the street who would speak a word to him.

"It is hardly to be wondered at that he deceived himself in this way, since he had deceived M. Dietisalvi and M. Agnolo in leaving them to support Piero—when perhaps had they remained close and united they would have dictated the terms to Piero that he imposed on them. And if nonetheless—fortune being against him—he had been sent away with the others, like the other exiles he would have retained a certain reputation and a good name and been able to make himself feared, as the others later did. He would not have been left at home in such a despised state, subject to the reproofs thrown at him, the villification and disdain. He would not have had to see his affairs turn sour under his own eyes, to his blame and discredit. . . .

"Piero's adversaries having been humbled in this way while he himself was raised up excessively, he did not, however, think it useful to treat them too harshly and give them reason for total desperation, because they were still men of great substance and worthy of much esteem; and for this reason they were apt to stir up great commotions. Piero thought, therefore, to ease their situation somewhat by suiting their confinement more to their own taste. On the 30th of October he had M. Dietisalvi's confinement change from Sicily to Lombardy, either at Novara or Alessendria whichever pleased him better. Francesco di Nerone his brother was confined to the Marches at Foligno or Todi or Orvieto as desired. With M. Agnolo nothing new was done because he was well placed from the beginning. They confined Gualtieri Panciatichi of Pistoia, the chief of his party, for 20 years outside of the contado and district of Florence, wherever he wished. . . ."[2]

The decisive contest, anticipated ever since the death of Cosimo, had finally come and gone. For everyone we have been concerned with—Piero di Cosimo, the defeated patrician leaders, the Strozzi family, and Marco Parenti himself—these early September days of 1466 marked a turning point with enduring personal as well as political consequences.

For Piero de' Medici, who had never before held undisputed authority, the outcome of the struggle was an unqualified triumph, both for himself and for his regime. On the sixth of September, when the fate of the opposition leaders was still in doubt, the Signoria was able to write to the duke of Milan that "by the grace of God and in large part (as is clear) by your help and the reputation of your soldiers, we have restored our city to unity between the citizens and great tranquility, putting an end to all civil discord."[3] To the king of France they wrote inveighing against citizens driven to sedition by their pride and avarice, and they congratulated themselves on having put a stop to the discord without any bloodshed.[4] And finally to all the world the Balìa pronounced its solemn sen-

[2] *Memorie*, pp. 74–98.

[3] A. Municchi, *La fazione antimedicea detta del Poggio* (Florence, 1911), app., doc. 12.

[4] Ibid., app., doc. 17.

tence against those who had wickedly summoned foreign arms and impiously put the liberty of the patria in such manifest danger—a crime worse than all others put together.[5]

The Florentine propaganda found a ready response in friendly courts. From France the Milanese ambassador reported that King Louis said the news showed God's wish to protect the duke of Milan—another sign of the close identification between the Sforza and the Medici. "It pleases me greatly," said Louis, "that the lilies have come out victorious and my fine cousin Piero di Cosimo, who was good enough to do me the great honor of accepting my arms." As for Agnolo Acciaiuoli, the king felt sorry for him but he was not too surprised, "because of his usual fickleness and instability."[6]

This assessment of Acciaiuoli's character would be borne out in the coming months as the exiles swung from dreams of reconciliation with Piero to schemes for armed reprisal. In mid-September, having only recently fled from Florence, Acciaiuoli stopped in Siena, and from there addressed to Piero a brief, proud letter whose purpose was to beg a favor but whose tone proclaimed the opposite:

> Spectabilis vir Frater honorande, I laugh at what I see. God has put it in thy power to cancel all the debts I have against thee, and you do not know how to do it. I lost my country and my estates for your father, you are in a position to restore all to me . . . be not tardy in showing you are not ungrateful; I do not say this for my belongings, although I have need of them, so much as for your reputation. I commend myself to you.

For his part, Piero answered by wrapping himself in the mantle of state, meeting Acciaiuoli's stiff plea with an impersonal severity:

> Your laughter is the cause of my not shedding tears, although I am sorry for your ill fortune. . . . Your guilt . . . is manifest

[5] Ibid., app., doc. 19.

[6] Letter of Panigarola and Emanuel de Iacopo, 8 Oct. 1466, in B. Buser, *Die Beziehungen der Mediceer zu Frankreich wahrend der Jahre 1434–1494* (Leipzig, 1879), pp. 434–36.

> and so great that neither my intercession nor that of any other person would be of any avail. . . . I have pardoned every offense; the republic cannot and may not lightly do so on account of the bad example, as you know better than I . . . I do not deny your friendship with my father and with us, which ought to have made you regard me as a son, and as such I considered myself. You were banished with my father and were recalled with him, according to the pleasure of the republic, which has full power over us.[7]

By this assertion of a total separation between private and public spheres, Piero de' Medici was able to dismiss his old ally's personal call on his compassion—and it must be said that there were others who wanted a fiercer retribution against the defeated party.[8] But in one sense, Piero's position was certainly a false one—or at least it was highly premature. For men of Acciaiuoli's standing it was not yet true to say that "the republic . . . has full power over us." This image of a state with impersonal power over all its subjects would become a reality of the modern world, but it was not yet one in fifteenth-century Florence. In fact, this could be said to be the deepest meaning of the events of 1466: a profound resistance by the patricians against any such claim to impersonal authority on the part of the Medici. Only when these patrician rebellions were securely a thing of the past would Tuscany become a "state" as we know it.

Agnolo Acciaiuoli and his principal allies were not simply private citizens in the modern sense. Like the Medici themselves, though on a lesser scale, they were public men. Their wealth and their diplomatic activities made them familiar figures in the courts and councils of Naples, Rome, Milan, Venice, and even France. But unlike the modern ambassador, Acciaiuoli or Neroni could speak in foreign capitals not only

[7] Both letters are printed in Fabroni, *Laurentii Medicis Magnifici vita* (Pisa, 1784), 2: 36, and translated in J. B. Ross, *Lives of the Early Medici as Told in Their Correspondence* (Boston, 1911), pp. 105–106.

[8] The king of France, for one, in the letter already cited; similarly Agnolo della Stufa wrote that if it were up to him he would have their house destroyed right down to the foundations (cf. Municchi, *La fazione*, app., doc. 31).

for the public, but for themselves—as the dozens of Florentine letters in the Milanese diplomatic archives clearly demonstrate. Just as the Milanese alliance was vital to the Medici, these foreign connections were an inseparable element of the patricians' power—and of the threat they posed to the regime from which they had become alienated. Beaten at home, the patricians were still not finally defeated.[9] As the *Memoir* put it, "they were still men of great substance . . . apt to stir up great commotions." Knowing this, the government in Florence watched their movements with anxiety. Reports soon accumulated from officials in the subject cities or from Medici agents further afield of the passage of small troops of armed men. Later, when open hostilities had broken out, there were rumors of raids or assassination plots—a threat real enough to bring Piero to write a warning to his sons at the villa at Cafaggiolo that they should keep themselves well guarded, talk little, see that the house was secure at night, and carefully scrutinize strangers.[10]

These were relatively minor alarms. More threatening signs

[9] In Acciaiuoli the sense of his own dignity perhaps went beyond simple patrician independence; in the very days of early September when his position was becoming untenable in Florence, he was offering himself as an intermediary between the king of Naples and the duke of Ferrara. Municchi publishes the minutes of a letter, unsigned, but apparently from Acciaiuoli to the duke of Modena. In it the author wildly schemes to redraw the entire map of Italy and states that "because I do not think that Florence can remain any longer in liberty," the duke should be given the "governo" of Florence. Municchi takes this letter as demonstrating the total insincerity of Acciaiuoli's many professions of zeal for liberty. This condemnation seems excessive. Even if the authorship of the letter were more certain, there is no warrant for extending the emotions of January 1467 back to 1465–1466. In addition, there is good reason to distinguish between *governo* and *signoria*; in fact Acciaiuoli himself makes the distinction in raising the specter of the Florentines calling in the duke of Anjou, "nonchè per governatore, ma per Signore." Similarly, it was possible to accuse the Medici of allowing Florence to be "governed" by Sforza, though Sforza was never in any sense the *ruler* of the city. See just such a protest from Luca Pitti, as reported by Nicodemo, in a letter of 14 Sept. 1465 in Buser, *Die Beziehungen*, p. 433.

[10] 11 Sept. 1468, in Municchi, *La fazione*, app., doc. 36.

were the unwillingness of the exiles to obey the terms of their "confinement" in specified locations and their gravitation to the cities and courts from which armed opposition to the regime might be staged—Rome, Ferrara, and Venice. These violations brought severe reprisals. In December 1466 and January 1467 the exiles were declared rebels and outlaws with a bounty on their heads, but by then they had succeeded in raising an army of their own. With the tacit support of Venice and the duke of Modena, they engaged one of the famous condottieri of the day, Bartolomeo Colleoni, normally a captain of the Venetian Republic. Consequently the battles that followed have been known as the Colleonic War.

Despite some successes, Colleoni was stymied by a coalition of Florence, Milan, and Naples and a peace was made in May 1468 that ended any hopes the exiles had of unseating Piero de' Medici. Even so, their ability to disturb the peace of Italy for two years after their defeat at home indicates again how precarious was Piero de' Medici's assertion that the "Republic has full power over us." The fact is that—in modern terms—there was an imbalance of private and public power in Renaissance society, and this was a continuing source of political instability.

The leaders of the abortive revolt never saw their homes again, but for the Strozzi and some of the others in exile since 1434, the complete Medici victory led to a swift rehabilitation—an ironic contrast to the scant results of their long, anxious months of maneuver. The recall of the old exiles was a sign of the new sense of security in the regime and it was designed as a token of its magnanimity. In their official decree the Signoria gave credit to God alone for saving the city from ruin in its recent troubles, brought upon it "by her own malignant and perverse citizens," and it was principally to thank Him that the priors undertook this action. The *popolo* has suffered a great deal, and it was hoped to bring them in exchange "some joy and comfort and pleasure." The descendants of the exiles were suffering "from the errors of the others more than their own," and the priors especially stressed "their patience and obedience and good conduct that they have always shown"—a lesson clearly directed at their successors in exile.[11]

Filippo Strozzi was quick to take advantage of the opportunity to revisit his family, though it was not until 1470 that he returned permanently to Florence. He set up a branch of his firm in Florence and a third in Rome in 1482. His wealth and his lack of political ambition eased his return to the front ranks of the Florentine patriciate. His first marriage was happy and fertile, and he married his children to the most prominent families of the oligarchy. Later came a second marriage and further children, including a son who became his biographer. In his son's biography we read the story of how Filippo was able to keep his ambition to build a magnificent family palazzo such a well-hidden secret that Lorenzo de' Medici actually urged him to the task in the name of civic beautification, thus smoothing the way for this ambitious plan which otherwise might have aroused a dangerous resentment in Lorenzo Magnifico. Filippo died in 1491, when his great monument was still in its earliest stages.

Lorenzo Strozzi's path was rather different from his brother's. After his exile was revoked he returned to Florence for a stay of two years, partly in order to find a wife. His choice was Marietta, the beautiful daughter of a Strozzi relation, but Filippo vehemently opposed the marriage. As an orphan and a Strozzi, the girl brought with her no relations, "in which we are much depleted." But his deepest concern was that her guardian was bankrupt and politically disgraced. The match was sure to "displease Piero and the others of the regime, even if they say yes; and at the first scrutiny we will see it."[12] Eventually Lorenzo turned to another girl, whom he married in San Lorenzo—a church closely identified with the Medici family—in June 1470, both Lorenzo de' Medici and Tommaso Soderini being present to bless the match. Shortly afterward

[11] The decree is printed by Guasti in *Lettere*, pp. 581–82.

[12] *Lettere*, pp. 594–95; Gregory, "A Florentine Family in Crisis: The Strozzi in the 15th Century" (Ph.D. diss., University of London, 1980), pp. 119–20.

he returned to Naples to take Filippo's place and he died there in 1479.

Alessandra, who as much as anyone was responsible for rebuilding the family, lived long enough to see her tenacity rewarded. She died in Florence in 1471. As for Marco Parenti, he continued in his customary role as informant and advisor as long as Filippo remained in Naples. We find him expressing his more benign view of Lorenzo's prospective match with Marietta, chiding Filippo not to be disappointed on the birth of a daughter—since girls marry younger, he wrote, you will be rewarded sooner with a fine *parentado* [kinship]—and reporting the quiet transition of power to Lorenzo de' Medici on his father's death. Marco had his own modest share in the rising fortunes of the Strozzi family. He served the republic in various financial and administrative posts, his son had his term on the Signoria, and Lorenzo de' Medici himself blessed the marriage of one of his daughters.[13] These and other signs of favor make it clear that by the time of his death on the ninth of June, 1497, Marco had secured his family's place in Florence's governing class.

★

Ironic confirmation of Marco's social achievement comes in one last fragment of biographical evidence. No more than a footnote, it still has a place among the memorials of Marco Parenti's life. In 1472 an anonymous Florentine, indulging a passion for lists, copied out the names of some leading Florentines (along with a few prominent foreigners) and appended to each a motto or proverb. These sayings are almost uniformly malicious. Obviously they were not intended as something these men would say; rather they are the sort of thing that might be said against them—a pointed remark or witticism that would bring a smile of recognition from the rest of the company.

We might think of the document as the guest list for an important party, with a little of the gossip thrown in. Several of the guests were men whom we have met. Lorenzo de'

[13] For Marco's late social and political successes, see above, ch. 2.

Medici is almost alone in his auspicious tag: "You will live long and happily." Most others are treated harshly: Pope Sixtus, "Soon you will meet your judgment"; Tommaso Soderini, "Your ideas will not succeed"; Iacopo Guicciardini, "He who fears too much is always distressed"; Donato Acciaiuoli, "You search for something you cannot find." We also find the two men in whom we are most interested. Next to Filippo Strozzi's names stands a familiar moralism: "Ill-gotten gains will not be inherited in the third generation." Marco Parenti received another: "The tongue lacks a bone, but it can break your back."[14]

It is an intriguing accusation, far more so than the envious slap at Filippo's wealth. It suggests a long list of negative images quite different from the confidential exchanges of the correspondence or the higher aspirations of the *Memoir*. And yet there is still a certain family resemblance. The man accused of being a back-biting gossip might be a family confidant as well. The historian who hoped to chronicle the downfall of a powerful regime might also seem to possess a wounding tongue.

There is no need to exaggerate the plausibility of an anonymous and malicious observer. But even such a splinter of evidence has its value as a reminder of how much is lost that contemporaries knew, of how even contemporaries never know each other whole.

[14] G. Corti, "Una lista di personaggi del tempo di Lorenzo il Magnifico, caratterizzati da un motto o da una riflessione morale," *Rinascimento* 3 (1952): 153–57.

PART III

HISTORY

Marco Parenti's

MEMOIR

★

RECENT HISTORIANS have cautioned against the habit of seeing Cosimo's coup in 1434 as a decisive break with earlier Florentine governments and the beginning of an undifferentiated epoch of Medici "rule." Certainly in its beginnings the Medici domination was little different from earlier coalitions of powerful families that had succeeded for a time in monopolizing power. Only gradually were the institutional structures of the republic modified to permit this new coalition a degree of stability never before achieved. Nonetheless Florence changed, and under Lorenzo it was a very different political society than it had been under his grandfather. If we must guard against the temptation to make 1434 more epoch-making than it was, it follows that more attention must be given to later moments of political decision that shaped the political consciousness of fifteenth-century Florentines.

Both logic and evidence suggest that the decade of Cosimo's death was a watershed in the history of the Medici regime. The great political coalition Cosimo built had survived the death of its founder and fought off a wide-scale defection from its ranks. As a consequence, there now seemed to be an acceptance of the fact that political power in Florence—however it was to be organized and defined—was an inheritance to be passed down in the Medici family. When Piero died in 1469, Lorenzo assumed the leadership of the regime with few signs of the difficulties that had nearly overwhelmed his father. This was not his own achievement. Just as Piero had inherited the backlash of Cosimo's greatness, Lorenzo started his political career with the new consensus gained by his father. And nine years later the Pazzi conspiracy proved the solidarity of the oligarchy behind its Medicean leadership. Spectacular though the assassination plot was, it gathered up very little of the force of patrician resentment, factional rivalry, or republican nostalgia that had filled the air in 1465–1466.

Clearly Medici leadership had become "routinized" by its successful extension into a second and altogether less charismatic generation. What is more, the rival assertion that others within the inner circle of the regime might be equally qualified to lead the same coalition had been decisively put down. We recall Machiavelli's judgment that from this point on legitimate opposition in Florence became impossible and only the path of conspiracy remained open.

Changes like these need to be understood in terms of the formal realities of how power was exercised and limited in fifteenth-century Florence, and recent studies have tended to emphasize these limitations. But the importance of formal structures and institutional change can be overstressed when seen in isolation. Time, habit, the passing of generations, the shaping in victory or defeat of new expectations about government and citizenship, these too are a vital part of any explanation of Florentine politics because they are bound up with the political consciousness of the active citizenry. The events of 1465–1466 were important not simply because they produced certain immediate effects—the exile of Neroni and Acciaiuoli, for instance—but because they were replayed in the minds of contemporaries and helped to shape the sense of citizenship Florentines brought to later moments of decision.

The duality of formal structures and subjective experience exists in all political systems, but the mixture of republican, oligarchical, and personal authority that Florence had evolved by the second half of the fifteenth century made this duality particularly problematic and open to manipulation from both sides. To foreign allies the Medici were fond of making the plea that they were only citizens, hemmed in by the multiple restraints of a republican constitution, while at home they bolstered their power by presenting themselves as the equals of princes in diplomacy, wealth, and standing. At the same time, it was open to Florentine citizens either to ignore the Medici and stress the uninterrupted operation of their republican institutions or—privately at least—to charge their leaders with usurpation and tyranny.[1]

[1] Alison Brown has noted that the "Florentine chronicles are strangely silent

Each of these ways of picturing the relationship between citizens and their government will enter into the discussions that follow. But as we look at contemporary descriptions of the upheavals of 1466 the goal will not be to assess the actual structures of political power in these decades. Rather, the views of Parenti and his contemporaries have a special interest as expressions of competing conceptions of citizenship. This competition had a long history in Florence, lasting well into the next century, and was in itself an important element of the contest that followed Cosimo's death.

---

about [Cosimo's] political role in the city and rarely mention his name after his return from exile in 1434 until his death thirty years later" ("The Humanist Portrait of Cosimo de' Medici Pater Patriae," *Journal of the Warburg and Courtauld Institutes* 24 [1961]: 186). Chroniclers following the bimonthly fortunes of the Florentine regime could easily content themselves with an entirely externalized account that tacitly preserved the fiction that the republican constitution stood unchanged.

CHAPTER II

A CRITIQUE OF MEDICI POLITICS: MARCO PARENTI'S VIEWS ON PIERO AND COSIMO

★

FLORENCE has been made famous by a long line of men, stretching from Dante, Compagni, and Villani to Machiavelli, Guicciardini, and Giannotti, who confronted political change with self-conscious articulateness. Within this succession, Marco Parenti has a modest but significant place as a sensitive witness to the growth of Medici power and its impact on the traditions of Florentine citizenship in the second half of his century. Before examining his critique of Medici politics, it may be useful to be reminded of the kind of witness he was and how his circumstances contributed to his sensitivity.

The broadest pattern of Marco Parenti's career is his slow ascendancy into the patriciate. His inherited wealth, his education, and his acquaintanceship brought him into the upper reaches of society, and the achievement was sealed by a certain degree of success in public office. His marriage, though risky politically, was socially advantageous for a man who began as a relative outsider; and after the repatriation of his in-laws, this marriage became an unambiguous asset.

Marco's acceptance into the upper stratum is important, because in his generation to be outside the patriciate was essentially to be excluded from any real observation of politics—or, to put it more accurately, the only alternate post of observation was from within the circle of functionaries and literati that the Medici government relied upon. But for all his success, Marco Parenti remained a figure on the edge of patrician life, and this too is part of his value as a witness. A man who was better placed would not have had to wait three hours to get Luca Pitti's attention or felt so acutely conspicuous in the antechambers of the Neapolitan prince. For an Acciaiuoli or Neroni, a Guicciardini or Soderini, such experiences of paying court or receiving favor were the stuff of political life, but for Marco they were essays into an untried part of his nature. Hence his need to admit that he alone was unfamiliar with Pitti's mansion or to comment ironically on "playing the courtier"; hence also his willingness to rethink each encounter and examine it for clues to success or failure. As a middleman and advisor, he was obliged to report his feelings and surmises, not to retain them for himself, and so he illuminates a world where others were more at home than he was.

These instances of "marginality" are taken from Marco's letters, but it is not far-fetched to see them also as standing in the background of his most sustained effort of observation, the *Memoir.* The impulse to record history is a complex one, and though we know a great deal about the context in which Marco began to write, we know almost nothing concrete about his goals or intentions. His comparative leisure and his literary education were certainly a factor, his political involvements and access to key figures through the Strozzi were surely another. But his only direct statement about his motives is that his memoir was meant to bear witness to the refounding of liberty in Florence after Cosimo's death, and that the failure of this expectation was bound up with his sense of the failure of the work. In this way he connected his inadequacy as a historian to a sense of exclusion—"the difficulty of knowing the truth when those who govern keep secrets to themselves drew me back from diligence and from the plan that I had formed." Yet what is remarkable is that he undertook the task at all.

Despite his criticism of the Medici, he seems to have avoided making a public demonstration of his feelings—a detachment or self-protection that might not have been permitted to a citizen whose voice counted for more in civic life. In the *Memoir* he describes being invited by the Neapolitan ambassador "to go with him to the house of M. Luca and the house of Piero in order to see the state of affairs in each and what they were saying." The ambassador, Marino Tomacelli, was working for a peace between the hostile camps and counted Marco as a well-informed friend:

> He thought that I, as a citizen knowing the citizens perhaps better than he, could help him to arrive at a truer sense of what he saw and heard in order to better advise the King. And I did it willingly so as to have this means of seeing and understanding for myself as well the directions things were taking without any blame from either party.[1]

These are not the words (or the actions) of a man who sees himself as engaged in the fight. Their spirit of inquiry needs to be remembered as we read the critique of Medicean politics that makes up so large a part of the *Memoir.* Clearly Marco did not regard himself as a partisan, except in the sense of being a friend of the Neapolitan ambassador whose king was the patron and protector of Filippo Strozzi. It may be tempting to dismiss this careful neutrality, but the personal history of Marco and his Strozzi relations over the previous several years provides another perspective. For all this time, he had engaged himself to represent the exiles, and it still remained unclear which camp would best protect their interest. By appearing at the ambassador's side in the houses of Luca Pitti and Piero de' Medici, Marco seems to have been showing that his family loyalty was fundamental and would have to come before all else.

★

Marco Parenti's account of Piero de' Medici's triumph over his enemies—the largest part of which is quoted in the preceding chapter—is both straightforward and comprehensive.

[1] *Memorie,* p. 84. Marco Parenti's name does not appear among those who signed the public oath of May 1466, a petition for unity and good government

He believed that the patrician leaders had lost their homeland out of a combination of miserliness, inactivity, disorganization and timidity. At the crucial moment when it was essential to organize for their own defense, each looked to the others to spend the necessary money, and so their side was badly provisioned. The result was that their supporters wavered, and many who were sympathetic hung back from showing themselves openly. Even so, Marco insists, there was still a possibility for decisive action, as the incident at the Medici palazzo proved. But when urged by Niccolò Soderini to round up their followers and attack Piero, they held back out of an overly prudent fear of provoking the lower classes to violence.

Of the four chiefs of the opposition party, Parenti only really characterizes two: Niccolò Soderini and Luca Pitti. (He was closer to Dietisalvi Neroni and Agnolo Acciaiuoli, but perhaps familiarity itself bred neglect.) Soderini stands out as the most vivid individual in the *Memoir*, an eloquent man with a passionate, powerful personality. He was an independent who was courted by the opposition and feared by Piero, but he muddled his chance to reform Florence by chasing his own interests. Yet in the final clash it was only Soderini who fully understood the need for immediate action; and when that moment had passed, it was Soderini who—before the rest—knew the game was lost and took flight.

In contrast to his balanced and sympathetic portrait of Soderini, Parenti's view of Luca Pitti was largely negative. Pitti was clearly the leader of the opposition cavalieri [knights], but this was the result of a politic concession on the part of Neroni and Acciaiuoli. They were Pitti's superior in prudence, but they frequented his house to increase his reputation at the expense of Piero's.[2] Pitti brought with him a past history of devotion to the Medici regime that colors Parenti's views, and at the end of the history Pitti is left powerless and forlorn.

These men—Neroni, Acciaiuoli, Soderini, Pitti—lost their

---

that was in effect a show of strength for the opposition cause. See G. Pampaloni, "Il giuramento pubblico in Palazzo Vecchio a Firenze e un patto giurato degli anti-medicei, maggio 1466," *Misc. di studi in memoria di G. Cecchini: Bulletino Senese di storia patria* 71 (1964): 212–38.

[2] *Memorie*, p. 75.

struggle by acting too timidly. The Mediceans, by contrast, showed all the opposing qualities of organization, energy, and a clear sense of self-interest. Their lesson was learned in the first cycle of the struggle, when Niccolò Soderini's reforms showed them the vulnerability of their position. At this point, according to Marco, the Mediceans began to organize for their own defense, even in default of leadership from Piero. Their strategy: a petition to which they got an ever-widening circle of men to subscribe (though we also know from other sources that there were *intelligenze* or secret pacts on both sides). Later, in the second and decisive cycle of the contest, Piero himself took charge. Aided and advised by Tommaso Soderini and Nicodemo Tranchedini, he moved rapidly to summon troops, fortify his palazzo, control the city gates, and provision his followers—tactics that gave him the initiative against opponents who simply trusted that time would bring them victory.

For Marco, the Medici victory in 1466 was explicable as a tactical triumph—preparedness winning out over confusion, discipline over indiscipline. Additional elements are also present that might point to other sorts of explanation, but these do not get the sort of emphasis we might have expected from one sympathetic to the losing side. The apostasy of Pitti does not lead to an essentially conspiratorial view, only to a certain satisfaction that the results brought him no happiness. We are left to feel that Pitti abandoned a side already headed in all likelihood for failure—with the important coda that there is honor in defeat, but none in treachery. Similarly, the prominence of Milanese soldiery might have led to an external explanation of the Medici victory as something forced on Florence. But, though Marco notes that the adversaries could make little use of their Neapolitan support and chastises their royal patron for his opportunistic rapprochement with Piero, the key point remains Piero's recognition of the danger he was in and his decision to do something about it. Finally, though luck or Fortune plays some part—especially in the selection of a Signoria favorable to the Medici—Marco quickly returns us to his tactical explanation by quoting the tag, "Fortune favors the bold." Piero had earned his luck, possibly by rigging the ballots.

Each of these junctures might have provided Marco with an opportunity to exonerate the noble victims and excoriate the victors for a triumph won not by right or skill but by stealth, force, or luck. But the historian's voice is surprisingly steady in dealing with both sides. Only once does it rise to a higher pitch and that is in consideration of a third group, whose support for the regime is calculating and opportunistic.

At the first outbreak of open hostilities, Parenti categorizes a variety of responses among the citizens. First there was the large group ("molti") who desired victory for the opposition "as the party dedicated to liberty against tyranny." But these people were held back from open partisanship by their knowledge of the unpreparedness in the opposition camp—a scruple that Marco seems to find understandable, perhaps because it was his own. On the other hand, "others" moved quickly to show their support of Piero. Here two motives operated. There were some who simply favored tyranny—"la vita tirannica sfrenata e rapace." But a more numerous group of Medici supporters drew real fire. These were the people, more "modest" than the first group, who were hungry for political office and prestige, and they feared that hesitation would cost them Piero's favor. Their judgment was that the Medici would triumph because now, as in the past, they were a well-organized party facing a disorganized and disunited opponent. These opportunistic Mediceans provoke Marco's anger. They acted only for their private advantage, "forgetting the city and the civil life, public honor, and the dignity of a free republic."[3]

Marco was convinced that he had witnessed a struggle between liberty and tyranny, and his anger was aroused because so many of his fellow citizens seemed prepared to deny this larger dimension of the conflict. The struggle had pitted the dignity of a free republic against the private advantage of these citizens, and calculating self-interest had won. It seemed that many Florentines would willingly forget their traditional political values and loyalties as long as the regime could satisfy their private ends. This was the legacy of Cosimo's long domination of the city and—contrary to Marco's initial expecta-

[3] Ibid., p. 80.

tions—the citizens had not taken the opportunity offered by his death to sweep it away.

★

Like many historians who have come after him, Marco found it difficult to deal with Piero de' Medici without continually looking back to Cosimo. Piero's time was too short and his father's influence too strong. But whereas Piero's rule was clearly irksome and tyrannical, his father's self-evident stature posed harder problems. What is more, Cosimo's domination had lasted thirty years, time enough for his oppressive greatness to take on a variety of colors.

The *Memoir* opens to Cosimo's eulogy. He was "the preeminent citizen of Florence, whether in wealth or prudence or authority or power," and these qualities seem to be emphasized not diminished by the simplicity of the funeral he had requested. At this early stage Marco says nothing of the negative implications of Cosimo's eminence, preferring to dwell instead on the opposition that was building up against Piero, who decided nonetheless to "assume the primacy [principato] like his father."[4]

The benevolent image of Cosimo early in the *Memoir* is shaped by Marco's need for a foil to his view of Piero and it underlines Marco's sense that Piero's power was both less secure and less benign than his father's.[5] Later in the manuscript, however, Marco presents a far more critical assessment.

[4] Ibid., p. 2.

[5] This is made particularly clear in a second favorable reference to Cosimo coupled with criticism of his son. It comes in connection with the economic instability of 1464 and the wave of bankruptcies that followed. Parenti was far from adopting the conspiratorial view of this event later popularized by Machiavelli, according to whom the bankruptcies were caused by Piero's calling in of his credits, as advised by a cunning and treacherous Dietisalvi Neroni. Marco believed more simply that Piero himself was financially vulnerable and would also have fallen had not others been afraid to demand their money. But, although Piero was not the cause of the financial crisis, he did appear to take pleasure in the troubles of the other merchants, "almost like one envious of the rich." And public opinion held that Cosimo, had he still been alive, would have put both his prudence and his credit to work to save the city from this disaster (*Memorie*, pp. 16–17).

Once again Cosimo appears in juxtaposition with other figures, but now these are calculated to bring out some of the negative features of his authority. The first is Francesco Sforza, Cosimo's powerful ally in Milan; the second is Neri Capponi, a leading Florentine politician regarded by many as Cosimo's only real rival.

These juxtapositions occur in a long digression on the rise of Francesco Sforza. Introduced as a "brief discourse" presenting "a memorable example of virtue and good fortune," this discussion in fact takes up almost a third of the manuscript as we now have it. Starting with the career of Sforza from soldier to duke, Marco is drawn into an extensive account of mid-century politics and diplomacy whose central subject is the Medici-Sforza alliance.[6] In this sense, the "brief discourse" proves less digressive than it first seemed, and it provides Marco an opportunity to reassess Cosimo's political legacy.

Sforza's remarkable career first presents itself to Marco's mind as an exemplary history of a man whose virtues triumphed over the misfortune of low birth.[7] This path, had Marco followed it, might have led him to something like Machiavelli's life of Castruccio Castracani. Instead, he outlines the wars and maneuvers that made Sforza the outstanding captain of his day and gave him the hand of the daughter of the last Visconti duke. With Visconti's death, a three-way struggle began between Sforza, the Venetians, and the Milanese republic, and Marco's view of Sforza becomes decidedly less heroic. Though contracted to defend Milan, Sforza se-

[6] The "digression" does not follow on the death of Francesco Sforza, which might have been more suitable if the purpose were simply an exemplary discourse on the life of an outstanding man. Instead Parenti launches into the lengthy retrospect in connection with the young Galeazzo Sforza's demand for a renewal of the Florentine subsidy to his late father, a demand that raised the issue of the future of the Florentine-Milanese alliance.

[7] "It seems to me a great thing to consider that a lordship so great and worthy as the dukedom of Milan should fall to the hands of a man of low birth, such as the Count Francesco, the illegitimate son of Sforzo of Cutignola, a humble castle in the Romagna, and Sforzo the son of a humble father from such a place. Therefore it occurs to me to write a brief discourse on the way in which Count Francesco came to be the duke of Milan as a memorable example of virtue and good fortune" (*Memorie*, pp. 40–41).

cretly came to an agreement with the Venetians: "setting aside good faith and loyalty which required him as their captain to protect the Milanese, he wrongfully turned against them to seize from them that liberty which he was obliged to defend in order to make himself their lord."[8]

These remarks made it clear how far Marco had moved from his stated purpose in presenting Sforza's history: the virtuous captain had revealed himself to be an ambitious and unscrupulous politician. But Marco was really less interested in the isolated figure of Sforza than in the significance of Sforza's rise for Florence itself. This point is made in an incident that immediately follows his unfavorable characterization of the count.

Venice, alarmed by Sforza's rapid military success, had proposed a new accord by which they would divide the Milanese territory between them. The proposal troubled Sforza and he turned to Florence for advice. He especially looked to his old ally Cosimo, "whose power in the city he had always supported by the force of his arms, while Cosimo did the same for the count. An abundance of public money was extended to him on the authority of Cosimo, who, because of his own great wealth, even drew on his own funds." Mutual assistance had made them great friends, "each one lending the other his power and money, by which they made themselves fearful to everyone else."[9]

It happened that Sforza's emissaries arrived in Florence to seek advice at a time when the city was troubled with plague and most of the citizens had taken refuge in the countryside. Scattered in their villas, the Florentines had time to ponder their own responses to Sforza's request. There were three schools of thought. Cosimo wanted Sforza to pursue his effort to take Milan, alleging that it benefited the city to have so powerful a friend in Milan who could be a brake on the power of Venice. Others maintained that Sforza should accept the pact because he would not be able to resist Venice on his own. But this argument, like Cosimo's, was really a cover. Their

[8] *Memorie*, pp. 54–55.
[9] Ibid., pp. 55–56.

true reasons had to do with the interests of Florence itself. Their hope was to diminish Sforza's power in order to strike at Cosimo's, which was "interlinked with his own." Cosimo's position was already "insupportable to many generous citizens," and they feared that to make Sforza the duke of Milan "would strengthen both of them so much that our city would be left in a state near to servitude."

A third group accepted the arguments of the second, but carried them still further in one respect. They believed

> that to secure a better form of rule and a more peaceful Italy it would be well to wipe out the tyranny of Milan and to assist the growth—already begun—of a third powerful free city; and it would be the third one between us and the Venetians. And since the space between Florence and Venice, and from Venice to Milan, and from Milan to Florence is quasi equidistant in the form of a triangle, in this way on every side, like a point, there would be a powerful city to keep the peace of Italy strong, the third one always counterbalancing the other two if they wished to clash.[10]

It is evident that in Marco's mind the first of these three views stood for nothing else but the self-interest of the Medici, while the second was subsumed in the third. The latter position, with the weight and elaboration Marco gives it, can safely be taken as his own. It is a splendid vision of liberty and peace in Italy protected by the counterbalancing (*contrapesando*) of the three cities. We recognize the doctrine that comes to be called "the balance of power." In diplomatic practice it has its roots in the success of the Peace of Lodi in 1454—the time of Marco Parenti's one term on the Signoria—and is particularly associated with the policies of Lorenzo de' Medici in his maturity.

The idea of the balance of power took some time to develop. Bernardo Rucellai is usually credited with its first full articulation, a half-century after Lodi.[11] But Marco had already grasped the essence of the idea, and in one respect he surpasses

[10] Ibid., p. 57.

[11] E. W. Nelson, "The Origins of Modern Balance of Power Politics," *Medievalia et Humanistica* 1 (1943).

even Rucellai. His image of an equilateral triangle of cities—each potentially a counterweight to the quarrels or ambitions of the other two—gives the idea extraordinary visual clarity and geometrical simplicity. It seems to be a projection on the map of northern Italy of the abstract vision seen in the ideal cityscapes of the same age.

It is worth noting that a similar linkage of liberty and the balance of power appeared in Venice during the late 1440s, the period Marco was describing. Francesco Barbaro, the Venetian patrician and humanist, wrote that with the death of the last Visconti duke, Venice faced a choice, "either to enlarge our dominion or to augment common liberty and save the peace of Italy." He hoped that Venice had not "called the people of Milan to liberty" for reasons of self-aggrandizement and he added that they had put their trust "more in the balance of things than in arms." Barbaro's words, when linked to Parenti's, suggest the sympathy that the "Ambrosian Republic" in Milan evoked in both sister republics. But in Barbaro's Venice as in Parenti's Florence harder heads won out.[12]

Marco Parenti himself was well aware that his vision of liberty and peaceful equilibrium represented a political ideal, not the ordinary plane of Medici rule. In fact he did what he could to dramatize this gap by moving with calculated suddenness from the free thoughts of Florentines scattered in their country homes to the depressing reality of their subservience once gathered again in Florence. Called together by the Signoria in a consultative council [Pratica] to make a reply to Sforza, "they all exerted themselves to guess the opinion of Cosimo and—little or nothing else being discussed—they turned their support to it so as not to displease him." Sforza was duly advised to press his war against the Milanese and given the financial assistance he needed to carry on.

[12] Barbaro's ideas are discussed at some length in H. Baron, *The Crisis of the Early Italian Renaissance* (Princeton, 1966), pp. 396ff. See also G. Pillinini, *Storia del principio di equilibrio* (Venice, 1973), and his earlier article, "Francesco Barbaro e l'origine della politica di equilibrio," *Archivio Veneto* 94 (1963): 23–28.

Thus Sforza got the expected advice and took the expected action. In this sense, the Pratica was a nonevent and a traditional chronicler might well have passed it by. But Marco, with his slow elaboration of the alternative views, wants to call attention to the road not taken in order to display the servility of the Florentines. Cosimo had succeeded in neutralizing their traditional institutions and smothering their political instincts. Assembled in the council chamber, they lacked the collective will to carry through the ideals that as individual citizens they might still contemplate in the privacy of the countryside.[13]

★

Marco was convinced that Medici domination threatened Florentines with "a state near to servitude." But, though the tendency of Cosimo's authority was to move toward tyranny, the actual balance of forces was not fixed. This would be shown most clearly by the reaction that followed Cosimo's death, but even while he was alive the balance had sometimes swung in the other direction. In those years there had been at least one leader—Neri di Gino Capponi—capable of counterbalancing Cosimo's authority and sustaining the old republican traditions.

We saw in an earlier chapter that Marco looked back on his brief period as a prior at the time of Lodi with a proud sense that he and his colleagues had challenged the regime by declaring an early end to the wars. The passage is worth repeating in this new context:

[13] The whole episode recalls a familiar one in the work of a slightly earlier Florentine historian, Giovanni Cavalcanti, in which Cavalcanti recounts his disillusionment at a *pratica* session. I have discussed Cavalcanti's disenchantment and its connection to a motif in Florentine historiography in my essay, "The Disenchanted Witness: Participation and Alienation in Florentine Historiography," *Journal of the History of Ideas* (1983): 191–206. Cavalcanti's conclusion was that "many were elected to office, but few to rule." Capponi's *Ricordi* includes a similar pronouncement: "Li uffici sono in più numero fussino mai: lo stato in meno" (Muratori, *Rerum Italicarum Scriptores* 18, col. 1149).

> It seemed to the citizens a recovery of some measure of liberty, being freed from the servitude of the accoppiatori, whom the priors that they themselves had selected were bound to support. The accoppiatori and those who backed them having lost their authority, the others lost their fear, and they dared from time to time to do something worthwhile on their own accord, without first asking those whom they were accustomed to regard as the chief citizens.[14]

In this sudden outburst of liberating energy we have a precise counterpart to the servility of the Pratica. It is evident that for Marco the renewal of liberty was first of all a recovery of political will. Only then did the constitutional reforms follow with the termination of the Balìa and the sealing of the electoral purses (*borse*).

The change in the political atmosphere after Lodi did not overthrow Cosimo's power, but it did bring "some measure of liberty." Though Cosimo remained preeminent (*principalissimo*), he held back, waiting for the "time and occasion" that would allow him to return to his "being feared" as before. For Parenti, this temporary weakening of Cosimo's position is an opportunity to introduce a rival politician whose prestige was a significant check against complete Medici domination. This was Neri di Gino Capponi. His portrait serves Marco—as it also did Cavalcanti and Machiavelli—as a way of casting an oblique light on some of the harsher features of Cosimo himself.[15]

At this time, Marco writes, there were in Florence a number of highly respected citizens with great skill in government. These men did not oppose Cosimo, "but they supported him only lightly, not being at all displeased with the recovery of a vigorous spirit among the people." The exception, and they

[14] Parenti, *Memorie*, p. 63.

[15] Machiavelli writes at the beginning of book 7: "There were in Florence, as we have frequently observed, two principally powerful citizens, Cosimo de' Medici and Neri Capponi. Neri acquired his influence by public services; so that he had many friends but few partisans. Cosimo being able to avail himself both of public and private means, had many partisans as well as friends" (*History of Florence*, intro. W. Dunne [New York, 1960], p. 311).

were only a few, were those whose standing depended entirely on Cosimo, men "much inclined to plunder and to exploitation of power." By contrast those whose nobility, virtue, and antiquity depended only on themselves welcomed the loss of Cosimo's reputation, thinking that it would increase their own. And among men of this type, Neri di Gino Capponi stood out, both "for the nobility of his house, the worthiness of his father, and his own virtue."[16]

As banker, magistrate, diplomat, and military leader, Neri Capponi combined in himself the whole range of civic duties. But Parenti's description of this outstanding citizen does not become an ideal portrait in the classical manner. Rather he celebrates Neri above all as a counterweight to the oppressive tendencies of Cosimo's power: Cosimo did not personally fear Neri, Marco writes, but held him in considerable esteem and "would not lightly have made him an enemy." Instead, Cosimo "supported him, and kept a certain brake on himself, if he had any ambition that might displease the others that might give them occasion to back Neri as a leader against himself."

All this is easily recognized as a buildup to Neri's death, which would give Cosimo the freedom to reestablish his complete dominance. Neri was deeply mourned by the populace, "to whom it seemed that they had lost a great shield of their liberty, as quickly proved true. Any doubts Cosimo had of resistance to his plans for governing the city were over, and

[16] Parenti, like Machiavelli, stresses Capponi's public services. His knowledge of the other Italian powers and his wide experience in dealing with *signori*, captains, and armies gave Capponi a key role in embassies, and as a military commissioner he was greatly respected by Florence's soldiery, "among whom he had such a high reputation that they revered and followed him no less than their own captains." But in times of peace he was no less valued. "A skilled merchant in commerce and exchange," Capponi served on magistracies dealing with such matters and was known for his prudence and judiciousness. Petitioners sought him out and he was expert in settling disputes, a skill that was useful to the Commune when money had to be raised in time of war. "All these qualities," concludes Parenti, "gave him much good will among the people and the men at arms" (*Memorie*, pp. 63–64).

he began to think how the *popolo* might be brought under his control as before." Even so, with the purses sealed, it took a year for a properly partisan priorate to emerge. In 1458, under the leadership of Luca Pitti, a virtual coup took place. A parlamento was staged and power was given over to a Balìa, but not before armed troops had poured through the city, "with much terror, passing by Cosimo's house on the way to the piazza, shouting '*Palle, Palle,*' which is the Medici crest, frightening everyone who heard it, not unlike a Signore when he seizes a town."[17]

Luca Pitti's stewardship was evidently the promised "time and occasion" for which Cosimo had been waiting since Lodi, and Pitti himself is seen as the embodiment of all that is wrong with factional politics.[18] He had been a poor man, but having been one of the priors who secured Cosimo's return from exile in 1434, his political and financial fortune was made. In consequence Pitti was "entirely devoted to Cosimo and therefore overbearing and prepared to do anything for Cosimo's government without respect for any other consideration." This description immediately recalls Marco's earlier division of the citizens into two groups: those whose "nobility, virtue, and antiquity depended only on themselves," against the others "every part of whose greatness depended entirely on Cosimo." Evidently, just as Neri Capponi had represented the patrician independence of the first group, Luca Pitti stood for the ruthless partisanship of the second, and the parlamento of 1458 was his triumph.

The parlamento of 1458 brings to an end the cycle of events that began with Lodi, and, in turn, closely parallels the central cycle of the *Memoir*, the rise and fall of liberty in 1464–1466. In each case, Florence swung from authority toward a partial liberty and back again; in each a combination of popular enthusiasm and patrician leadership won some victories but could not sustain itself against the superior energy, organi-

[17] *Memorie*, pp. 65–66.

[18] A view that is revived in Machiavelli's account of the factional excesses of Cosimo's last years when the old leader's authority waned. See *History of Florence*, p. 313.

zation, and outright coercion of the Medici party. How conscious was Marco of this parallel? Possibly his "brief discourse" was intended as nothing more than what he calls it, "this digression to fill in the background of the acquisition of Milan by Duke Francesco and the succession of Galeazzo, his son."[19] Even so this doubling of a major element in his account shows the consistency of his preoccupation with Florentine liberty.

Yet if Marco's view of Medici power was steadily critical, it did not rigidify into simple polemic. This is most evident in Marco's treatment of the last chapter of Cosimo's life, the years from 1458 until his death in 1464. To Machiavelli this seemed a time of unbridled factionalism when the regime became "unbearable and violent, because Cosimo, already old and weary and weakened by bad health, was not able to be present at public business in his usual way: hence a few citizens plundered the city."[20] But perhaps Cosimo's contemporaries found it easier to acknowledge his greatness in these final years. Vespasiano's admiring and nostalgic portrait seems to reflect this late period and Marco himself presents an unexpectedly benign view, not simply of the man himself, but of his fatherly, protective influence on the times.

In the aftermath of the disturbances of 1458, Marco writes, men stood in suspense, "waiting to see how Cosimo wished to use his power, since it seemed he could decide to move things in any direction he wished." Reforms in the distribution of taxes and offices—the two principal parts of the city, Marco calls them—quieted their fears, and the Florentines turned with relief to their own lives and businesses. Here Marco echoes a long line of Florentine chroniclers for whom the reopening of the workshops is a sure sign of the restoration of peace to their industrious city. But Cosimo, great businessman that he was, had it in his power to stimulate business as well as protect it. The threat to his position having been overcome, "it seemed that ill will was put aside, and he turned himself toward the good of the city." He favored the merchants

[19] *Memorie*, p. 70.

[20] *History of Florence*, p. 313.

and quickly brought order to the Monte so that, after many unprofitable years, it became lucrative again to its investors. The consequence was an abundance of money and the quickening of commerce.[21]

Here Parenti, with admirable pragmatism, reverses an earlier argument. Where previously he had seen Capponi's reputation as balancing and containing Cosimo's to the benefit of the city, he now argues that undisputed enjoyment of power made Cosimo benevolent. But whatever the explanation, Marco was sure of the effect: "Merchandise of every type and from everywhere abounded. Houses and possessions rose in value more than one could ever remember. The Monte rose from a very depressed price—for a long time it had been as low as 12, 11, or 10 percent—to as much as 30 percent." Not for a long time, he concluded, had anyone seen the city in such prosperity.

As a man whose cast of mind was fundamentally traditional and mercantile, Parenti found it easy (easier than Machiavelli did, for instance) to celebrate these economic achievements, and he went on to list the signs of the city's commercial prosperity: the profusion of festivals, jousts, plays, weddings, balls, and dinners, all graced by splendid decorations and women outfitted in silks, embroideries, pearls, and jewels, the youths attending in the richest liveries, and the older men dignified by robes of rose-colored, purple, or black wool, along with silks of every color and the richest linings.

The responsibility for all this was not Cosimo's alone: "This prosperity was owning to the goodness of the times, due to the league and the peace that held throughout Italy." Even so, Parenti was willing to give Cosimo every credit for being an architect of the league and a protector of the peace. He insisted, nonetheless, that Florentines believed they had lost more than they had gained under Cosimo's tutelage, however benevolent. He was sure that Florence set a higher value on its liberty than on anything else:

> And nevertheless, on his death everyone rejoiced, such is the

[21] *Memorie*, pp. 67–68.

love of and desire for liberty. It appeared to the Florentines that from his way of governing they had experienced a certain subjection and servitude, from which they believed his death would liberate them. This they desired and in this they delighted, putting off thought of any other good that they enjoyed.[22]

Marco Parenti found Cosimo a larger and more troubling figure than his son. With Cosimo there was room for some shifting of emphasis over the different stages of life, for a complexity in the final assessment reached at his death, that Piero did not require. The difficulty with Piero was simply that his story could not really be separated from his father's. As a result—though in a somewhat clumsy fashion—the history had to expand itself to incorporate the repeated cycle of liberties won and lost, and the *Memoir* acquired an extra dimension that Marco probably had not at first envisaged.

★

Marco had begun his work "in the belief that in the future it would be our task to write about the affairs of a free city and of men who would become better citizens because they were tired of the servitude of previous times." It would be easy to consent to his own sense of frustration and emphasize the obvious limitations of the work. But Marco had taken up this ambitious task with a good deal of energy, one sign of which is his willingness to pursue the earlier history of Francesco Sforza and Cosimo de' Medici—that is "the servitude of previous times." His sincere attachment to threatened civic traditions gives the *Memoir* a sense of conviction without the narrowness of simple partisanship. The result is a better understanding of the sources of resistance to Piero de' Medici's authority as well as the reasons for his ultimate victory.

We have assigned Marco Parenti a modest place in the long line of Florentine historical writing and political thought. But against the rather barren background of the second half of the fifteenth century, when the traditional commitment of Flor-

[22] Ibid., p. 69.

entine citizens to writing the history of their own times seemed to be flickering, the *Memoir* deserves more interest. Only Alamanno Rinuccini, whose priorista will be examined in the next chapter, produced anything comparable. Otherwise, the most articulate voices of the time were committed to praising the Medici and rationalizing the changes that were transforming Florentine citizenship.

For whom, then, does Marco Parenti speak? In part the value of the *Memoir* lies simply in its dissent from the general chorus of praise—a resistance that points to later renewals of republican feeling in the last decade of the century and beyond. But even in its own time and despite its relative isolation, the *Memoir* convinces us of its centrality. Marco's whole biography is evidence that his was hardly a voice crying in the wilderness, and his book has nothing of the eccentricity or rage that marked Cavalcanti's histories a generation earlier.[23] On the contrary, Marco was firmly grounded in the common sense of his society. His *Memoir* shows how troubled Florentines continued to be by the growing threat to their traditional sense of citizenship. Other, more scattered signs can be found elsewhere—in the minutes of debates in the Pratica, in the occasional private letter, or simply in the events themselves. But the virtue of Marco's history is that it articulates these feelings at some length even while representing the crisis that brought them to the fore.

[23] See D. Kent, "The Importance of Being Eccentric: Giovani Cavalcanti's view of Cosimo de' Medici's Florence," *Journal of Medieval and Renaissance Studies* 9 (1979): 101–32.

CHAPTER 12

THE "CONSPIRACY" OF 1466: OTHER VIEWS

★

EVERY MAJOR upheaval in Florentine history produced its flurry of records and commentaries. A scattering of partisans, participants, ordinary citizens with an eye for politics or a diary to fill, as well as those who for one reason or another had committed themselves to longer narratives about their city, recorded their own version of events. This impulse had slackened in the mid-fifteenth century, in part because of the widening gulf between the ordinary citizen and the inner circle of government, in part because of a comparable literary gulf between the language of everyday life and the new, exalted conception of historiographical prose. Even so, the disturbances following Cosimo's death were too important to go unrecorded. The events of 1466 are traced in a small group of *ricordi* and histories, largely written from the perspective of the winning side, and these contemporary views became the basis for a long tradition of pro-Medicean accounts. The reconfirmation of Medici power in 1466 can also be felt, though more subtly, outside of the immediate historiographical reactions. Two philosophical dialogues that debate the value of active citizenship in the new climate provide a further perspective on the political experience of Marco Parenti's generation. Like the *Memoir* itself, these writings—ricordi, histories, and dialogues—express the preoccupations of a time of transition, when Florentine political consciousness was registering but also resisting the force of new realities.

The only real companion to Marco Parenti's *Memoir* is the chronicle kept by his friend Alamanno Rinuccini. The two men belonged to the same patrician intellectual circle that gathered around Argyropulos, but Rinuccini, a member of an old and prominent family, possessed social and educational advantages well beyond Marco's. In the mid-1450s his home was a gathering point for these young men—the same ones who met in Franco Sacchetti's villa for days spent in "discussion of literature or of the governing of republics." Marco's correspondence shows that two decades later the two men retained the acquaintance begun at this time.

Rinuccini's chronicle took the form of a *priorista*—a listing of the names of successive slates of priors, followed by brief notations of memorable items that occurred during their two-month term of office. It might be thought that so traditional, even primitive a form of history writing would have no appeal to a man of Rinuccini's classical taste. But the chronicle had been begun by his father, and he himself kept it faithfully for thirty years before handing it on to his brother. In Alamanno's hands the family chronicle became a place to record the iniquities of Medici power. Its brief, uncomplicated form and semiprivate character gave him free reign and the result is a dry record intermittently illuminated by flashes of patrician anger.

Rinuccini was both prouder and more self-confident than Marco Parenti, but he recorded a version of events that—though far more sketchy—is very similar. For Rinuccini too the contest was between Piero de' Medici and those who wanted "to return the people to liberty." Piero "was impatient with the freedom [vivere libero] of the city; his opponents had the support of "all the good citizens and the people." But Piero acted more decisively and made better provision. He alleged that troops were being collected by the other side, but it was clear that he had planned some time ahead to bring in arms. In this way he showed that he had "a spirit more tyrannical than civil." It was believed that he tampered with the electoral purses, ensuring the victory of his own men, and he secretly persuaded Luca Pitti to change sides. Without the authority of the Signoria, he took control of the gate of San Gallo, guarded the piazza, and continually brought in armed men, further signs of tyranny.

This could stand as a summary of Marco Parenti's longer and more complex narrative. Only in one way does Rinuccini take his account further and that is in his insistence on underlining the lesson of the story. Citing evidence that Piero de' Medici had long wanted to stage a parlamento, he concluded that:

> one can see that the spirit of Piero and of his followers was not content to live as a citizen, but always desired to rule [signoreggiare]. Because of which, if anyone should ever read these things, I urge and admonish you if you want to live in liberty never to allow any citizen in the republic to grow so great that he is more powerful than the laws. The appetite of man is so insatiable that if a man is more powerful than is proper, the more he will want and desire what is not legitimate.[1]

The anti-Medicean views of Marco Parenti and Alamanno Rinuccini had no immediate echo in Florentine historiography. Instead the disturbances of 1465–1466 have been seen through the eyes of the victors. From the outset there was an "official view" of the upheavals, shaped by the triumphant party, embellished by apologetic histories written in the subsequent decades and carried into the mainstream of Florentine historical writing by both Guicciardini and Machiavelli. These accounts projected a view of the "Pittian conspiracy" compounded of dark ambition, premeditated violence, and conspiracy in foreign places.

The elements of the Medicean case are all present in a manuscript containing some brief memoranda (ricordi) of the affair set down by Iacopo di Niccolò di Cocco Donati, a committed Medicean who sat on the priorate of July and August 1466. For Iacopo the upheavals were quite simply the result

[1] Alamanno Rinuccini, *Ricordi storici di Filippo di Cino Rinuccini dal 1282 al 1460 colla continuazione di Alamanno e Neri suoi figli*, ed. G. Aiazzi (Florence, 1840), pp. 100–104.

of a conspiracy between ambitious men and their foreign backers. Three-quarters of the politically active citizens supported Piero, but Luca Pitti allowed himself to be drawn into opposition by "unbridled passion and the importunities" of his co-conspirators. Together they plotted with the duke of Modena to "overthrow the government and expel the aforesaid Piero di Cosimo and many of his principal supporters, among whom I was one." Fortunately warning came to the Signoria from Bologna, so that they were able to prevent the manifest danger of "the destruction of the city and the loss of liberty."[2]

[2] B.N.F., Strozziane VIII, 1439, fols. 68v–71r. The text begins: "Ricordo come io scriptore Iacopo di nicholo di chocho donati mi trovai del numero de' signori chi entrorono a dì primo di luglio 1466." In addition to his brief memoir of the tumults of 1466, Iacopo records the public oath of May 1466 (on which see G. Pampaloni, "Il giuramento pubblico in Palazzo Vecchio a Firenze e un patto giurato degli anti-medicei, maggio 1466," *Misc. di studi in memoria di G. Cecchini: Bulletino Senese di storia patria*, 3d ser., vol. 22–24, pp. 212–38). He also includes two sonnets of his own composition dedicated respectively to Piero de' Medici and Mona Lucrezia, Piero's wife. The final couplet of the former reads, "Che s' una volta ci venissi errato / Firenze perderia suo bello stato."

Three other manuscript chronicles should be noted. The first is A.S.F. *Manoscritti* 120, "Copie di note scritte in un priorista fatto da Bernardo Lotti." The account is typically brief and bare, but it does contain an outline of events and a sharp remark on the arrogance of Piero de' Medici. Lotti was in the Signoria during this period, and Marco Parenti considers him an anti-Medicean. In fact Lotti takes a centrist position in which the main concern seems to be the restitution of order:

> Al tempo dei Signori di Luglio e Agosto Piero di Cosimo de' Medici aveva poca intelligentia con Mess. Luca Pitti, et essendo 2 potenti Signorili cittadini, havevano divisa la città, e digià per ambitione venuti all' arme che ciascuno di loro teneva in casa . . . li veniva per la città et in piazza soldati a loro devotione e per diligentia che con loro usassino, e' Priori non si poteva reprimer' la loro forza, per il che furono forzati e' priori a far' venir' gente che guardassino la città. Et ciascuno era in sul arme et era tanta la licentia o grandezza di Piero de' Medici che se bene la Signoria mandava per lui, non vi andava, et a sua posta haveva la chiave delle porte.
>
> Achadde che addì 29 di Agosto havendo fatto la Signoria disarmare Luca Pitti, detto M. Luca andò a visitar' Piero de' Medici a casa, e stettono assai insieme soli e si tiene che rimanessino daccordo intra di loro, e che Mess. Luca ne andasse indietro alla volontà di Piero per quello che poi successe, perchè mai Piero di disarmò la sua casa per diligentia che facessino e' Priori.

This was the first indictment against the anti-Mediceans and it was repeated in the Signoria's decree of exile: namely, that the opposition had conspired with foreign powers against Florentine liberty. But Iacopo—unlike the Signoria—coupled

---

E stando la citta [ ] dì cosi, finalmente la Signoria ordinò che alli 2 di settembre vedendo i molti amutinamenti, Gio. di Cardinale di Piero Rucellai e Filippo di Ser Francesco di Ser Filippo da (?) e Bartholomeo di Niccolò d' Ugolino Martelli, [e Bernardo di Francesco di Bernardo Paganelli], signori tutti cogniti di tal confusione et huomini di somma prudenza e governo, risolverno [volseno] si facessi publico parlamento, al quale questi sopradetti 4 grandi republichisti avevano già provvisto e fatto venir quietamente circa 4 mila fanti acciò che guardassino la piazza e la città . . . (fols. 246ʳ–248ʳ; bracketed phrases are interlinear).

Lotti's account needs to be treated with caution since there are some evident interpolations; even so, it does seem useful as a voice from the palazzo.

Another manuscript source of some interest is the "Diario di Goro di Giovanni, donzello della Signoria di Firenze" (B.N.F., Strozz. XXV, 518). According to the "donzello," the cause of the disturbance was the attack on the Council of 100: "e questo era solo per volere levare via il chonsiglio del 100, overo la balìa e dimenuire alchuna alturità aveva detto consiglio." Here again the perspective is that of the palazzo, and Goro has some particular information on the division of the priors. Like Lotti, he emphasizes the unwillingness of Piero's side to disarm: "La Signoria mandò molti aspri bandi per la città sotto pena delle forche a qualunche che avesse presa l'arme la dovesse posare giù e dare licenza a tuti i forestieri e chontadini. En questo modo istettoro per che lla nuova signoria ebe preso l'uficio sanza ubidire a veruno bando mandato, ma tutavia veniva gente nuova i' favhore di piero di chosimo; e venuto a dì 2 di settembre e a ore 18 vene in sulla piazza de' signori molti fanti forestieri e presono tutte le bocche della detta piaza, e di poi a ore 19 venono i' piaza molti ischuadre di fanti a piedi balestieri e i schoppettieri palvesini e lancie lunghe bene armati di numero di più di 3000 fanti. . . . e fermi tutti i battaglia i' sulla piaza, chominciò la champana a sonare a parlamento" (fol. 152).

A third account, which sees these events from a very different vantage, is the diary of Ser Giusto d'Anghiari: B.N.F. II, ii, 127, entitled "Cronica o memorie dal 1437 al 1487," fols. 33–140. This is a seventeenth-century copy by Sen. Strozzi and seems more complete than another version of this diary found in B.N.F. NA 982. Ser Giusto, who was secretary to one of the territorial nobility, records news of events in Florence as well as interviews and contracts with Luca Pitti and Piero and Lorenzo de' Medici. In late August when events came to a head, he records receiving a letter from Piero de' Medici asking Giusto's master for help, thus giving us a brief glimpse of the way in which manpower was mobilized in the countryside to fight the factional battle (cf. fol. 85).

it with a second allegation of violence. It seems that Dietisalvi Neroni maneuvered to have Piero withdraw to his villa at Careggi (and did the same himself) while the new Signoria was being drawn. Piero was deceived by "false and wicked oaths and a simulated peace," he wrote, "since it is held certain that they had arranged to assassinate him at Careggi." But since God did not want to see such wickedness, Piero soon decided to return to the city, thus evading the plot.

The certainty that the anti-Mediceans had planned to murder Piero on the road from Careggi to Florence became a prominent part of the case against them. Piero himself wrote in a letter that Francesco Neroni had confessed as much when he was captured. In fact Neroni's confession speaks only of wanting to exile Piero, not kill him, and the absence of the charge from the official condemnation increases one's skepticism. Marco Parenti, as we have already seen, knew the story, but vehemently rejected it. It was a ruse, he wrote, deliberately concocted by Piero to justify his sudden return to Florence surrounded "with many armed men."[3] But true or false, the existence of such a plot became part of the common knowledge of the day. Luca Landucci, a contemporary diarist whose political knowledge went no further than what could be seen or heard in the marketplace, refers to the assassination plot with simple matter-of-factness and later, more sophisticated observers showed no more hesitation.[4]

Iacopo di Cocco Donati's ricordi express the essentials of the Medicean case. But Iacopo wrote simply as a witness to the events, giving testimony to God's favor and his party's virtue. It did not occur to him—in contrast to Marco Parenti—to claim the larger role of historian. In an earlier age extensive narratives were often composed by ordinary citizens like Iacopo, but in the second half of the quattrocento this was seldom the case. The prestige of classical culture was such

[3] See his account in ch. 10 above. See N. Rubinstein, "La confessione di Francesco Neroni e la congiura anti medicea del 1466," *Archivio storico italiano* (1968): 373–85, for a discussion of the truthfulness of the alleged murder plot.

[4] Luca Landucci, *Diario fiorentino dal 1450 al 1516*, ed. I. del Badia (Florence, 1883), p. 9.

that history writing had become a specialist art, best undertaken by those trained in composition. In fact, two Latin histories of the upheavals of 1466 were composed in the following decades and both were strongly pro-Medicean. They stand in useful contrast to Marco Parenti's vernacular memoir.

The first (and more considerable) of these two histories is *De discordiis florentinorum liber—A Book Concerning the Dissensions of the Florentines*. It is a little-known work of the minor humanist Benedetto Colucci, and it was given its first and only publication in the mid-eighteenth century. Colucci came from a relatively poor family in Pistoia, a neighboring town long under Florentine control. In typical humanist fashion, he earned his living as a teacher and functionary, pursuing a somewhat itinerant career in Pistoia, Empoli, Florence, and Bologna. He had neither the range nor talent of a Cristoforo Landino, nor the political and bureaucratic usefulness of a Bartolomeo Scala, but like them and so many others he cultivated letters and wealthy patrons—including the Medici—in search of advancement. Though little is known specifically about the composition of his history, clearly it grew out of this context.

Colucci's history belongs to the growing literature of praise for Cosimo de' Medici and his family. According to an excellent study of this tradition, the eulogistic literature on Cosimo grew up in three clear stages. In the first half of the century, humanists like Bruni and Poggio praised Cosimo as "a practical Roman statesman." This was in sharp contrast to the "epic praises" humanists elsewhere in Italy lavished on their patrons.[5] A similar restraint also marked the second generation, which came to prominence in the 1450s and 1460s. These were the literary patricians of Marco Parenti's own circle and they exalted Cosimo for his embellishment of the city and his support of learning. For Alamanno Rinuccini, Cosimo was the man who had brought Argyropulos to Florence out of his "incredible love of learning," and for Donato

[5] A. Brown, "The Humanist Portrait of Cosimo de' Medici, Pater Patriae," *Journal of the Warburg and Courtauld Institutes* 24 (1961), pp. 188, 204.

Acciaiuoli he was the father of learned men, their patron, friend and helper.[6] But a younger generation of poets, philosophers, and humanists—men like Marsilio Ficino, Cristoforo Landino, or Bartolomeo Scala—lacked the independent social position of the patricians. Influenced by Neoplatonic ideas, they refashioned the image of Cosimo: he was a ruler to be compared to Augustus, a modern Maecenas, "the cultivator of religion and patron of philosophy."[7]

The impulse behind this rising chorus of praise was primarily literary and philosophical rather than political. But in this more and more courtly intellectual environment it was inevitable that historical writing too would take on an apologetic role, as it does in Colucci's narrative. His vision of the Medici family is uniformly exalted. At the outset Colucci expresses his feeling that Cosimo's greatness was such he might have been inspired to write Cosimo's biography, were it not that he felt inadequate to the task. Instead he limited himself to an idealized portrayal of Cosimo's final hours. First there is the gathering of the leading citizens at the villa at Careggi. To them Cosimo spoke so eloquently about the need for peace that even his secret enemies wished him a longer life. Then the dying man spoke privately with his son, giving him instructions for the simple funeral he desired, though what else "such a great father told such a great son" is not known to mortals. Finally, Cosimo gathered the churchmen around him. He had done with worldly talk, he said, and "spoke of divine matters so divinely that those who were present thought of him not as a politician but as a most fertile metaphysician."[8]

[6] Ibid., p. 198.

[7] Ibid., p. 186.

[8] B. Colucci, *De discordiis florentinorum*, ed. L. Mehus (Florence, 1747), pp. 6–8. On Colucci's career, see A. della Torre, *Accademia Platonica* (Florence, 1902), pp. 706–712, 805–808; and A. Frugoni, *Scritti inediti di Benedetto Colucci da Pistoia* (Florence, 1939). I am grateful to Alison Brown for first having drawn my attention to this little-known work as well as to my student and research assistant Mary Belgraver for many stimulating and useful discussions of this text. Some of the points I develop here were first brought out in her seminar paper on Colucci.

This deathbed scene amounts to representing Cosimo as something more than simply a great man or hero, as Machiavelli, for instance, would do. Machiavelli's hero is a man of pragmatic shrewdness and "utmost prudence"; Colucci's is one who sheds the dross of politics as he faces death, to become a man of peace and a saintly metaphysician. His death is virtually an apotheosis.

Colucci recognized a strain of saintliness in Piero too. Piero is idealized as a man both innocent and long-suffering. He "bore with heavy mind" the hostility of Pitti, Acciauoli, and Neroni, knowing that they had been raised up by Cosimo's favor and were indebted to him "as if he were their good father." "Between his funeral tears," Piero tried to dissuade them from plotting, and he repeatedly warned the Neroni against actions that would bring destruction on their own house, "which owed so much to Cosimo."[9] While Pitti gathered around him a factious crowd, so that he became "a place of refuge for the wicked," Piero stood aloof from faction. He flattered no one, and he bore abuse against himself with equanimity.[10]

In Colucci's account there is no question whatever of Piero's innocence or the violence of his enemies. The patrician leaders filled their houses with friends and arms, and from the countryside came reports that they had collected troops in the territories of the duke of Modena. But it is said, writes Colucci, "that by his innocence Piero de' Medici prevailed upon the living God to save his fatherland and his blameless house." Praying before an image of Christ, Piero vowed that if victory were given to him, he would not spill the blood of any citizen.[11]

Piero's remarkable clemency becomes the central theme of the history. In political terms, his overriding desire for peace is stressed because it helps to prevent a great, destructive war amongst "the Latins"—though true to the humanist interest in diplomacy and battle, Colucci actually gives more space to

[9] Colucci, *De discordiis*, p. 11.

[10] Ibid., p. 13.

[11] Ibid., p. 23.

the ensuing war than to the civic upheaval. Just as important, Piero's humaneness is central to the moral teaching of the history. Clemency is Piero's distinguishing virtue, the quality that makes him exemplary and renders his life and these events memorable. Thus, at the start of the work the author writes that it would be wrong to pass over Piero's remarkable actions in silence, because "when he had his most terrible enemies in his hand, he sent them away unharmed." Piero was more afraid that he might be accused of cruelty, Colucci writes, than of "the fact that they were plotting to murder him."[12]

Colucci's history is relatively restrained. Though he took as his model the bitter and dramatic short histories of Sallust, his work lacks a large and central villain in the style of Sallust's Catiline. Two reasons for this may be imagined. First, there is the obvious problem of who was to play the role of Catiline—a man described as "reckless, cunning and treacherous," one "seized with a mighty desire of getting control of the government, recking little what manner he should achieve it, providing he make himself supreme."[13] The role seems written for Luca Pitti, but Pitti's last-minute reconciliation with Piero ruled him out. The second reason is more general. Sallust exhibited the twisted greatness of Catiline as a figure of the corruptions of the age, the public sickness that led the author to retire from political strife. Colucci, on the other hand, wrote in a mood of celebration. Neither a citizen nor a patrician, he had no sense of the city's communal or republican traditions and was little concerned to lament them. Rather, like the other literary eulogists, he looked forward to an age of Augustan harmony under Lorenzo.

The value of Colucci's restraint becomes clearer when we turn to a second apologetic account of the events of 1466. This is the *Libri de temporibus suis* of Fra Giovanni di Carlo, a Dominican friar who taught theology at the university and served as prior of Florence's great friary of Santa Maria No-

[12] Ibid., p. 3.

[13] Sallust, *Catilinae Coniuratio*, trans. J. C. Rolfe, Loeb Classical Library (Cambridge, Mass., 1960), pp. 9–11. For this interpretation of Sallust, see R. Syme, *Sallust* (Berkeley, 1964), ch. 6.

vella. This work, written between 1480 and 1482, has never been printed and only recently has drawn the attention of scholars. In its own way, however, Fra Giovanni's history—or at least that part of it devoted to 1466—has had a considerable influence on Florentine historiography, because it was the source of some of the more bizarre elements in Machiavelli's account of this period.

Fra Giovanni entitled the first of the three books of his history a "Defense of Cosimo," and the second is no less favorable to Piero. But Fra Giovanni gave his account the personal tension and drama missing in Colucci's by stressing or (as far as one can see) inventing a number of new elements. The most prominent of these has already been mentioned in an earlier chapter: the cunning and deliberate plot of Dietisalvi Neroni to discredit Piero and—in twentieth-century jargon—"destabilize" the regime. Apparently, Dietisalvi took advantage of Piero's trust to examine financial records and then persuaded Piero to call in his credits. This was a deliberate scheme to precipitate a financial crisis and it succeeded in creating a wave of bankruptcies that helped to undermine the regime. Similarly, Agnolo Acciaiuoli's enmity toward Piero is attributed to a personal grudge against Cosimo, who decided against Acciaiuoli in a family dispute over a large dowry. On the other side of the conflict, Fra Giovanni dramatized Piero's role in an eloquent speech in which he unmasked the ingratitude of the Neroni. Piero also took care to pacify the populace after the bankruptcies by holding a great joust, which is elaborately described—though in fact the joust in question had no relation to these events since it did not actually take place until after Piero's death.[14]

Because it appealed to Machiavelli's sense of drama, Fra

[14] I have followed the analysis of Fra Giovanni in R. Hatfield, "A Source for Machiavelli's Account of the Regime of Piero de' Medici," *Studies on Machiavelli*, ed. M. Gilmore (Florence, 1972), pp. 317–334. The account remains puzzling, but the recent researches of S. Camporeale show that Giovanni di Carlo is a larger and more interesting figure than has been suspected. See Camporeale's important study, "Giovanni Caroli e le *Vitae Fratrum S.M. Novellae*: Umanesimo e crisi religosa (1460–1480)," *Memorie Domenicane*, N.S., 12 (1981): 14–268.

Giovanni's account had considerable influence on later histories, but Colucci's more sober rendering is certainly closer to the "official" perspective of the time.[15] This was the view carried forward by Florence's other great historian of the sixteenth century, Francesco Guicciardini, in his *History of Florence.* In this youthful work, written in the republican interlude that followed the ouster of the Medici, Guicciardini speaks for the patrician interest, not the Medici, and he is broadly critical of Lorenzo's "tyranny." Nonetheless, this son of one of the leading figures of Piero's regime shows no sympathy at all for the patrician opposition and presents an image of the upheavals that is a summary of the pro-Medicean position, including the plot to murder Piero on the road from Careggi. Most striking is his insistence that Piero, "not following the style of Cosimo his father, was most clement in these upheavals, and would not allow anyone to be punished other than those who could not without great danger be left unpunished." Piero certainly lacked the outstanding qualities of his father or his son, but in mercy and clemency he exceeded both.[16]

★

The intellectual climate of Florence was changing. This was the age we associate with Ficino's platonic feasts, with Botticelli's fragile and wistful nudes, with Lorenzo Magnifico's collection of ancient jewels and the elegance of his pseudo-popular "songs." Political values also shifted. Among intellectuals the confident classical republicanism of Bruni or Palmieri was being replaced by a new vision that was less individualistic, less striving, less egalitarian, a vision that focused instead on the creation of a harmonious order symbolized and presided over by the virtuous ruler.

This new outlook is reflected in the pro-Medicean historiography of the upheavals of 1466 we have examined, but more direct expressions of the new political philosophy are

[15] In addition to Hatfield, "Source," see G. M. Anselmi, *Ricerche sul Machiavelli storico* (Pisa, 1979).

[16] Guicciardini, *Storie fiorentine* (Bari, 1931), pp. 17, 80.

to be found in two contemporary political dialogues. In the first—Bartolomeo Platina's "On the Best Citizen"—the new hierarchical order is embraced and idealized. In the second—"On Liberty" by Alamanno Rinuccini—the new political order is deplored, but its reality is grudgingly accepted; the effect is that the emphasis is shifted to the resulting tensions and accommodations for those schooled in older values. Platina and Rinuccini take us still further from the actualities of 1466 or the partisan world of Iacopo di Cocco Donati. But they too are a part of Marco Parenti's generation, a part of the background against which we must try to understand his one brief attempt to give expression to what seemed a faltering tradition of political feeling.

Bartolomeo Platina was a north Italian humanist whose career is primarily associated with Rome. He spent four formative years, however, in Florence from 1457 to 1461. He went there to study Greek with Argyropulos and made friendships with several prominent Florentines of that circle—including Alamanno Rinuccini, Donato Acciaiuoli, and Pierfilippo Pandolfini. He also seems to have been welcomed by Cosimo and Piero de' Medici, and he dedicated "On the Best Citizen" to Lorenzo.

The dialogue belongs to a recognizable type of humanistic literature called the "mirror of princes"—didactic works concerned with the education, virtues, and duties of rulers.[17] Platina carefully adapted his dialogue to a Florentine setting, where a discussion of princely rule as such would have been out of place. The philosophic conversations he records take place at Careggi at the time when Platina was living in Florence and sometimes enjoyed the hospitality of the Medici villa.[18] In the conversations Platina himself says very little,

[17] See F. Gilbert, "The Humanist Concept of the Prince and the *Prince* of Machiavelli," in Gilbert, *History, Choice and Commitment* (Cambridge, Mass., 1977).

[18] On Platina's connections to Florence, see Della Torre, *Academia*, pp. 530–37. The editor of the dialogue, F. Battaglia, assumes that the work dates from 1457 to 1461, the period of Platina's residence in Florence. See *De optimo cive di Bartolomeo Sacchi detto il Platina*, ed. F. Battaglia (Bologna, 1944), p. xxxiii. This seems unlikely, however, given the emphasis on Cosimo's ex-

leaving Cosimo—whose age and frailty are emphasized—to represent as well as articulate his political ideal. The old man has become a philosopher (he even quotes a little Greek), passing on his teaching to the future leader of the city, the attentive and deferential Lorenzo.

As a philosophic teacher—"a second Socrates" Platina calls him at the conclusion of their conversations—Cosimo need not appear too princely.[19] His recommendations are all for moderation, manly self-restraint, abstinence from distracting pleasures, and a strictly civil manner of life. Once again we find ourselves in the presence of the pater patriae—that convenient republican evasion. But for Platina it is not simply an evasion; it is an idealized description of the relationship between Florence and its leading family, an ethical and political ideal for Lorenzo to inherit and imitate.

Like so many fifteenth-century humanists, Platina believed that true nobility is a matter of personal virtue rather than inheritance. This view was not incompatible with a hierarchical conception of society—it simply put pressure on the leader or leaders of society to live up to a moral ideal. Hence the ambiguities of the dialogue's title: the "best citizen" in the sense of the "select citizen" must also demonstrate the innate virtues that make him worthy of his high position. In particular, he must practice the virtues that go with leadership—charity, generosity, justice—and abstain from the vices—especially *superbia*, pride—that would make him hateful to the people. In turn, the "best citizen" should reward worthy men with public honors, thus encouraging virtue in the city.[20] In this way Platina continued a vital theme in Bruni's thought, which tied the growth of virtue to "the hope of honor."[21] But

---

treme old age and frailty—surely a tactless strategy if Cosimo were still alive—and the virtual disappearance of Piero di Cosimo from the line of succession. These aspects of the dialogue suggest that Platina was looking back to an idealized image of Cosimo's last years from the vantage of the late 1460s or early 1470s, when Piero was already dead and the young Lorenzo, the dedicatee, was in power.

[19] Platina, *De optimo cive*, p. 285.

[20] Ibid., p. 278.

[21] This formulation of Bruni's thought is taken from Q. Skinner, *The Foundations of Modern Political Thought* (Cambridge, 1979), p. 80.

Platina deals with this topic under the rubric of generosity—an indication of how far he has moved from Bruni's comparatively egalitarian concept of a society that encourages virtuous men to compete for glory toward Castiglione's courtly world in which they vie for the prince's eye.

Platina prefaces the dialogue with praises of the active life—again a common humanist theme. Nature presses us to want to serve our fatherland and our friends, a duty that cannot be fulfilled by those who retire into solitude and "separate themselves from humanity."[22] The life of the "best citizen" is strenuous and active. He must exert himself to see that everyone feels secure in the possession of his own goods and that the city "becomes every day more remarkable for its morals, industriousness, glory, and wealth." It is a "grave burden" that the "best citizen" carries on his shoulders—"to keep the city flourishing in fortunate times, and to protect her from dangers and disasters in adversity."[23]

Platina's enthusiasm for the active life is a familiar inheritance of the political literature of early fifteenth-century Florence, where the same Ciceronian ideals of active virtue were revived in Bruni's works and publicized in Matteo Palmieri's "On the Civil Life." In fact, Platina's dialogue has been cited as a continuation of this strain of Florentine civic humanism in the less favorable conditions of the second half of the century.[24] In this respect it is coupled with Alamanno Rinuccini's nearly contemporary dialogue "On Liberty"—the major protest from within the patriciate against Medicean "tyranny." And yet this coupling points to something problematic in both works, because Rinuccini's dialogue, far from a praise for the active life, is framed as an apologia for the author's choice to live in tranquil solitude.

Rinuccini's dialogue is the mirror image of Platina's, not its twin. Here the preface argues for a "life lived far from the crowded city and innumerable anxieties associated with the greed and ambition which it fosters." Again the setting is

[22] Platina, *De optimo cive*, p. 239.

[23] Ibid., p. 258.

[24] See Baron, *The Crisis of the Early Italian Renaissance* (Princeton, 1966), p. 437.

rural, but the place is the author's own farm, where he is living frugally in modest independence. The mood is one of grief, due to the recent loss of Rinuccini's only son—and that sadness is soon extended to the wider loss that is the subject of the dialogue.

In the body of the dialogue Rinuccini renames himself Eleutherius, the lover of liberty, and he is visited in his rural retreat by two friends, Microtoxus, the shortsighted, and Alitheus, the truthful.[25] The friends come to inquire about Eleutherius' retirement into solitude, and Microtoxus presents the conventional arguments, familiar from Palmieri or Platina, for a return to the city and the active life. The philosophic Alitheus—who is identified as a student of Argyropulos—is initially sympathetic to arguments that would draw their mutual friend back to Florence. But it falls to him first to define liberty and then to lament its disappearance from the city. For Alitheus, as for Microtoxus, liberty and action are connected, but Alitheus understands that the connection has been battered by a corrupt and coercive state. The equality of citizens—"the basic principle of all liberty"—no longer exists, and noble minds now wear "the yoke of servitude." Alitheus strengthens the point by contrasting present conditions to a capsule history of Florence emphasizing its past freedom.

The arguments of the two visitors occupy the first book of the dialogue. In the second it is the host's turn, and he speaks for the outraged Florentine patriciate, protesting against the usurpation of their privileges. "Who could justly reproach me for having enough pride to refuse to become a suppliant," he asks, "begging from those wicked usurpers for my rightful inheritance and that of other good citizens."[26] As proof he recounts his own experience as an emissary of the city and Lorenzo de' Medici's refusal to see the distinction between public duties to the republic and private obligations to himself. This violation of the traditional boundaries between private

[25] Rinuccini, *De libertate*, ed. F. Adorno, in *Atti Colombaria*, 22 (1957): 265–303; translated as "On Liberty," in *Humanism and Liberty*, ed. R. N. Watkins (Columbia, 1978), pp. 193–222.

[26] Rinuccini, "Liberty," p. 219.

and public spheres is a sign that Florence was governed tyrannically. Lorenzo "accepted tyranny as a legacy from his grandfather, but exercised it much more severely than his grandfather did. He was more insolent than his father. . . . He did everything according to the impulses of his willful spirit."[27]

The dialectical movement of the dialogue as a whole is clear, and the "lover of liberty" draws the necessary conclusions. Without liberty public activity is not an expression of virtue, but an experience of degradation: "Not my country but the criminals whose force took over all her laws and authority ignored my willingness to render good service. . . . Since that was so, why waste my time and effort?" This conclusion is not a renunciation of effort, Eleutherius insists: "I would take on work, and danger too for my country. But the truth is that I cannot peacefully tolerate our ungrateful citizenry and the usurpers of our liberty. I live, therefore, as you see, content with this little house and farm."[28]

Eleutherius' protests notwithstanding, the effect of his argument is to substitute reading and writing and healthful exercise (when it is not raining) for the public life of the city. Citizenship in the sense that was traditional to men of Rinuccini's class remains only as a potential. And even in the literary sphere he is unprepared to make a strong claim for persuasiveness, which is another form of engagement. "I am not telling you what others ought to do," says the "lover of liberty," "but simply what I have done and for what reasons."

"On Liberty" is a work of philosophy, not autobiography. We need not read it as defining a final position either for Rinuccini or his patrician circle. But the dialogue has great historical value in locating a powerful tension between the political interests of the patricians and their humanist ideals. For much of the century the Ciceronian conception of active civic virtue had seemed to coincide with the ambitions of politically minded Florentine citizens. Their inherited political and social roles took on a new depth and decorum. Their

[27] Ibid., p. 221.

[28] Ibid., p. 222.

vision expanded, their history was enlarged. At the same time, the new "civic humanism" functioned as an ideology for a stabilized political order that was restrictive enough to exclude disruptive popular forces, but inclusive enough to favor the flexible participation of their own class of prosperous, civic-minded citizenry. But this Ciceronian culture had other potentials as well. It could encourage service to the patria by men whose qualification was literary rather than social—functionaries and courtiers like Scala or Poliziano. Like all ideologies, it could also mask realities and blind the patriciate to its loss of power. This is the danger Rinuccini presents in Microtoxus—a man sincere in his belief that nothing in Florence had changed to diminish the "civil life" that Palmieri had glorified.

When we place Rinuccini's work side by side with Platina's a larger dialogue results. Together the two pieces do in a sense demonstrate the continuation of earlier civic concerns into the later fifteenth century, but it is striking to see the reversal of positions, that has occurred. Now the advocacy of the active life comes from one committed to a hierarchical order culminating in a semiprincely figure. In this world—and Rinuccini bitterly agrees that this is so—only those prepared to embrace this hierarchy will be able to exercise the virtues of citizenship. Ultimately, in fact, only the "best citizen" can be a citizen at all in the full sense of the word.

★

In the opening pages of his history, Benedetto Colucci writes that the enemies of so exceptional a man as Piero de' Medici showed they could not understand "how much stability the life of this unique man might bring to us." As if framing a direct reply, Rinuccini, near the end of his dialogue, quotes a line from Hesiod: "Often the whole city suffers through one bad man."[29] These were the poles of feeling around which Florentines were having to redefine the changing political realities of their republic.

[29] Colucci, *De discordiis*, p. 4; Rinuccini, "Liberty," p. 221.

Marco's views cannot be fully identified with the ideas of any single contemporary. The gulf between him and Colucci, for instance, is obvious, but even Rinuccini offers no simple parallel. Marco was neither so short-sighted as Microtoxus (though often as earnest), nor so philosophic as Alitheus, nor so patrician as Eleutherius. Marco's renunciation took another form than rural independence, and his confession that he could not sustain his memoir when its spirit no longer fitted the times acquires a deeper meaning when set against the works of the pro-Mediceans. Colucci, Fra Giovanni, Iacopo di Cocco Donati, Microtoxus, Alitheus, Eleutherius, the "Cosimo" and "Lorenzo" of Platina's treatise, Vespasiano da Bisticci, Marco Parenti himself—all are voices in a larger debate on the limits and possibilities of citizenship in the second and third generations of Medici domination.

CHAPTER 13

HISTORIOGRAPHY AND THE PUBLIC WORLD

★

THE DIFFERENCES that separate Parenti's account from Benedetto Colucci's bear the stamp of two distinct historiographical traditions marked by characteristic attitudes toward political conventions as well as literary ones. On one level, the two texts are divided by the extent to which they are affiliated to the classical tradition in historiography; on another, they are separated by the way in which each construes the relationship between the private or social world and the public sphere.

Florence had an old and well-established historiographical literature. Its first outstanding work was the early fourteenth-century chronicle of Dino Compagni, but it was the massive chronicle of Giovanni Villani (d. 1348)—self-consciously written to provide a benchmark for future generations—that really established the foundation of a continuous local tradition of vernacular writing. This tradition did not die out in the fifteenth century, but it suffered a great loss of prestige when Leonardo Bruni and his humanist followers reworked the chronicles in a more elevated, classical style. Though Florence, like other Italian states, did not acquire an official historiographer until the next century, Bruni's career as chancellor set a kind of public stamp upon his work, which was ratified by the decision of the republic to commission Donato Acciaiuoli to translate Bruni's history into Italian. This association between the chancery and classically minded historiography was reinforced by the writings of Poggio and Scala, and the commission that Machiavelli received to write the history continued the same tradition. By contrast, the vernacular works of the same period were the products of private individuals—men like Cavalcanti or Parenti—and these works were often reduced in dimension to subliterary and semiprivate documents, like the priorista of Rinuccini.[1]

By the mid-fifteenth century, then, two distinct paradigms of historical writing existed in Florence—though in practice individual works might borrow from both. The humanist school built on a self-conscious, literary imitation of classical models, especially Livy and Sallust. Latin was preferred to Italian, and with the choice of language went a series of rhetorical devices and literary values learned from Roman historiography and oratory. Perhaps the most fundamental feature was the preference for a linear and causal narrative. History had become both a search for explanations and an instrument of secular instruction. Accordingly narrative had to be disciplined to carry—as far as events permitted—a single, lucid story. Narrative had taken on some of the power and some of the responsibilities of argument. It must be consequent, firmly outlined, and eloquent. So endowed, history would be a means of public instruction: philosophy teaching by example.

The vernacular paradigm was looser and is more difficult to define. Much of this writing appears to be naive and unconscious of its inherited models, and it has often provoked a reading that is equally naive and insensitive to tradition. The language itself, with its familiarity and wide spectrum of use, both private and public, did not challenge chroniclers and diarists to define their genres or to adopt an appropriate linguistic decorum. And yet it is also true that vernacular writers were often deeply influenced by classical values, as the whole

[1] These pages summarize arguments I have made at greater length in two essays: "Machiavelli, Guicciardini, and the Tradition of Vernacular Historiography in Florence," *American Historical Review* 84 (1979): 86–105; and "Representation and Argument in Florentine Historiography," *Storia della storiografia* 10 (1986): 48–63.

of European culture inevitably was. Vernacular historiography was open to classical ideas on one side and to quotidian practices on the other—a position lying somewhere between the record keeping of ricordanze and the art of Sallust.

The central impulse of vernacular historiography was mimetic, and the consequence was an episodic, eventful narrative structure. Chronicles emphasize representational inclusiveness over argumentative clarity. Often they are encyclopedic, capable always of finding room for another entry—a remarkable occurrence, a moralized tale, a bit of news or rumor from far-off places. The chronicler's first concern was to produce an attestable record. He was generally more concerned with witnessing the truth of particular occurrences than with arranging events in clear explanatory sequences. For a writer like Villani such secular sequences were inherently less meaningful because the deepest significance of events lay outside of time. Others, further removed from the Augustinian framework, continued the impulse to historical record keeping as a sort of civic equivalent to family diaries. The priorista, with its bimonthly lists of priors, is the clearest instance, but chroniclers in general were much given to lists: the dimensions of the cupola of the cathedral, entries of foreign dignitaries, the names of families exiled or repatriated, the provisions of *balìe*. Such items could be offered without explanations, not because there were none, but because the writer and his audiences shared the intimacy of their city. Neither language nor tradition required them—as humanists writing in the language of distant Rome were forced to do—to turn their world inside out and reconstruct it in public and universal terms. As a result the memoirs and chronicles of these times have a way of tumbling from the most public to the most private events without any sign of transition.

These brief generalizations help characterize the gap between the histories written by Colucci and Marco Parenti. Colucci's history fits unambiguously into the classical paradigm. His story focusses on an image of the virtuous ruler unjustifiably attacked by ungrateful and vicious enemies, and this simplified psychological and moral framework endows the work with the clarity of outline and instructive purpose dictated by its tradition. An essentially similar presentation could be found in Sallust's Catiline, Bruni's chapter on the duke of Athens, or Poliziano's apologetic history of the Pazzi conspiracy.

Parenti's *Memoir* is more equivocally placed. In most respects it seems a work governed by the styles and assumptions of the vernacular tradition. The most pervasive sign is the language itself, not much more formal than the style he used in his letters and less literary, for instance, than that of Vespasiano's *Lives*. Another clear sign is the presence of lists, which speak to the documentary impulse of chronicle literature. Like a number of other vernacular accounts, the *Memoir* records the names of individuals and families exiled or repatriated in 1466. The long list of the signori of Italy—including a separate listing of the noble houses of Venice—is certainly closer to the spirit of Benedetto Dei, that obsessive maker of lists ("the proven friends of Benedetto Dei," "the bitter enemies of Benedetto Dei") than to the topographical surveys of the humanist Flavio Biondo.[2]

Marco Parenti's *Memoir* shows something of the power of the classical paradigm as well. The outstanding example is the "brief discourse" introduced in the middle of the *Memoir* to explain the rise of Francesco Sforza from mercenary captain to duke of Milan—a "memorable example of virtue and good fortune." The classical influence goes deeper than adherence to the conventional formula of a heroic life. The larger purpose of the digression is to explain the connection between Sforza and Medici fortunes. By employing this retrospect Parenti obeys the fundamental impulse to clarity of the classical spirit and is able to bring into the foreground of his history material that the ordinary chronicler would have had no way of accommodating.[3]

[2] B. Dei, *La cronica*, ed. R. Barducci (Florence, 1984), pp. 137–38.

[3] My argument, as will be evident, owes a great deal to Erich Auerbach's *Mimesis: The Representation of Reality in Western Literature*, trans. W. Trask (Princeton, 1953). Auerbach deals with historiography only briefly and in the opening chapters, but it seems to me that his study is very illuminating

Parenti's narrative is a sometimes unstable combination of elements from both historiographical traditions. In places—seemingly where events provide a central focus—the account proceeds with great consistency, sustained by the brief positioning phrases and conjunctions that are essential to a linear narrative.[4] More often, the episodic principle reasserts itself, and even the best-developed incidents terminate abruptly, with nothing to connect one episode to the next. Similarly, through much of the *Memoir* the chronicler's typical spirit of localism holds sway. It is "our" city, they are "our" ambassadors.[5] Ambassadors are appointed "here" and foreign dignitaries pass through the city on their way to other parts.[6] But a more universal outlook also makes itself felt. When Parenti troubles himself to explain the Medici arms or the office of the accoppiatori, he is giving thought to the possibility of a wider audience for his history.[7] Such an audience would require a more public style of address and could be expected to appreciate the universals underlying the transience of history. For these readers Parenti enlarges events by drawing on the rhetorical or psychological generalizations sanctioned by classical historiography. As we have seen, he describes the rise of Sforza as an exemplary case, and it is no more than an extension of the same principle to explain the actions of great men in terms of universals of character and situation. For instance, the duke of Milan's desire to rid himself of a potential rival is explained in terms of considerations that are at once his own thoughts and general maxims of politics. The duke understood, Parenti writes, the ambition of great men, the variability of fortune, and how time and occasion had the power to change men's minds.[8]

---

for historical writing, which in some ways is the most mimetic of literary genres.

[4] For instance: "Mentre che queste cose erano in combustione . . ." (*Memorie*, p. 49). Similarly: "In queste tante diversità di guerre fra il Duca e la lega . . ." (*Memorie*, p. 43).

[5] *Memorie*, p. 32.

[6] Ibid., pp. 14, 2.

[7] Ibid., p. 66.

[8] Ibid., p. 22. A second instance may be quoted for its Guicciardinian tone:

These generalizations would have been as recognizable to Tacitus as to Hume; more to the point, they can be found at work in Machiavelli or Guicciardini. But Parenti knew very clearly the limits of his ambitions as a writer. Sforza's life, he wrote, "would make an important history [storia] in itself and one worthy of a most eloquent writer, but my intention is not this, but only to tell how it happened that [Sforza] from being a most excellent captain succeeded to the most worthy lordship of Milan." In this way he declined to write a "history," with its demand for eloquence, and at the end of this same disgression he refers to his work simply as "nostri ricordi"—our memoir or memorials. In the same spirit his friend Vespasiano, concluding his life of Cosimo, wrote: "Many other things might be told of Cosimo by one who purposed to write his life, but I am not set on this task. I have only set down matters concerning him which I myself have seen or heard from trustworthy witnesses."[9]

As Vespasiano attests, the chronicler or diarist thought of himself less as an author than as a privileged witness. The same spirit speaks in Parenti's statement of his hopes and failures, quoted at the opening of the Introduction. He had begun to write in the expectation of liberty, but the failure of his hopes had weakened his spirit, and his chosen role of witness had been frustrated by "the difficulty of knowing the truth when those who govern keep secrets to themselves." The result was that "these memoirs are very uneven and discontinuous in describing all that occurred, though sometimes more and sometimes less according to the times."

Parenti's expectation of continuity in his narrative, even if unfulfilled, marks him as an unusual diarist and can be taken as one of many signs of a movement toward a synthesis of the vernacular and classical traditions. This cross-fertilization

---

after his victories, Sforza wished to enjoy in peace the dukedom won by his efforts and good fortune, "but the manner of acquisition and the condition of human affairs would not suffer such tranquility to exist without a measure of disturbance" (ibid., p. 59).

[9] Ibid., pp. 41–42; Vespasiano, *Renaissance Princes, Popes, and Prelates*, trans. W. George and E. Waters (New York, 1963), p. 234.

was of the utmost importance to the future of Florentine historiography, because out of it would come the histories of Machiavelli and especially Guicciardini. But Marco Parenti's most immediate successor was another well-educated vernacular diarist, his own son Piero Parenti, whose lengthy memoir is the outstanding documentary witness to the period of Savonarola and Soderini.[10] In the two Parenti we see how naturally the acute political sense of the Florentine governing class was channeled into historical narrative. But in this period of transition there remained an instability in the forms of historical narrative, as writers struggled to find the necessary distance from events. Before the quick but fitful observation of a Marco Parenti could be transformed into the sustained historical vision of Guicciardini, the historian would have to find a way to represent even the most intensely felt episodes in the life of his community in a fully public language. Profound political changes as well as literary ones lay between the generations of Marco Parenti and Francesco Guicciardini.

★

Marco Parenti's *Memoir* shows every sign of having been intended for "publication." From internal evidence it seems clear that he wanted to give public voice to his views of Florentine politics and that he wrote to be understood by readers unknown to himself personally. The anonymity of the text belongs to its subsequent history and not to its author's first

[10] Pampaloni describes the "diary" as "one of the most reliable and best-informed sources." See his "Piero di Marco Parenti e la sua 'Historia fiorentina,' " *Archivio storico italiano* 113 (1959): 147–53. On the historiographical significance of Piero Parenti's memoir as a bridge to the work of Guicciardini, see Gilbert, *Machiavelli and Guicciardini: Politics and History in Sixteenth-Century Florence* (Princeton, 1965), esp. pp. 60–70. With regard to the continuities of Florentine vernacular historiography, which I have stressed somewhat more than Gilbert, the existence of Marco Parenti's *Memoir* helps to explain the otherwise puzzling fact that Piero began his account with the murder of the Milanese duke in 1476, though he quickly jumps ahead to start a record of contemporary events surrounding the French invasion. Marco's account goes no further than 1466, but the assassination of 1476 is briefly mentioned. See the Appendix.

intention—though by the time he had completed his first seventy pages that hope was already faltering because of the disappointments and political inhibitions that eventually cast the manuscript into a safe obscurity.

As a would-be public statement, the *Memoir* completes the movement from private to public suggested by the focus of each of the three principal sources for Marco Parenti's biography—the ricordanze, the letters, and the *Memoir*. The same pattern could be read in a hundred other lives—if we still had the documents to guide us—because men of Marco's class were expected to be seriously engaged in both realms. In a sense, this overlap of private and public was *the* characteristic of the patrician class, one that had long governed their unconscious assumptions about their privileges in the political and social order. But in Parenti's generation this vital point of self-definition was coming under pressure from great changes, both in the actualities of politics and in the tendencies of political thought—changes in which the Medici triumph of 1466 (as Parenti only half-consciously registered) played a very large part.

It would be hard to offer a portrait of the Florentine political class in which public and private spheres are clearly separated, but it was also a legacy of communal political tradition to attempt to do so. Civic institutions had been shaped by the urgent need to prevent the common good from being subverted by private power. The very strength of this effort testified to the natural tendency for the two interests to become "confused." By the second half of the fifteenth century the alignment of the two spheres had certainly changed since the days when the primary threat to public order came from great families of feudal origins. Now the principal danger came from the growing domination of the Medici family, bolstered by a financial and military alliance with the Milanese dukes.

There is good evidence that in Marco's generation the conduct of the Medici was forcing the patricians into a heightened awareness of the boundaries between private and public—not defined in terms of personal and property rights as liberal tradition would later do, but as a matter of direct political participation. Access to office was at the center of the patriciate's political consciousness and it was threatened by any sign that the Medici regarded themselves as more than the first among equals. Rinuccini's *Dialogue* provides an apt illustration of this patrician irritability and defensiveness. Rinuccini claims that on a mission to Rome he had done "the duty of a good envoy and a loyal citizen," but that Lorenzo "complained that I wrote publicly to the magistrate on great affairs of state, rather than privately to him." Rinuccini's protest is an attempt to save the essential distinction between private and public that allowed men of his class to participate in public life as equals: "I shall always remember and declare that I was sent forth, not by one private individual but by the whole people, by the highest public office, by the Republic itself."[11]

A closely related example can be found in the ricordanze of Francesco Gaddi, another patrician who combined literary interests with a career in politics and administration. The ricordanze show a remarkable sensitivity to the public/private division. Gaddi set aside one section of the notebook for his public duties, rather than mixing these in with his own affairs.[12] For each trip he carefully noted the source of his commissions, specifying whether he traveled in behalf of the republic or of Lorenzo personally.[13] The reasons for this

[11] Rinuccini, "Liberty," in *Humanism and Liberty*, ed. R. N. Watkins (Columbia, 1978), p. 200.

[12] The Gaddi ricordanze is to be found in the Biblioteca Laurenziana, *Acquisti e doni*, 213. Gaddi says at the opening that he will set aside the first part of the notebook for debts and credits relating to his stay in Rome, the next for those relating to his stay in Florence after 1485. Pages 90–120 were reserved for "più gite facte in diversi tempi e delli offici." A final section is taken up by a listing of his possessions, including the inventory of his library; only this part of his ricordanze has been published. On Gaddi see L. Sozzi, "Lettere inedite di Philippe de Commynes a Francesco Gaddi," *Studi di bibliografia e di storia in onore di T. de Mariniis*, ed. R. de Maio, vol. 3 (Vatican, 1964), pp. 205–262.

[13] Here is a sampling of such notations in Gaddi's recordanze. He traveled from Rome to Naples "per ordine di Lorenzo de' Medici," and later to France "per ordine di Lorenzo con commissione dal publico" (fol. 91). Later we read that he was "mandato dal publico" (fol. 91). Again, "partì da firenze per a

scrupulousness become apparent on two occasions when his "public duty" clashed with Lorenzo's "private commission." In one instance Lorenzo became so enraged that the public interest had been served before his own that he sent his son to Gaddi's door to demand a return of his commission and ciphers.[14] In another, Gaddi took pains to record his objections to a supposed debt incurred while traveling on Medici business in France. Lorenzo had insisted that he should recover the money from the public purse. But this he could not rightly do, Gaddi protested, "since I was not sent by the public but by Lorenzo."[15]

These instances demonstrate clearly that Gaddi's sensitivity to the division of the public from the private domain was no abstract matter. His scrupulous notations were self-protective, and they strongly suggest that his sensitivities—and by extension Rinuccini's—were sharpened by Medici encroachments. But Gaddi's ricordanze have yet another lesson for us, since at one point—still writing in this same section of his notebook—he made a sudden deviation into the realm normally regarded as private. In 1485 he was selected for the priorate, and he wrote as follows: "On the 22nd of March, I being one of the priors, took a wife, as urged by relatives and friends. She is Noretta, daughter of Carlo di Iacopo di Messer Niccolò Guasconi, with a dowry of 1,200 florins, with 1,000 florins on the Monte, making 2,200 between money and gifts."[16]

In normal circumstances marriage was a personal, not a public, concern—and even now Gaddi was careful to make a second record of the dowry settlement in another part of his

---

roma mandato dal Magnifico Lorenzo per tornare nel bancho suo e per attendere alle cose sue dello stato e altre particolarità secondo conventione facto con lui" (fol. 92).

[14] Here he glosses his entry with this marginal note: "con commissione publico e di Lorenzo de' Medici" (fol. 93). But Gaddi discovered how difficult it was to be the servant of two masters; when he returned the Ten commended him but Lorenzo was extremely irate "per la sua particular commissione" (fol. 93).

[15] Gaddi, *Ricordanze*, fol. 96.

[16] Ibid., fol. 93.

notebook.[17] But the implication seems to be that high office could transform private acts by placing them in a public context. As prior Gaddi had become a public person, and for the two months he and his colleagues occupied the palace, their private selves were dissolved in their public trust. In this light Gaddi's resistance to Lorenzo's willful blurring of private and public roles takes on an added meaning: it amounted to a defense of Gaddi's own right as a magistrate to join the two spheres together. In the end the patriciate could only continue to be a class of public men if no single citizen or family was permitted to establish an exclusive claim to the public sphere.

Rinuccini's *Dialogue on Liberty* and Gaddi's ricordanze were written after Marco Parenti's *Memoir* and in a strict sense cannot be used to document the moment of its composition. Nonetheless, these were men of Marco's own generation and cast of mind and their reactions seem to parallel his own. For his part, Marco had maintained a strictly private decorum in his ricordanze, where no public offices were recorded unless they involved financial obligation, until the sudden irruption of public concerns at the time of his priorate. In the *Memoir* his concern that public proprieties be maintained against Medici usurpation is one of the underlying themes. It is evident in his complaint that Piero's illness diverted public business to the Medici palace and again in his description of Medici troops marching through the city "just as is done by a Signore when he seizes a city." But his most effective protest against the degradation of public life is his dramatization of the contrast between the clear-sightedness of Florentines scattered in their villas and their unseemly rush, once called to a public forum, to submit themselves to Cosimo.

When we ask why Marco Parenti gave so different an account of 1466 from Benedetto Colucci, it seems essential to point to these issues of private and public. Colucci wrote with a professional writer's distance from events in which he had no personal stake. His humanist Latin was a language that had exclusively public uses, and the same clear separation of

[17] Ibid., fol. 20.

the public from the private is assumed in the substance of his account. To Colucci it seemed obvious that Piero de' Medici in his person embodied a stable public order. This placed Piero in a unique position, well above the other combatants. No grounds, therefore, could be imagined for opposition to Piero except personal ones. His opponents were driven by a combination of petty spite, ingratitude, and vicious character—a reduction of political conflict to personal antagonism that also marks Poliziano's apologetic history of the Pazzi conspiracy.

The pattern of Marco's life—and the place of writing within that pattern—was very different. For him writing was an act of citizenship, and citizenship involved a complex overlap of political and social commitments. In the *Memoir* these are apparent in his proud references to his relationship with the Strozzi and the prominence that he gives to the story of their repatriation.[18] But these signs of his personal loyalties are not simply trivial; underlying his personal stake in events is a view of politics that makes it impossible—or at least highly undesirable—to separate the state from society. His analysis of the political conflicts of his day was built on a natural division between two social groupings. On the side he placed those whose "nobility virtue and antiquity depended only on themselves." These were the traditional patriciate and their attractions were self-evident. Best embodied in the figure of Neri Capponi, they were represented in 1465–1466 by those "generous" citizens who found Piero's rule insupportable. On the other side stood men whose "standing depended entirely on Cosimo." Lacking the independence required for virtue, they were "much inclined to plunder and to exploitation of power."

In short, Marco's views identified political virtue with social leadership and held that political power separated from a tradition of social responsibility led to greed, exploitation, and the loss of liberty. This was hardly an original view. It goes back to Aristotle's definition of aristocracy as government by

[18] It is revealing that in the Gaddi priorista the list of the families restored to Florence in 1466 mentions Filippo and Lorenzo Strozzi seventeenth—approximately halfway down the list. Marco, of course, had listed the Strozzi first. See British Library, MS Egerton 3764, fol. 196.

the best, while oligarchy, its perverted double, is rule by the self-interested few. Similar ideas lie behind Rinuccini's *Dialogue* and Vespasiano's eulogy of the virtuous self-sufficiency of Franco Sacchetti. These men spoke to the natural self-conception of the Florentine patriciate. Only in the radically altered conditions of the next century would the patriciate finally come to accept that republican disorder and popular rule posed a greater threat to their social privileges than did Medici autocracy.

In Marco's generation these half-spoken assumptions of the patriciate were also being challenged by a new orientation in political thought. Earlier in the century the revival of classical republicanism had given new emphasis and clarity to the public realm. The traditional public roles of the political class acquired dignity by the opening of Florentine experience to the wider theater of Roman history, a fact that helps to account for the ready acceptance of Bruni's program. But the influence of Argyropulos and the revival of Platonism brought a more hierarchical conception of the public sphere that focused on the virtues of the ruler.[19] The carriers of this new, philosophic vision of politics were not the educated patricians who had made up the Sacchetti circle, but the professional literary men who grouped around the Medici—Scala, Ficino, Poliziano, and Landino. Like the humanist chancellors before them, their primary connection to the city was through its government and leading house, and they naturally tended toward a more "statist" conception of politics.

It is now generally agreed that Renaissance Florence never really saw the birth of what Burckhardt called "an objective treatment and consideration of the State." But the enlargement and clarification of the public sphere, which was one of the principal effects of the classical revival—especially in its later, more hierarchical guise—was certainly an important step in

[19] This side of Florentine political tradition is surveyed in A. Brown, "Platonism in 15th-century Florence and Its Contribution to Early Modern Political Thought," *Journal of Modern History (forthcoming).* I am most grateful for the opportunity to see this essay before its appearance in print.

this direction. And in this respect Machiavelli, a displaced citizen turned functionary, carried forward the humanist impulse. His whole program can be considered an attempt to meet a desperate challenge to the political order by radically discounting private virtues in favor of public ones.

In a famous passage in his letters, Machiavelli wrote that "since I don't know how to talk about the silk business or the wool business, I have to talk about government, and I must either make a vow of silence or discuss that." In Florence, a city of textiles, this amounted to a renunciation of interest in the social world—the world of trade and talk about trade. Machiavelli knew very well that few of his fellow citizens could be expected to make such a radical choice. In fact, his disclaimer only has impact in a setting where other choices would be expected. Marco Parenti's life and ideas illuminate just this context. In his world many individuals were inclined to prefer silk to politics; nonetheless they held to a broad expectation that the patriciate as a class was vital enough to exert a dominating interest in both. Through his marriage, education, and political interests, Marco had identified himself with this class. For a brief time he had even aspired to be their historian, until—caught by the contradictions between being a partisan of liberty as well as of the Strozzi—he retired in dismay.

But it would be wrong to reduce men like Marco Parenti to a background against which to measure greater and clearer thinkers to come. Ever since Burckhardt, historians of political thought have been eager to trace the progressive clarification of the boundaries between private and public spheres that resulted in the modern conception of an impersonal and sovereign state. The "acquisition of the concept of the state" should not be spoken of as an abstract intellectual conquest; it is necessary to ask who gained and who lost by the imposition of this increasingly impersonal view of authority. The multiplicity of meanings that the fifteenth century attached to the word "stato"—state, regime, status—can be disorienting. But the confusion, it should be remembered, is ours, not theirs. For Parenti and his peers these overlapping layers of meaning precisely reflected the several dimensions of their own lives. Thus when Alessandra Strozzi described the Parenti as having "un poco di stato," she was able to condense into a few words a reality that much of this chapter and large parts of this book have labored to recapture.

APPENDIX

A NOTE ON THE MANUSCRIPT OF MARCO PARENTI'S *Memoir*

MARCO PARENTI'S *Memoir* survives in an anonymous, untitled copy in the manuscript collections of the Biblioteca Nazionale in Florence. Catalogued as Magliabecchi XXV, 272, it is described as containing "Diverse notizie istoriche d'Italia, delle potenze che la dominavano nel 1464 e delle cose seguite in Firenze contro la fazione de' Medici fino al 1467." The work as we have it fills 107 pages and is written in a hand probably belonging to the sixteenth century.[1] The loss of the original manuscript makes the identification and dating of the work more problematic as well as obscuring much that we might want to know about its composition. In this respect Marco Parenti was less fortunate as a historian than his son Piero, whose "diary" can be read partly in the autograph as well as in an early copy.

Marco Parenti's original manuscript had already lost the marks of authorship by the time it fell into the copyist's hands. Fortunately, two self-references in the text make its identification secure. To authenticate his information on the death of Count Iacopo Piccinino, the author cites "Filippo Strozzi mio cognato gran mercante et accettissimo al re. . . ."[2] The same link is repeated later when he describes himself as Strozzi's brother-in-law and most trusted relative in Florence.[3] The second autobiographical detail is the author's statement that

[1] See M. Phillips, "A Newly Discovered Chronicle by Marco Parenti," *Renaissance Quarterly* 31 (1978): 153–60.

[2] *Memorie*, p. 26.

[3] Ibid., p. 93.

he was a member of the Florentine Signoria for April of 1454, the time of the ratification of the Peace of Lodi.[4]

The dating of the work is less sure. In concluding the long digression on Francesco Sforza and Cosimo de' Medici, Parenti writes that "what followed we have already narrated at the start of these memoirs [ricordi], which we began at the death of Cosimo de' Medici in the belief that in the future it would be our task to write about the affairs of a free city."[5] This appears to mean more than that narrative per se began with the death of Cosimo, since he speaks of nursing an expectation that was later disappointed. In other words, when he began his work as a diarist, Parenti knew only that the events were likely to prove memorable, but he did not yet know the disappointing outcome, and he goes on to blame this disappointment for the unevenness of the composition.

The narrative of events after the decisive parlamento of September 1466 is certainly uneven. Even so, Parenti continues to follow events down to the summer of 1467: the completion of the famous cupola of Florence's cathedral, the dispatching of ambassadors, and especially the alliances and maneuvers that made up the Colleonic War. The final event spoken of in the manuscript as we now have it is the departure of the duke of Milan, after a lavish welcome, on the twenty-eighth of July, 1467. There is no indication at all why the manuscript breaks off at this time. Like so many chronicles and memoirs, it simply comes to an end.

The fact that Parenti began composing the memoir not long after the death of Cosimo is confirmed by some brief and enigmatic references in his correspondence: "Di que' signori quando gli ai mandamegli—concerning those seigneurs, when you have them send them to me." This curt and initially puzzling pharse closes Marco's letter of May 18, 1465.[6] A month later comes a second, fuller reference: "All the signori of the kingdom should be sent here. And if some are still missing from the plan [disegno] I requested, it should be easy

[4] Ibid., p. 61.

[5] Ibid., pp. 69–70.

[6] CS ser. 3, 180, fol. 58.

for you to inform yourself about them. But regarding those very small ones, do not worry" (June 22, 1465).[7] The difficulties must have been larger than they seemed, since in December Marco was writing again with some agitation: "Those signori that you have, send them to me as you have them; perhaps they will be enough as it stands (December 14, 1465).[8] Finally, there was relief and a little humor. "You say," Marco wrote in February of the following year, "that my work is almost finished and that you will send it by the first wagon. I am amazed that it should be of a weight to need freighting, since I thought it would be a piece of paper to be slipped into a letter" (February 1, 1466).[9]

With the text of Parenti's *Memoir* in hand, it is easy to sort out this otherwise perplexing and disconnected subtheme in the correspondence. Marco's repeated requests relate to the long listing of the powers of Italy that occupies several early pages in his history—"tutti e' signori d'Italia che si trovavano vivi in questo tempo."[10] Having already mentioned the pope and the cardinals, Parenti sweeps the entire length of Italy. But Marco's little joke with Filippo about the bulk of the expected list seems to have misfired, since when he comes to Naples, "for the sake of brevity" he records only the name of the king—promising to list the rest of the nobility in a separate notebook inserted "in this book."[11]

Marco's repeated requests in his letters for the signori are the only reference in Marco's correspondence to his activity as a historian. It is the slenderest of bridges, but these requests make it clear that Parenti was speaking literally when he wrote that he had begun the memoir after the death of Cosimo de' Medici. It is worth noting, too, a request in the autumn of 1465 for details on the royal wedding in Naples,[12] though in the *Memoir* Parenti writes that he has good description of the festivities, but will pass it by for the sake of brevity.[13]

Within the text of the *Memoir* there are further indications

[7] CS ser. 3, 131, fols. 156–57.
[8] CS ser. 3, 180, fol. 27.
[9] CS ser. 3, 180, fol. 76.
[10] *Memorie*, p. 7.
[11] Ibid., p. 10.
[12] CS ser. 3, 131, fol. 169.
[13] *Memorie*, p. 30.

of the date of composition, though their value is always qualified by the possibility of interpolation. In discussing the reform measures of late summer and early fall of 1465, Parenti includes the imposition of a tax to commence in 1467, "but it was not carried out because of the upheavals that later occurred before the said time, as will be described in due course."[14] Similarly, in discussing Luca Pitti's disillusionment over the promised marriage alliance with the Medici, Parenti writes that Piero wished to "reserve" Lorenzo for a marriage with signori, which he later did by marrying Lorenzo to "one of the Orsini."[15] This event did not take place until 1469. In another place, we find a reference to Nicodemo Tranchedini as the ambassador of the dukes of Milan, "both past and present."[16] This indicates that Parenti was writing during the reign of Galeazzo Sforza, who became duke after the death of Francesco Sforza in March 1466. More puzzling is a reference to the "example" of the assassination of this same Galeazzo in 1476—"killed with a knife by Giovan Andrea da Lampognano, gentleman of Milan, as in its place we will describe more fully."[17] Presumably this reference to an event a full decade later than the main narrative is an interpolation that the copyist has simply incorporated into the text—a process that can be observed many times in comparing the autograph and copy texts of Piero Parenti's diary. If the interpolation was truly Marco's it is evidence that he still had the manuscript in hand ten years after the "conspiracy" of 1466; it would also indicate that he once envisioned a narrative on a much larger scale than the surviving fragment—an ambition also implied by the length of the "brief discourse" on the rise of Francesco Sforza. There is also the possibility that the interpolation was the work of Piero, Marco's heir and successor as Florentine memorialist. The manuscript must have passed into Piero's hands, and it is worth noting that his own diary begins with a brief reference to the Lampognano assassination.

It is not easy to draw all this together into a single definitive

[14] Ibid., p. 34–35.

[15] Ibid., p. 96.

[16] Ibid., p. 76.

[17] Ibid.

statement about the dating of the work. It seems clear that Parenti's ambition to chronicle the events after the death of Cosimo came quite early and that he was already collecting information and probably composing in 1465. It also seems very probable that most of the first two-thirds of the manuscript as we now have it was written before the decisive events of September 1466 brought disillusionment—as he confesses on pages 69–70. Despite this slackening of interest, Parenti continued to attempt a sort of narrative until the summer of 1467. The discontinuous, chronicle-like account probably indicates that events were being recorded more or less as they came. Finally, unless a portion of the original manuscript has been lost, Parenti must have abandoned his efforts, except for the revisions or interpolations noted.

INDEX